HUMAN DIGNITY IN BIOETHICS AND LAW

Dignity is often denounced as hopelessly amorphous or incurably theological: as feel-good philosophical window-dressing, or as the name given to whatever principles give you the answer that you think is right. This is wrong, says Charles Foster: dignity is not only an essential principle in bioethics and law; it is really the *only* principle. In this ambitious, paradigm-shattering but highly readable book, he argues that dignity is the only sustainable Theory of Everything in bioethics. For most problems in contemporary bioethics, existing principles such as autonomy, beneficence, non-maleficence, justice and professional probity can do a reasonably workmanlike job if they are all allowed to contribute appropriately. But these are second order principles, each of which traces its origins back to dignity. And when one gets to the frontiers of bioethics (such as human enhancement), dignity is the only conceivable language with which to describe and analyse the strange conceptual creatures found there. Drawing on clinical, anthropological, philosophical and legal insights, Foster provides a new lexicon and grammar of that language which is essential reading for anyone wanting to travel in the outlandish territories of bioethics, and strongly recommended for anyone wanting to travel comfortably anywhere in bioethics or medical law.

'I never had any respect for the concept of human dignity. I thought it was a motherhood concept, empty of real practical import. But Foster converted me. Foster, uniquely, goes the right way round, identifying real human problems and trying to solve them, rather than starting with philosophical problems and theories and creating a concept of dignity that fits them. This is a book for people and progress. It's the best book on dignity I know.'
Julian Savulescu, Uehiro Chair of Practical Ethics, University of Oxford

'This book is the perfect antidote to the unseemly polemics that have dominated recent debates about the concept of dignity in bioethics. Foster takes the notion of dignity seriously and argues that it is indispensible to deliberations about pressing issues in bioethics such as informed consent, abortion, euthanasia, cloning, enhancement, and the use of body parts. He argues that the concept is more fundamental than our concepts of autonomy, rights, and justice, and requires us to think hard about more substantive issues such as what it means to be human and what it means to flourish as a human being. He presents an excellent overview of the current literature on dignity in bioethics, usefully collecting together in one place sources from philosophy, clinical bioethics, law, international conventions, and the blogosphere. While scholarly, it is accessibly written in lucid and lively prose. *Human Dignity in Bioethics and Law* is a substantial contribution that moves the debate on this contentious but important issue up to the next level.'
Daniel P Sulmasy, Kilbride-Clinton Professor of Medicine and Ethics, University of Chicago

'In *Human Dignity in Bioethics and Law* Charles Foster sets out an argument that is provocative in its simplicity: dignity is the 'bioethical theory of everything', the value by which all bioethical disputes should be adjudicated. Drawing extensively from both philosophical and legal debates, this book makes an important contribution to a central issue facing societies in the 21st Century. It deserves to be highly influential for academics and practitioners alike.'
Suzy Killmister, Massey University

'Wide-ranging and erudite, Foster's book 'Takes Dignity Seriously'. Dignity is shown to be a core value in law and bioethics, foundational, a lens through which to project hard cases. It is a rare book which finds a common thread to questions as disparate as euthanasia, sado-masochism, enhancement, cloning, abortion, refusals of medical treatment by children, and numerous other areas of controversy. But this is achieved thoughtfully, entertainingly, and persuasively, in the process throwing new light on many leading cases in the UK , USA, Germany and Israel. It is bound to provoke debate, even controversy. It will be a great assignment for university seminars.'
Michael Freeman FBA, Professor of English Law, UCL

'Charles Foster's *Human Dignity in Bioethics and Law* sets out clearly the state of the question regarding the basis of personal dignity. It also advances an original argument to defend a substantive content for the concept of dignity. It is worthy of study and re-study.' **Patrick Lee, John N and Jamie D McAleer Professor of Bioethics. Director, Institute of Bioethics, Franciscan University of Steubenville**

'Charles Foster has written a remarkably thoughtful and eloquent book, arguing persuasively that 'human dignity'—not 'autonomy' or any other narrow principle—is the indispensable lens through which to view the perplexing moral landscape of contemporary bioethics. I learned much from this comprehensive, open-minded, and deeply humane volume.'
Adam Schulman, co-editor of *Human Dignity and Bioethics: Essays Commissioned by the President's Council on Bioethics*

'This is a spirited study, engagingly written, deeply immersed in the relevant literature, and rich in insight. A valuable contribution to the study of human dignity from a bioethical perspective.'
George Kateb, William Nelson Cromwell Professor of Politics, Emeritus, Princeton University

'Charles Foster's analysis and defence of the concept of dignity as fundamental in medical law and ethics is to be welcomed warmly by scholars and students of the field. It is written with his characteristic verve and panache, yet is at the same time thoughtful and scholarly. We are all in his debt for his analysis of the philosophical, historical, sociological and legal accounts of dignity. And even if you do not accept all his normative conclusions, his demonstrations of dignity-based reasoning in law and ethics are genuinely illuminating and helpful.'
Richard Ashcroft, Professor of Bioethics, Queen Mary College, London

'Respecting patients' *dignity* is one of the most commonly used ideas in bioethics: whether in professional guidelines, in legal judgments or in casual conversation. And yet philosophers, on the whole, don't like it. Many argue that it is too vague and that it can be replaced by other, better concepts, such as autonomy. Indeed this was my position. Foster, however, swims strongly against this philosophical tide and has forced me to rethink. Those who want to sideline dignity will need to read this book and engage with Foster's arguments. Those more open to the importance of dignity will enjoy Foster's company as he informs and amuses the reader with bizarre legal cases and forceful analyses.'
Tony Hope, Professor of Medical Ethics, University of Oxford

'Dignity has long been considered the most protean of ethical concepts—shape-shifting, frustratingly elusive, impossible to pin down—but in this invigorating book, Charles Foster argues powerfully for dignity to be reinstated at the heart of thinking about ethics in medical practice. Dignity is, in Foster's hands, a richly empirical concept concerning the embodied and socially embedded moral lives of real people and what it is that makes it possible for them to 'flourish': the normative force of dignity being provided by empirical evidence about the interpersonal conditions under which humans either do or don't thrive. Through an analysis of real and hypothetical cases, Foster argues that ethics should be concerned with the encouragement (the *maximisation* even) of such relationships. Foster believes that the normative force of dignity 'is best appreciated in the wild places', illustrating this through a number of worked examples concerning 'places' such as reproductive choice and 'enhancement'. But ultimately, perhaps, it is in the interactions between human beings in the quotidian settings of health care practice, discussed in earlier chapters, in which dignity is shown at its most powerful as a way of knowing the difference between ethical and unethical practices and where dignity is or is close to being, as Foster argues—at the heart of everything.'
Michael Parker, Professor of Bioethics, University of Oxford

'This brilliant, erudite, and yet common-sensical book is written by a moral philosopher and lawyer who reasonably hates Kant, sees clearly the limits of autonomy in describing who we are, and defends ably the dignity of the embodied, relational beings we are. I certainly agree that dignity has a substantial meaning that can be deployed by real people making challenging decisions, and I now know a lot more about why that is so.'
Peter Lawler, Dana Professor of Government, Berry College, Georgia and author of *Modern and American Dignity*

Human Dignity in Bioethics and Law

Charles Foster

·HART·
PUBLISHING
OXFORD AND PORTLAND, OREGON
2011

Published in the United Kingdom by Hart Publishing Ltd
16C Worcester Place, Oxford, OX1 2JW
Telephone: +44 (0)1865 517530
Fax: +44 (0)1865 510710
E-mail: mail@hartpub.co.uk
Website: http://www.hartpub.co.uk

Published in North America (US and Canada) by
Hart Publishing
c/o International Specialized Book Services
920 NE 58th Avenue, Suite 300
Portland, OR 97213-3786
USA
Tel: +1 503 287 3093 or toll-free: (1) 800 944 6190
Fax: +1 503 280 8832
E-mail: orders@isbs.com
Website: http://www.isbs.com

British Library Cataloguing in Publication Data
Data Available

ISBN: 978-1-84946-177-1

Typeset by Compuscript Ltd, Shannon
Printed and bound in Great Britain by
TJ International Ltd, Padstow, Cornwall

All human beings are born free and equal in dignity and rights. They are endowed with reason and conscience and should act towards one another in a spirit of brotherhood.

Universal Declaration of Human Rights, Article 1

The account of human dignity we badly need in bioethics goes beyond the ... dignity of 'persons' to embrace the worthiness of embodied human life, and therewith of our natural desires and passions, our natural origins and attachments, our sentiments and repugnances, our loves and languages. What we need is a defense of the dignity of what Tolstoy called 'real life', life as ordinarily lived, everyday life in its concreteness. Our theories about human dignity need to catch up with its widespread, not to say ubiquitous, existence.

L Kass, 'Defending Human Dignity', in E Pellegrino, A Schulman and T Merrill (eds), *Human Dignity and Bioethics* (Notre Dame, IN, University of Notre Dame Press, 2009) 313–14

Dignity is a vacuous concept. The notion of dignity should be discarded as a potential foundation for rights claims unless, and until, its source, nature, relevance and meaning are determined.

M Bagaric and J Allan, 'The Vacuous Concept of Dignity' (2006) 5 *Journal of Human Rights* 257, 269

'If I am not for myself, who will be for me? And if I am only for myself, what am I? And if not now, when?'

Hillel, *Pirkei Avot* 1:14

For Aharon Barak

FOREWORD BY LORD JUSTICE MUNBY

Three years ago, Charles Foster wrote an important book, *Choosing Life, Choosing Death: The Tyranny of Autonomy in Medical Ethics and Law*, which, in his own words, was an assault on the presumption that autonomy ought to be the only voice heard in medical ethics and law. In that book, the idea of dignity made honourable appearance, though his primary focus was on non-maleficence, beneficence, justice, professional integrity and rights and duties as other contenders for a voice in the debate.

Now, he has written an even more significant book, *Human Dignity in Bioethics and Law*, which gives pride of place to dignity. He makes a very large and important claim: "dignity is the key that, properly wielded, unlocks all problems in medical ethics and bioethics. It is the bioethical Theory of Everything." What does he understand by dignity? He summarises it as *being human*. It is, he says, objective human flourishing. Every transaction must be managed so as to maximise the amount of dignity in it. But, as he emphasises, and this is a vital point, the dignity interests of all parties to the transaction—all the stakeholders—must be taken into account. One must, as he puts it, conduct an audit of dignity in general rather than the dignity of a particular patient.

How well does this ambitious claim fare?

On one level the argument is immediately attractive and indeed arresting. Only the autonomous can exercise autonomy, and the young, the demented and the mentally incapacitated are not autonomous. But every human being is entitled to dignity. Dignity is a universal principle. Indeed, being given pride of place in the Universal Declaration of Human Rights it is arguably *the* universal principle—something that autonomy can never be.

Moreover, and unlike that other familiar principle, the best interests of the individual (which itself, as our author points out, demonstrates the inadequacy of autonomy alone), dignity carries within it a meaningful concept and identifies the goal at which we strive. The best interests test does neither. As was famously said in the High Court of Australia, even though English judges seem immune to this painful truth, to assert that something is in the patient's best interests is merely to record the result of a process in which what may be a complex moral and social question is transformed into a question of fact. The best interests approach does no more than identify the person whose interests are in question; it does not assist in identifying the factors which are relevant, it offers no hierarchy of values, "much less any general legal principle which might direct the difficult decisions to be made".

So dignity avoids the problems inherent in both autonomy and best interests. It identifies a principle of universal application which is, indeed, the ultimate legal value. So far, so good. But if dignity is the overarching principle in play, what implications does this have for best interests and, in particular, for autonomy?

In relation to best interests there is no particular problem. On the contrary, the identification of dignity as the ultimate legal value provides the rationale for a best interests test and a benchmark for a best interests evaluation. So there is no conflict between dignity and best interests; the one merely complements and gives content to the other. As our author says, implicit in any holistic determination of best interests is a notion of the Good Life, of human thriving.

In relation to autonomy, on the other hand, matters are surely very different. Dignity, as our author explains it, and autonomy, at least as traditionally understood in this country, stand potentially in stark conflict with each other. Can dignity trump autonomy? He asserts that it must and shows that it can. This is powerful medicine indeed.

Whereas many jurisdictions in the United States of America take a more nuanced view, in this country autonomy is seen as absolute. The competent patient has an absolute right (now or by way of advance directive) to refuse treatment, for reasons good or bad, or indeed no reason at all, and even if the certain consequence is death. Now this is rather curious, for the absolute right which autonomy gives to *refuse* consent is not matched by an equally absolute right to *give* consent. There are some things that the law forbids us to consent to. I cannot consent to be killed. And as *Brown* shows, I cannot consent to be subjected to certain extreme forms of sado-masochistic sexual behaviour. That, says our author, was a case soluble only by the application of the notion of dignity. The persuasive conclusion which he draws is that since it is dignity which ultimately defines what we can consent to; so also dignity should be able to impose limits on what we can permissibly refuse consent to. If I cannot consent to be killed, why should I be entitled to bring about my death by refusing consent to life-saving medical treatment? After all, my purpose, my motive, my intention, may be the same in each case: I want to bring my life to an end. Why should the one means be licit, the other illicit?

Although, as our author comments, any decent dignity analysis will regard autonomous prior expressions of refusal very highly indeed, he suggests it is not inconceivable that there may be cases where the patient's countervailing dignity interests can trump an advance directive. He asserts that since dignity is a deeper concept than autonomy, which is merely a *manifestation* of dignity, so where autonomy is in conflict with other second-order principles, such as justice, it is to the parent principle of dignity that we must have recourse in resolving the conflict. The argument is powerful and compelling.

But if dignity is to serve these important ends, is the concept of dignity sufficiently robust to bear the burden? Is it, as a concept, adequate to do the fundamental legal work which our author demands of it? Can it be more than a mere rallying call for basic decency, important though that obviously is? After all, and he does not shirk this, a common view, pervasive in the literature, is that dignity is merely a slogan to which resort is had when there is no better tool to hand, a makeweight or rhetorical flourish, a meaningless incantation designed, for example, to comfort the living or to assuage the consciences of those involved in making life and death decisions.

Can dignity survive that most challenging and testing of all environments, the battle fought out in the court-room? An English judge, referring to what he called the purifying ordeal of skilled argument on the specific facts of a contested case, observed that argued law is tough law. Is dignity tough enough to pass the judicial assay? Our author asserts that it is, and, as it seems to me, succeeds in making good his case. He refers to decisions in a variety of jurisdictions, including what for a European lawyer are probably the most significant cases of all, if, as I fear, too little known to too many lawyers in this country: the decision of the French Conseil d'Etat in the 'dwarf-throwing' case and the opinion of the Advocate General and the decision of the First Chamber of the European Court of Justice in *Omega*. When one also remembers what the European Court of Human Rights has said about dignity, for example in *Pretty*, it is surely clear that dignity is increasingly seen by judges not merely as a fundamental principle of European law, and thus of our domestic law, but also as a practical and workable forensic tool.

The European Convention on Human Rights and Fundamental Freedoms surely provides, as our author suggests, more than adequate tools with which to give meaning and content to the concept of dignity. There is now a rich and subtle jurisprudence, developed both by the European Court of Human Rights and in our domestic courts, giving detailed texture to the basic principles laid down in Articles 3 and 8 of the Convention, and it is there that we can find, readily to hand, much of the straw with which to makes our bricks. Article 3, with its prohibition of inhuman or degrading treatment, sets the minimum required to avoid obvious assaults on human dignity. Article 8, with its obligation on the State to "respect" private life, points the way to the more positive and aspirational manifestations of dignity; for, as the Strasbourg case-law shows, Article 8 embraces the protection of an individual's dignity, mental health, mental stability and moral and psychological integrity. Moreover, as our author points out, and this must be correct, Article 8(2) demands that the dignity interests of all stakeholders be assessed and a decision made in the light of that assessment.

He tests his thesis in a number of bioethical or medical contexts and, it may be thought, succeeds triumphantly in making good his thesis.

We are all indebted to Charles Foster for giving us the privilege of pondering the implications of this profoundly important and, as it seems to me, ultimately convincing book.

My only regret is that, writing as a medical lawyer, philosopher and ethicist, he concentrates mainly, though not exclusively, on the role of dignity in the medical or bioethical context. The criticism is, of course, unfair, because he has done what his title shows he set out to do. But I make the point because dignity, as he has analysed and explained it, has ramifications for many other equally important areas of our law. The dignity of the vulnerable is surely central to judicial and local authority decision-making in relation to what the Mental Capacity Act 2005 calls personal welfare matters. Dignity surely has a crucial role to play in the context of community care and adult social care, contexts in which, too often it might be thought, proper regard for the dignity of the vulnerable and disabled is sacrificed to economics. And, most scandalously of all, as continuing exposes of conditions in too many of our hospitals, care homes and other institutional settings disgracefully reveal, dignity at even the most elementary level is too often lacking.

Is it too much to hope that our author may yet be persuaded to add to this remarkable achievement by embarking in another book upon an examination of dignity in these wider contexts?

James Munby
13 June 2011

PREFACE

In *Choosing Life, Choosing Death*[1] I criticised the hegemony of autonomy in medical ethics and law. I resented at length the pervasive presumption that autonomy could give all the necessary answers.

That was an easy book to write. It is easy to say what the answer to something is not. This was not an easy book. It is much harder to do what I have tried to do here: to say what the answer is. And of course I have failed.

I set out my thesis in Chapter 1, and I will not repeat it here. But it is worth saying that this is a book about dignity rather than about, say, the right balance between Beauchamp and Childress's famous Four Principles,[2] or about respect for persons, or about professional probity. And that is because whenever I burrowed down into a bioethical problem of any type I eventually, if I went far enough, hit something that looked very similar to the substance I see when I look at a grand landscape, gave the sound I knew from listening to a piece of eternal music, and gave the sensation I get when I read something really moving. This was very strange to me. I did not expect it. I did not have a high, romantic view of the business of bioethics.[3] Indeed *Choosing Life, Choosing Death* is, at one level, a rough, pragmatic appeal for a bit of common sense in bioethical discourse. Anyone reading that book would know that I come from Yorkshire.

But I do, I suppose, have a high, romantic view of humans. The fact that this was not reflected in my thinking about bioethics is an indication that my bioethics was rigidly and dangerously separated from the rest of my reflection. I expect that's a fault common in lawyers, for whom compartmentalisation is often the only way to stay sane. But there's a price to pay for it, as their families and their readers know.

The President's Council on Bioethics commissioned a number of reflections on the term 'human dignity'.[4] Those reflections make up a substantial, learned and highly polemical volume, full of sound and fury, signifying that no one agrees about anything at all except that dignity—whatever it is—is important. The

---

[1] Oxford, Hart, 2009.

[2] See T Beauchamp and J Childress, *Principles of Biomedical Ethics* (Oxford, Oxford University Press, 1994), Although, as I argue in ch 1, there is a sense in which my contentions here might be said to amount to a plea to listen properly to the conversation between those principles.

[3] Throughout this book I use 'bioethics' and 'medical ethics' more loosely than some would like. Nothing turns on the distinction.

[4] E Pellegrino, A Schulman and T Merrill (eds) *Human Dignity and Bioethics* (Notre Dame, IN, University of Notre Dame Press, 2009).

religious excoriate the reductionists for their shallowness, and the reductionists lambast the religious for their credulity.

I wanted to get beyond all this: to try to communicate some of the sense of what I found at the end of my own bioethical tunnelling; to connect it with my own experience of sick children, exhilarating talk, palliative care wards, old Burgundy, infected wounds, forgiving friends, Do Not Resuscitate decisions, and surf.

The chapters may seem to be arranged rather eccentrically. It may seem more logical to have set out my stall and then gone through human life chronologically, as I did in the earlier book, from before conception to after death, taking in consent, confidentiality, enhancement and so on en route. But bear with me. The topics are taken in the order they are in order best to develop a cumulative argument.

Until we get to enhancement and cloning, I look at how dignity analyses might be used to describe various types of medical actions and omissions. I continue that look in the following chapters on the unborn, end-of-life decision-making, and the use of body parts, but in the enhancement and cloning chapter I use a dignity analysis to question fundamentally whether medical therapy itself is ethically acceptable. This chapter concludes most of the *argument* of the book, and sets the tone for the remaining chapters. These remaining chapters are accordingly shorter than many might expect them to be. They are principally concerned with illustrations of the way that the courts have wielded the notion of dignity in these areas. There has been a lot of wielding, but it is not terribly interesting.

Chapters 2 to 5 are primarily concerned with the history of the notion of dignity, and with the meanings it has in today's literature. Those chapters will be frustrating and trite to philosophers and experts in the history of ideas, and hard going for lawyers. The alternatives were to leave them out (which would have left me having merely to *assert* that my notion of dignity fell exegetically within the meanings given by others), or to write a much longer book, which would have pleased nobody other than the sort of people I do not want to please. I anticipate that the most significant criticism of my thesis will be that I am not writing about dignity at all, but am simply making some suggestions as to how, in various bioethical situations, I might give beneficence some workably substantive content, or how 'respect for persons' might work. The defence to that allegation is primarily exegetical.

Since writing *Choosing Life, Choosing Death*, my dislike of Kant has deepened—which is saying a lot. I would like to think that this is the sort of book he would have loathed: that is to say, an *embodied* book, marked, and perhaps characterised, by the flaws that come from messing round unscientifically, and in defiance of Pure Reason, in playgrounds, hospitals, courtrooms and graveyards. Only an embodied book can deal properly with humans, who are, I've now reminded myself, the real substrate of bioethics.

Charles Foster
Green Templeton College
Oxford

ACKNOWLEDGEMENTS

Many people prodded me along the road that led to (but did not end with) this book. It is invidious to name names, but some of the most important are Professor Tony Hope, Professor Michael Parker, Professor Julian Savulescu, Dr Mikey Dunn, Dr Dominic Wilkinson, Dr Mark Sheehan, Dr Jane Kaye, Dr Karen Melham, Dr Paula Boddington, Dr John William Devine, Mr Jonathan Herring, Professor Roger Crisp and Professor Aharon Barak. Many of the thoughts and illustrations spilled out in the course of conversations. I haven't always been able to trace their origins: sorry.

To the Principal, Fellows and students of Green Templeton College, Oxford: thank you so much. The college is a happy crucible where some very exciting intellectual syntheses occur.

The manuscript was read in draft by Professor Timothy Endicott, Professor Tony Hope, and Jonathan Herring, all of whom made penetrating and often depressing comments. If the book isn't completely incoherent, a lot of the credit is theirs. And if it is completely incoherent, it's because I didn't hear them properly.

Richard Hart and the team at Hart Publishing have been tremendous. It was brave to take on a book like this, which doesn't fall neatly into any established genre within legal publishing, but they have kept their nerve and their cheeriness throughout it all. I'm very grateful.

This book has been more than usually onerous for my family. I feel ever more acutely the debt I owe to them all. As well as not moaning at my moodiness and absence, they have also taught me most of the little I know about how to be a human being. Which is the subject of this book.

CONTENTS

TABLE OF CASES

Table of Cases

TABLE OF LEGISLATION

UK Legislation

International Legislation

1

Beginnings

This book has several contentions. Together they form an argument.

The argument goes like this:

1. There are some situations in medical ethics and bioethics with which existing analytical tools are wholly unable to deal.
2. The notion of human dignity is sometimes the only concept that is any use.
3. The role of dignity in the really hard cases suggests that it might be useful in the easier cases too, if we only knew how to use it properly.
4. Using it properly entails:
   (a) giving dignity a substantive meaning; and
   (b) proposing a practical model for its deployment.
   The substantive meaning of dignity can be derived from a look through an anthropological lens at what makes humans thrive.
   I propose a transactional model. One should ask of every proposed solution to every problem in bioethics or medical ethics (every 'transaction'): 'Is that the solution that maximises the amount of dignity in the world?' That will involve considering the dignity not only of the patient, but also the clinician or researcher, and the wider community.
5. A thorough survey bears out the suggestion in point 3, and indicates that dignity is the key that, properly wielded, unlocks all problems in medical ethics and bioethics. It is the bioethical Theory of Everything.
6. Looking back at the road we have travelled, we are surprised that we are surprised at this result. The result accords very neatly with our intuitions. We have outlawed the use of those intuitions during the journey (if indeed they needed to be outlawed: they have probably been systematically suppressed or perverted by our academic training), but it is reassuring that they were nudging us in the right direction all along.

I enlarge a little on each of these steps below.

Steps 1 and 2: Sometimes Existing Tools Won't Do, and Dignity has to Step In

A teenage girl with profound learning disabilities is admitted to hospital. She is undressed ready for a surgical procedure, but is left naked on a hospital trolley for several hours in full view of some male youths. They do nothing but look at her and lust. She enjoys the attention.

What has happened here is wrong. But it is not condemned by any of the usual canons of medical ethics or law. Think, for instance, about Beauchamp and Childress's four principles:

(a) Autonomy can hardly object. If the girl is capable of autonomous thought or action at all (so making autonomy relevant), she autonomously wishes to be an object of desire.

(b) Non-maleficence: do no harm. What harm has been done here? The girl herself sees her exposure as a good. So, no doubt, do the ogling boys. And what, other than dignity, can say that they are wrong? If we suppose, as is likely, that neither the girl nor the boys have been corrupted by the experience in such a way as is likely to cause subsequent harm to themselves or others, it is hard to see any harm here other than harm that has to be described using the language of dignity.

One can see dignity at work here in a slightly different but related way. The rule 'first do no harm' is generally thought of as being the primary rule in medical ethics—eclipsed though it often is in rhetoric by autonomy. But, as Neuhaus has pointed out, it begs a question. It is an enjoinder to protect and maintain something that is recognised as good.[1] But what might that thing be? In the contexts in which the principle is wielded, it is plainly not always bodily or psychiatric integrity. Only dignity can describe adequately all the 'goods' that healthcare professionals are pledged to protect.

(c) Beneficence? Most would agree that this is not relevant here. But if it is, it too, like non-maleficence, has nothing substantive to say unless and until dignity feeds it its lines.

(d) Justice? Again, not engaged here.

Some might invite other notions to contribute. But on examination they all prove to be parasitic on the big four, or on dignity. Privacy, and 'respect for persons', for instance, turn out to be special ways of framing autonomy claims. Professionalism is important, but its concern for the well-being of the patient is classic Beauchamp and Childress and/or dignity territory, and its concern for the integrity of the

---

[1] R Neuhaus, 'Human dignity and public discourse', in E Pellegrino, A Schulman and T Merrill (eds) *Human Dignity and Bioethics* (Notre Dame, IN, University of Notre Dame Press, 2009) 217.

healthcare professional herself fits more neatly into dignity than it does into anywhere else.

All this will convince many that their misgivings about dignity are justified. Here, they will say, is a classic case of dignity being used as a name for whatever principles are necessary to produce the answer that one thinks is right. It is only capable of being used that way because it is hopelessly amorphous. Why not just say: 'The girl should be covered up', and admit frankly that we can't give a very rigorous philosophical justification for it? At least that has the virtue of honesty. Dignity, here, is just a fig leaf to cover our philosophical embarrassment.

These are powerful criticisms. Indeed they are criticisms justly levelled at many of the sloppy usages of dignity in the academic, legal and lay literature. In order to contend that dignity is not only useful but essential, I have to be harder on those usages than are most of dignity's traditional opponents. And that is hard indeed. But I will be. For the moment I will simply assert, without arguing the point, that it is possible to give dignity a meaning that makes it effective at the bioethical and medico-legal coalface, and that that meaning can be empirically derived from a broadly anthropological look at what makes human beings thrive. I am aware that in deriving normative conclusions from empirical observations, some philosophers will think that I have fallen naively for the naturalistic fallacy. I will defend myself against that charge in due course.

Step 3: Usefulness in Hard Cases Suggests Usefulness in Easier Cases

This is a matter of demonstration. And that demonstration will come. In an earlier book[2] I contended that autonomy alone (all too often the only principle brought into the discussion) was manifestly inadequate to deal satisfactorily with even the most trivial of problems in medical ethics. It needs help. The modest and even banal suggestion was that you could only get ethically good results if you listened to the voices of all of Beauchamp and Childress's principles. I was happy to place autonomy at the head of the table, and even to give it the casting vote in the event of deadlock. But I have now listened more critically to the chorus of those voices. The sound of a good choir is greater than, and different in quality from, the sum of its parts. And my suggestion here is that the sound of a well-tuned Beauchamp and Childress choir is the voice of dignity. Often, in practice, it will be impossible to step back far enough from the choir to hear the harmony as it is meant to be heard. One part will tend to drown out the others. But there is a way of broadcasting the harmony directly into our ethical earphones. It is by pressing the button called 'dignity'. Dignity is the direct route to the right answer in most of the cases commonly surveyed in bioethics. Its utility is all the more obvious when we come to the outlandish frontiers of bioethics.

[2] C Foster, *Choosing Life, Choosing Death* (Oxford, Hart, 2009).

To be perfectly honest, in most of the common, ward-round problems in medical ethics, we don't need a solution as sophisticated as that given by dignity. Properly deployed, the other principles, slightly distorted though our apprehension of them might be, will give perfectly workmanlike solutions. The real necessity of dignity is best appreciated in the wild places—and particularly in the realm of human enhancement and reproductive cloning. But that doesn't mean that we shouldn't use dignity to give the more satisfactory, more nuanced, and downright easier answers to everyday problems too. It does mean that it is worthwhile learning how to use dignity (at first in intellectually less strenuous places, such as consent to treatment and clinical confidentiality), before we are forced to use it in the places to which the other principles clearly won't reach.

Step 4: (a) Dignity's Substantive Meaning, and (b) a Transactional Model of Deployment

(a) What is Dignity?

Lawyers and ethicists need to be anthropologists, and anthropologists need to be neuroscientists, archaeologists, sociologists, Shakespeare scholars and classicists. It would also help if they had a nodding acquaintance with the Torah, Talmud, New Testament, Koran, Upanishads, the myths of Old Iceland, and the Walmart catalogue. From these texts, as well as from their own experience of testy judges, departmental bickering, broken marriages, sick children, red wine, mountains, and celebration, they would get some idea about what humans are; what makes humans tick, and what makes them tick well: what makes them *thrive*.

I contend that thriving is connected to human dignity. But the connection is not immediately obvious. It is one thing to say that dignity-enhancing laws will tend to be laws that help humans to thrive (a proposition with which I agree): it is quite another to equate human dignity with human thriving in the simple and obvious sense.

Dignity is a slippery notion. In trying to grasp it, it is best to start with the concrete and then work to the philosophical. To try it the other way round is disastrous.

Some aspects of dignity are like the proverbial elephant: we know them when we see them, but they are difficult to describe. Let's try describing some obvious examples and see where that takes us.

A woman is dying of cancer. She is fearful of dying, and is in intense pain. Nonetheless she shows great fortitude. She is far more concerned about the welfare of her carers than she is about her own needs. She greets pain, fear and death with a smile. Whatever dignity is, she has it and displays it.

A political prisoner is daily raped and tortured by his captors. He refuses to give the names of his dissenting friends, and prays daily for those who persecute him, expressly forgiving them after each act of violation. Whatever dignity is, he has it and displays it.

4

What do these examples tell us? They suggest that dignity is not necessarily connected with bodily integrity. One can be physically compromised or brutally violated, and still have dignity. Indeed the compromise or the violation may be the soil in which dignity (whatever it is) flourishes most gloriously, or the background against which it is seen most clearly. They might also suggest that dignity consists in, or at least may be manifested in, these individuals' responses to the hand that life has dealt them. The patient and the prisoner refuse to abandon something that they are—something that they stand for—in the face of vicissitudes. In their cases, their dignity begins to look like an attitude of mind.

But what about people who don't have minds, or who have minds that are incapable of forming these admirable attitudes? What about the patient in PVS whose cerebral cortex has been wiped out by anoxia? Does she not have dignity in any sense? Surely she does. Would it be acceptable to invite medical students to practise their vaginal and rectal examinations on her? Surely not: and surely the reason why consists, in some way, in some residual dignity.

Or consider the profoundly mentally disabled girl lying naked on the trolley, enjoying the lustful attention of other patients. Is it acceptable for her to be there undraped? No: and again dignity—her dignity—has something to do with this. The dignity of the lusters also falls into the balance.

Or consider a patient who has given his body to be dissected by medical students. One of the medical students cuts off the patient's ear and takes it home to be used as an ashtray. Why not? Dignity again, most would say. But how?

If we are right to say that dignity is engaged in the case of these three patients, does this mean that we are talking about something different from the dignity of the cancer patient and the torture victim? Many have thought so. The difficulty of seeing that we might be meaning the same thing has propelled many dignity-sympathisers into the belief that dignity is just one useful principle amongst many, or to distinguish between dignity as an inalienable status (often seen as suspiciously theological) and dignity as a quality that is evinced by people who are dignified. On this latter analysis, the 'mind-less cases' would have status-dignity but no quality-dignity, and the prisoner and the cancer victim would have both.

This distinction is wrong. The error arises because the attributes associated with dignity (fortitude, patience, consideration for others, and so on) are wrongly seen as akin to chattels that we might possess and then lose; as something separate from us; as instruments that we use in order to do life. In fact they are a corollary of the status possessed by the 'mind-less' cases. They are a way of *being*, not of *doing* life. The 'mind-less' cases are human (if they're alive) or were human (if they're dead). The dead human is still alive in the minds of many people, whose views matter. Why should the PVS patient not be subjected to unnecessary rectal examinations? One important reason is (and I come to another in a moment), because being human *in the sense splendidly demonstrated by the prisoner and the cancer victim* means that one should not be treated that way. The italics are significant. All the patients I have discussed are going about the same enterprise: that of *being human*. They are participating in the human adventure.

5

Being human doesn't necessarily entail *doing* anything, or having done anything, or even (although this will be more controversial, having the potential to *do* anything).[3] It follows from the human ear ashtray example that it need not even involve breathing or having a beating heart. So: doing the right thing ethically in each of these examples entails facilitating the full humanness of each person: of encouraging flourishing. The fact that someone doesn't have the neuronal hardware necessary to appreciate that their own flourishing is being maximised is neither here nor there. Flourishing is primarily about *being*, and only secondarily (although often more spectacularly) about *doing*. The cancer victim is flourishing, although her body is crumbling, because it is of the essence of human beings to use their status of existence to laugh at the void. It's what humans do, and therefore in doing it, she is being human, which is a high calling.

Catherine Dupre invites us to consider that 'dignity is not only about being, but also, very importantly, about the process of becoming. An understanding of human dignity as time-inclusive would acknowledge the fact that an individual's personality is never finished and keeps evolving throughout their life'.[4]

I am sympathetic to the core of this idea, but reject it in the form in which she presents it. If the evolution of personality is a crucial ingredient of dignity, then the patient in PVS has no dignity. His personality will never evolve. And yet his *story* goes on; there is a continued unfolding; his *being* continues.

At the end of his life, Peer Gynt hadn't been good enough to go to heaven, and hadn't been bad enough to go to hell. He begged to go to one or the other, rather than being melted down in a spoon with other men who were too insubstantial for either. He was too light for the super-dense reality of heaven, and he didn't taste of enough for a demon's meal. He was asked to point out one time in his life when he had been truly himself: truly human. He couldn't. The main challenge for humans is to avoid his fate. The challenge for bioethics is to help humans to heaviness and tastiness—in other words to be themselves. Part of being oneself is to be a member of the species *Homo sapiens*; the other is to be a member of the species wholly distinct from all other members. To be both is to be dignified.

What is dignity, then? It is objective human flourishing. Anthony Duff prefers to use the word 'dehumanisation' to denounce that which is contrary to human dignity.[5] To recast the idea of dignity in those terms might sometimes be helpful. There is nothing significant separating me from Duff. But his formulation need

---

[3] Ronald Dworkin comes to a similar conclusion. Although he says that a person's dignity is normally connected in some way to her capacity for self-respect, he notes that seriously mentally incapacitated people will also possess dignity because what continues to happen to such a person colours the whole of her life: R Dworkin, *Life's Dominion: An Argument About Abortion, Euthanasia, and Individual Freedom* (New York, Oxford University Press, 1993) 237.

[4] C Dupre, C 'Unlocking Human Dignity: Towards a Theory for the 21st Century' (2009) 2 *European Human Rights Law Review* 190, 201.

[5] R Duff, 'Harms and wrongs' (2002) 5 *Buffalo Criminal Law Review* 13.

not always be negative. Dignity-enhancement is the process of humanisation.[6] That's what we should be aiming at in our lives, loves, and laws.

This formulation works (and I shall apply it) to 'dignity' as a noun and to 'dignified' as an adjective. It is vital that it should. Many of the discussions in the literature are pointless, with people talking about 'dignified' as something slightly different from 'of or pertaining to dignity', or referring to 'dignified behaviour' as behaviour in concordance with dignity in a sense other than that understood by the other party to the debate.

My formulation does not rely on any idea of dignity as a status that humans have as a result of membership of the species *Homo sapiens*. Yes, part of being myself is being a member of my species, but my species is simply the only possible vehicle for my particular mode of *being*. For the purposes of my argument, it's the being that matters: not, essentially, the human being.

This shouldn't worry religious people, although it will. If humans do have some form of special status (and I do not at all exclude the possibility), we can't begin any non-theological discussion by asserting it as an axiom. It needs to be demonstrated, and it can only be demonstrated by looking at its corollaries. Not only that, but the corollaries will be the practically important things about the status: the things that should govern our ethical and legal thinking. What will those corollaries be? They will be the things that make humans thrive. So if and to the extent that the religious are correct in saying that humans are qualitatively different, by adopting a 'thriving' formulation we will be *enacting* the idea of special status, although without expressly uttering its controversial name.

Let's test this idea against some of our difficult examples.

Why should I not use a human patient's ear as an ashtray? The answer, if I'm right, must be that to do so does not promote human flourishing. But what can that mean? Is it not nonsensical to talk about the flourishing of a dead person?

There are several possible ways in which the statement might make sense. It might mean:

(a) That part of the dead person's human *being* survives her death. She continues to live in the minds of others. For that part of her that survives to flourish, the remnants of her body must be treated with respect.

(b) That another part of her being survives her death—namely her wishes. A wish not to have one's dead body abused can be presumed. Even if the dead person in fact had no such qualms, from a regulatory perspective the presumption is a sensible basis for rule-making.

(c) That if the possibility of her ear being so abused had occurred to her while she was still alive, this would have interfered with some part of her flourishing —for instance her peace of mind. An assurance embodied in a legal or

---

[6] There will also be a significant overlap between my version of dignity and 'authenticity'. I will not try here to map their relationship.

7

ethical code that this would not happen is therefore a flourishing-promoting assurance.

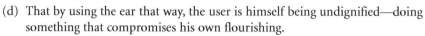

(d) That by using the ear that way, the user is himself being undignified—doing something that compromises his own flourishing.

(e) That a set of societal rules prohibiting such abuse enshrines a principle of respect for persons that will facilitate human flourishing in society generally. To use an ear in that way instrumentalises humans, and instrumentalisation metastasises fast and widely.[7]

I adopt all these meanings. My understanding of dignity lies beneath them all. Note that meanings (a), (d) and (e) illustrate the transactional nature of a proper dignity analysis, which I refer to below. One should conduct an audit of the net amount of dignity left at the end of the proposed transaction, taking into account, suitably weighted, the dignity interests of all the relevant stakeholders, including, here, the ashtray user, potential ashtray users, persons whose ears may in future be used as ashtrays, the relatives of the ear-owner, relatives of people who in the future may have their ears used as ashtrays, society generally, and so on.

A second troubling example: the naked girl on the hospital trolley, willingly receiving the ogles of the Casualty waiting room. How is objective human flourishing at stake here? Again, there are several possible ways. Having seen in the ear example how an analysis might work, we can conflate them here. Broadly, the boys are using the girl. It is classic Kantian instrumentalism. She is a thing, not a person: a means to the end of their gratification, not an end in herself. That enhances the flourishing neither of her, nor of the boys, nor of other girls they might see, nor of society at large.

The mention of the species name and the specific reference to 'human' flourishing might imply species-ism. I am not guilty. I see nothing in my conception of dignity that might not be a characteristic of a dolphin or a tree.[8] When it

---

[7] Ruth Macklin would object that I am invoking in each of these elements not a real idea of dignity, but the idea of 'respect for persons': see R Macklin 'Dignity is a useless concept' (2003) 327 *British Medical Journal* 1419, 1420. I deal with that objection in ch 4.

[8] I adopt without caveat the analysis of Debes: 'A proper account of dignity must pick out a distinctive value belonging to humans. This is not equivalent to demanding a value that belongs distinctively to humans, which demand would not only arbitrarily rule out a shared space of dignity between different humans and other entities but also risk ruling out the best substantive options for humans. For example, if rationality should after all turn out to be the most defensible basis for a theory of human dignity, we wouldn't want to yield it simply because we discovered that chimps and whales were rational or that Martians really have been trying to communicate with us for millennia. At least, at the formal level we don't want to force such a decision. Thus we don't want to condition the 'distinctiveness' of dignity (at the formal level) on its being something only humans have. That is the wrong sense of distinctiveness, formally speaking. This does not contradict the background qualification that human dignity, not dignity simpliciter, is our object of study. Human life remains the limiting factor (the theory must fit humans) and the heuristic lens (it is our experiences, intuitions, and history that provide the basic material for conjecture). The point at hand is simply that we cannot justify loading the formal account against non-human entities, by fixing the criteria of success as whatever would do precisely that': R Debes, 'Dignity's Gauntlet' (2009) 23 *Philosophical Reflections* 45, 61.

comes to advancing my 'transactional' model of dignity, that has some potentially important consequences.

A related point: Talk of the 'high calling' of being human might lead some to fear that I'm smuggling in the *Imago Dei*. I'm not, although as a matter of fact you may be able to get to my conclusion by that route. But there may be problems doing so. In the next chapter I suggest that the notion of the *Imago Dei* can helpfully supply a list of quintessential human characteristics, also possessed by God as he is described in the Judaeo-Christian tradition. But God, in that tradition, is conscious and cognate, and so if I am right in reducing the doctrine to a list of qualities, the doctrine might not be much help in the case of the PVS patient.

If I argue, as I do, that there are some human states of being that represent better than others what humans *are,* I must import two notions, neither of which is uncontroversial. The first is that there is a state of human being (and, by extension, human doing) for which we are suited. (I don't say 'designed', of course.) The second is that it is possible to describe that state with sufficient precision to make the discussion worthwhile.

There is little between me and many modern virtue ethicists. Like them, I rely on Anscombe to defend me from the charge that my interest in the nature of human being makes me a practically irrelevant marketer of self-indulgent philosophical reverie.[9] I am with Aristotle, as against Plato and the Stoics, in holding that virtue is a necessary but not sufficient condition of flourishing,[10] but would not follow Aristotle in saying that the missing elements, not supplied by virtue, essentially consist of the fruits of good luck. I have already disowned that position: the cancer patient and the torture victim are both unfavoured by luck, but misfortune allows their virtue to be all the more obvious, and their objective flourishing all the more florid.

Virtue ethicists have long battled against the allegation that virtue and vice are so culture-bound that it is impossible to talk meaningfully about either.[11] But the objection has been overstated: the surprise from the anthropological literature is the amount of agreement about right and wrong.[12] In any event, the cultural variation that there is is not so much of a worry for me as it is for a straightforward traditional virtue ethicist. There is universal agreement about the common defining features of ethically good humanness—those moral characteristics that mark flourishing humans: no one at all thinks that it is good to lie, kill indiscriminately, be cowardly or selfish, and so on.

---

[9] G Anscombe, *Intention* (Oxford, Basil Blackwell, 1957); G Anscombe and P Geach, *Three Philosophers* (Oxford, Basil Blackwell, 2002).

[10] For accessible summaries of this view, see M Nussbaum, 'Non-relative virtues: An Aristotelean approach' in M Nussbaum and A Sen (eds), *The Quality of Life* (New York, OUP, 1993) 242–69; and J Gentzler 'What is a death with dignity?' (2003) 28 *Journal of Medicine and Philosophy* 461, 476–80.

[11] The classical expression of this view is in A MacIntyre, *After Virtue* (London, Duckworth, 1985) especially ch16.

[12] See M Nussbaum, *Frontiers of Justice: Disability, Nationality, Species Membership* (Cambridge, MA: Harvard University Press, 2006).

This reliance on consensus might sound like deciding on one's philosophical position by asking for a show of hands. Were that the case, the objection based on the naturalistic fallacy might have some bite. But that is not what is going on. The consensus only exists because it has been found empirically, by bushmen and bankers alike, that acting in a certain way promotes their flourishing. The show of hands is merely evidence that those forms of acting are enflourishing.

Even if it is true that the prerequisites of human flourishing are culturally determined, that is only a practical problem—not one that goes to the root of my thesis. It would simply mean that, in devising ethical and legal strategies based on flourishing, one would have to be culturally sensitive, which is hardly a novel proposition. It would mean that the empirical basis of one's ethical or legal action or inaction might vary between groups. Nobody ever pretended that pluralism was easy. My proposal doesn't make it any harder.

Virtue ethicists have been unnecessarily defensive in seeking to justify the origins of their moral rules. The problems they face in that respect are no greater than those of their opponents, and indeed they can often call in their opponents' help. If a virtue ethicist gives a utilitarian justification for a particular rule, she can hardly be mocked coherently by a utilitarian. Virtue ethicists' defensiveness has sent them counterproductively into the arms of Rawls, where they will find little comfort or security.[13] A scientifically informed Aristotelian naturalism is a far more promising partner.

It has been rather unfashionable to seek to justify my sort of neo-Aristotelianism by reference to what the sciences can tell us about human nature. In some ways this is strange. If one is searching for the principles that should govern human thought and action, one might think it more sensible to start by looking at humans, than by blowing the dust off the syllogisms in a university library. The unfashionableness of the notion itself suggests that it might be where the truth lies. And there are some major thinkers who are tending in that direction.[14] There may be some (surprising) aid from the neurobiological reductionists—those who think that we are nothing but the changing polarities of our neurones. Unless they are to smile on obvious depravity, surely they must agree that the content of whatever ethical rules they propose is dictated to some degree by something that might conveniently be labelled 'human nature'.[15]

So: what is good human *being*? What does the evidence tell us about how best to be human?

---

[13] See Rawls' notion of coherentism, discussed well in M Slote, 'Virtue Ethics and Democratic Values' (1993) 14 *Journal of Social Philosophy* 5, and C Swanton, 'Profiles of the Virtues' (1995) 76 *Pacific Philosophical Quarterly* 47.

[14] See, eg, P Foot, *Natural Goodness* (Oxford, Clarendon Press, 2001); J McDowell, 'The role of *Eudaimonia* in Aristotle's *Ethics*', reprinted in A Rorty (ed) (1980) *Essays on Aristotle's Ethics* (Berkeley, CA, University of California Press, 1980) 359–76; J McDowell, 'Two sorts of naturalism', in R Hursthouse, G Lawrence and W Quinn (eds), *Virtues and Reasons* (Oxford, OUP, 1995) 149–79; A MacIntyre, *Dependent Rational Animals* (Chicago, IL, Open Court, 1999).

[15] See, eg, S Harris, *The Moral Landscape* (London, Bantam, 2011).

I am not so presumptuous as to think that I know the answer. My main point here is that the questions: 'What makes humans thrive?', and therefore 'How can we maximise human dignity?', and therefore 'How can we make ethically correct decisions?', are empirical questions. When you tunnel down as far as you need to into the basics of bioethics, you find that the empirical and the normative are identical.

Because I do not know the answer to these questions, anyone coming to this book looking for assertive answers to questions like 'Should we allow cloning?', or 'Is cognitive enhancement wrong?', will be disappointed.

Critics of my tentative suggestion that the empirical may be the normative may say that I'm guilty of a naive scientism—an assumption, of the sort fashionable amongst the semi-educated of the 1950s, that science will one day give us all the answers to all the questions of life, including how best to live.

But I'm not guilty. However much science, anthropology and sociology do, we will still need moral philosophers. However, there are reasons to expect that observations about what is good for humans will inform our ethical, and hence legal, conclusions. Take a fanciful example. One might contend that the question of mixed-gender hospital wards is ethically fairly uninteresting. If a patient objects to going onto a mixed ward, one might think that his refusal is culturally conditioned, and that the only morality in play is the notion that, resources permitting, particularly fastidious patient should be accommodated on a single-sex ward if possible.

But suppose that it is conclusively demonstrated that patients on mixed wards have very significantly worse outcomes that those on single-sex wards. Then, if the issue is financially neutral, it would be ethically wrong not to seek to have single-sex wards. And I daresay, since popular culture and morality track best interests fairly closely, one would soon have little difficulty persuading patients that single-sex wards were culturally desirable too. Certainly the lawyers would snap quickly at the heels of any hospital that continued to have mixed wards, barking '*Bolam*'.[16]

There are many questions pertinent to bioethics and law that are in a similar category.

Critics of my suggestion (about the identity of the empirical and the normative) might also say that I'm guilty of banality—of saying nothing more than: 'It is the business of ethics and law to work out the best way of treating people.' I offer an extended defence to this charge in Chapter 10, but would merely point out here that if one purports to identify the most fundamental stratum on which law and ethics stand, a fair amount of one's description of that stratum will inevitably refer to the whole point of law and ethics. If ethics and/or law already adopt my definition of their objects, I see that as reassuring, not damning.

---

[16] The *Bolam* test is the touchstone of liability in clinical (and other professional) negligence cases. It asserts that a doctor (for instance), will only be found negligent if what he has done would not be endorsed by a responsible body of opinion in the relevant specialty: see *Bolam v Friern Hospital Management Committee* [1957] 1 WLR 583; cp *Bolitho v City and Hackney Health Authority* [1998] AC 232.

Having said that I did not purport to say what makes humans thrive, two broad points can be made. The first is that we are not human in a vacuum. We exist in our bodies, and we exist in a social, political and physical environment. This is obvious, but in fact many speculations in contemporary bioethics are conducted as if the patient were an isolated organism floating in a petri dish.

Humans are embodied animals. Any sensible scheme of bioethics has to take this fully into account. Very often, and particularly in those systems inspired or contaminated by Plato or Kant, bodies have been ignored. There are many reasons for this. One is that bioethics has often been done in libraries by philosophers, rather than by clinicians over a bedpan, or by lawyers over a description of real injuries. Another is that, if there is such a thing as original sin, it surely consists in an intrinsic warp towards Manichaeism, and academics are particularly warped.

What happens to the bodies of humans affects all elements of them. If a Pope's brain doesn't have enough serotonin surging through it, he will lose his faith, although he might keep on mumbling the creed, experientially unconvinced of its propositions. But give him Prozac, and colour and faith will flow back into his world. A previously sweet child will become uncontrollably violent if she develops a limbic system tumour. Excise the tumour and the playground will be safe again. Bodily integrity has metaphysical consequences.

Does this mean, then, that the depressed Pope lacks dignity? Or that a torturer succeeds in his objective of robbing his victim of dignity by stealing his bodily comfort?[17] Or that a cancer victim, bearing her illness with fortitude and cheerfulness, has no dignity, or truncated dignity? It cannot. On the contrary, dignity is often much more prominently visible in people facing bodily hardship than in the comfortable, healthy slumper.

The second point is that humans don't do well by themselves. At bottom they are social animals. Not only do they smile more, but they do more and do better when they are part of a community. That means that the most accurate description of an individual will be in terms of the nexus of relationships in which she exists.[18,19] When

---

[17] Rene Jules Dubos observed that: 'Among other living things, it is man's dignity to value certain ideals above comfort, and even above life. This human trait makes of medicine a philosophy that goes beyond exact medical sciences, because it must encompass not only man as a living machine, but also the collective aspirations of mankind.' In *Mirage of Health*, cited by R Richardson, 'Endpiece' (2003) 326 *British Medical Journal* 1077.

[18] This is acknowledged by writers on relational autonomy (see, eg, P Benson, 'Feminist intuitions and the normative substance of autonomy' in Taylor J (ed), Personal Autonomy: New Essays on Personal Autonomy and its Role in Contemporary Philosophy (Cambridge, Cambridge University Press, 2005) at 124–42; C Mackenzie, 'Relational Autonomy, Normative Authority and Perfectionism' (2008) 39 *Journal of Social Philosophy* 512; C Mackenzie and N Stoljar (eds), *Relational Autonomy: Feminist Perspectives on Autonomy, Agency, and the Social Self* (New York, OUP, 2000); C McLeod and S Sherwin, 'Relational Autonomy, Self-trust, and Health Care for Patients who are Oppressed', in MacKenzie and Stoljar, *Relational Autonomy* 259–79; M Oshana, *Personal Autonomy in Society* (Aldershot, Ashgate, 2006)), and also by writers on dignity in a legal context: see, eg, C Dupre, 'Unlocking Human Dignity: Towards a Theory for the 21st Century'(2009) *European Human Rights Law Review* 190. She comments: 'In reality ... people live at the intersection of several spheres and are not just enclosed in their private bubble with a few incursions into the public sphere' (196).

[19] This is illustrated well in a legal context (a challenge to a ban on physician assisted suicide) by Stevens J: 'The State has an interest in preserving and fostering the benefits that every human being

we look at the reports from the nursing homes and the palliative care wards, we see that the people denied the luxury of illusion—the people for whom the metaphysical chips are down—often define themselves explicitly in this way. Reciprocity isn't just one of the rules of the human game: it's the game itself. If you're not a reciprocal creature, you're not playing at all.[20] We know, too, that active caring is good for you: that altruism confers a startlingly measurable benefit: that the more tightly you slot yourself into the social nexus, the more you will thrive.[21]

We are all, for better and for worse, interrelated. This is obvious at many levels. We all had a common ancestor a few million years ago, and it would be surprising if Jung were completely wrong about us all sharing, and potentially meeting in, a massive cognitive hinterland.

It is hard to overestimate the importance of the nexus. When a flock of birds or a shoal of fish turns as one, or a line of chorus girls high-kicks in unison, the speed of reaction of the group is neurologically inexplicable in terms of the speed of reaction of the individual. The speed of transmission along the neurones of the individual is simply insufficient for the flock to wheel.[22] But wheel it does. There is something mysterious and crucial happening at the level of the group that does not happen at the level of the individual. The group is not only more than the sum of its parts, but qualitatively different.

We all recognise this mystery, although it is rarely put this way. We accept the utility of society, and sign up to a social contract, enforced by legal bailiffs, which alters the shape of our selves. We are defined by our necessary neighbourliness, just as the physical boundaries and the internal environment of a cell are defined

may provide to the community—a community that thrives on the exchange of ideas, expressions of affection, shared memories and humorous incidents as well as on the material contributions that its members create and support. The value to others of a person's life is far too precious to allow the individual to claim a constitutional entitlement to complete autonomy in making a decision to end that life.' *Washington v Glucksberg* (1997) 521 US 702.

[20] CS Lewis wrote: 'The golden apple of selfhood, thrown among the false gods, became an apple of discord because they scrambled for it. They did not know the first rule of the holy game, which is that every player must by all means touch the ball and then immediately pass it on. To be found with it in your hands is a fault: to cling to it, death.' CS Lewis, *The Problem of Pain* (London, Geoffrey Bles, 1940).

[21] See, eg, SL Brown, DM Smith, R Schulz, M Kabeto, P Ubel, J Yee, C Kim, and K Langa, 'Caregiving and Decreased Mortality in a National Sample of Older Adults' (2009) 20 *Psychological Science* 4, 488–94; SL Brown and RM Brown, 'Selective Investment Theory: Recasting the Functional Significance of Close Relationships' (2006) 17 *Psychological Inquiry* 1–29; SL Brown, R Nesse, AD Vinokur, and DM Smith, 'Providing Support may be More Beneficial than Receiving It: Results from a Prospective Study of Mortality' (2003) 14 *Psychological Science* 320–27; P Dulin and R Hill 'Relationships between Altruistic Activity and Positive and Negative Affect among Low-income Older Adult Service Providers' (2003) 7 *Aging and Mental Health* 294–99; C Schwartz et al 'Altruistic Social Interest Behaviors are Associated with Better Mental Health' (2003) 65 *Psychosomatic Medicine* 778–85; D Shmotkin et al 'Beyond Keeping Active: Concomitants of being a Volunteer in Old-old Age' (2003) 18 *Psychology and Aging* 602–07; N Morrow-Howell et al (2003) *Journals of Gerontology: Psychological Sciences and Social Sciences* 58B, S137-S145; A Harris and C Thoresen 'Effects of Volunteering on the Well-Being of Older Adults' (2005) 10 *Journal of Health Psychology* 739–52).

[22] See, eg, R Sheldrake, *A New Science of Life: The Hypothesis of Formative Causation* (London, Icon, 2009).

by a sometimes uneasy mechanical and electrochemical negotiation with its immediate environment.

Going back to thriving: it is impossible to talk simply about 'my' thriving. My thriving is affected by and affects a multitude of other organisms, and by the super-organism (analogous to that wheeling flock). (If anyone wants to hunt for the real meaning of a special status for the *species*, I'd suggest that they start with those high-kicking, impossibly co-ordinated chorus girls.) In practice this means, as the law recognises (at least when it exercises its expressivist function, or looks shrewdly at slippery slopes), that it is not even desirable (even if it were practicable) to legislate purely for the individual. You'd be aiming your legislative arrows at a target (the individual), that hardly exists, or is in any event so gloriously diffused amongst the Brotherhood of Man that it would be hard to know when you'd hit the bull's eye. Medical law is at its very worst when it is motivated purely by a desire to placate the autonomous man. That's because there is no such thing as the autonomous man.[23]

If thriving is dignity, dignity is held in a joint account. Any coherent exposition of dignity will be a communitarian exposition. The transactional approach to analysis is therefore a consequence of the substantive definition. It follows that any properly thought-through expression of self-interest will be an expression of the dignity interests of the species.

The fact that, in this definition of human thriving, and thus dignity, we are determining empirically what is good for humans, means that we can lay to rest many otherwise wholly legitimate fears about the potential tyranny of dignity as a legal idea.

David Feldman has influentially written that:

> we must not assume that the idea of dignity is inextricably linked to a liberal-individualistic view of human beings as people whose life-choices deserve respect. If the state takes a particular view on what is required for people to live dignified lives, it may introduce regulations to restrict the freedom which people have to make choices which, in the state's view, interfere with the dignity of the individual, a social group or the human race as a whole ... The quest for human dignity may subvert rather than enhance choice ... Once it becomes a tool in the hands of lawmakers and judges, the concept of human dignity is a two-edged sword.[24]

If dignity has a meaning that is tied to objective findings in the neuroscientists' laboratories and the sociologists' methodologically impeccable papers, there is no need for Feldman to worry.[25]

---

[23] A conclusion buttressed by the studies cited, inter alia, by Onora O'Neill, which demonstrate that, although autonomy is often the main thought in the minds of the drafters of legislation and professional guidelines, it is well down the list of patients' priorities: see O O'Neill, *A Question of Trust* (Cambridge, CUP, 2002).

[24] D Feldman, 'Human dignity as a legal value: Part 1' (1999) *Public Law* 682, 685.

[25] His worries seem to have infected, amongst others, Beyleveld and Brownsword: see their reliance on Feldman in *Human Dignity in Bioethics and Biolaw* (Oxford, OUP, 2004) 25–27.

(b) Deploying the Notion of Dignity: a Transactional Model

All this philosophising is vain unless we can *use* the notion of dignity we have identified.

Ethicists and lawyers are collectively guilty of a sort of tunnel vision. In deciding whether something is right or wrong, we tend to focus on one subject. That subject is usually the patient. We typically ask: 'Is it a good thing for X that X is treated?'Sometimes other competing interests are brought into play, and the spotlight momentarily moves away from the patient. The best example is the interest of a doctor who conscientiously objects to doing the treatment proposed. When a competition like this arises it is resolved in a messy, ad hoc, unprincipled way. Sometimes the analysis is supplemented by a nod to other societal factors—for instance the fact that, resources being limited, treating X will mean denying treatment to Y. And sometimes, too, it is acknowledged that in deciding whether or not a proposed treatment is a real benefit to X, one has to look at other people to whom X relates. Such acknowledgements are typically couched in the language of relational autonomy.[26]

But sometimes, (and especially if the analyst is a consequentialist), the question will be more holistic: 'Looking at the net amount of good and bad that will result to the world from the proposed treatment, what should be done?' The holism of that question should be applauded and adopted. But there are, of course, potent objections to the question as a whole. Those objections are the stuff of the basic textbooks.

I propose a version of the consequentialist approach. The consequence to which one should look is the net amount of dignity—the net amount of objective human thriving—left by the proposed action or inaction. One should view the subject of one's ethical or legal analysis not as the patient, or the doctor, or society, or anything else, but as the *transaction* that constitutes the whole bioethical encounter.[27] Almost every imaginable transaction is one to which there are many parties. This view, then, is a corollary of the realisation that we need to consider not atomistic entities (because there are no such entities), but the nexus in which each entity exists and of which she consists.

One should then ask: 'How can this transaction be managed so as to maximise the amount of dignity in it?' The dignity claims of all parties to the transaction are of course taken into account. In practice, those of the patient are likely to be predominant. But that does not mean that the others are ignored. This is not, or not necessarily, a 'first past the post' system. It will often be possible to negotiate a solution that allows for the preservation and expression, within the confines of practicality, of the dignity of all or most of the stakeholders.

There is nothing new about the idea that dignity describes more than the status or the interests of the patient. Mountfield and Singh talk about dignity as

---

[26] See the references at n 18 above.

[27] This view has something in common with views advanced by Stephen Wilkinson (see *Bodies for Sale: Ethics and Exploitation in the Human Body Trade* (London, Routledge, 2003)) and Martha Nussbaum (see *Frontiers of Justice*).

'Janus-faced'—looking at both the inflictor and the inflictee of an action.[28] Ronald Dworkin notes that:

> if ... objective importance cannot be thought to belong to any human life without belonging equally to all, then it is impossible to separate self-respect from respect for the importance of the lives of others. You cannot act in a way that denies the intrinsic importance of any human life without an insult to your own dignity ... Kant insisted that if you treat others as mere means whose lives have no intrinsic importance, then you are despising your own life as well.[29]

Baroness Hale observes: 'Respect for the dignity of others is not only respect for the essential humanity of others; it is also respect for one's own dignity and essential humanity. Not to respect the dignity of others is also not to respect one's own dignity.'[30] Debes concludes, after his vigorous analysis of the pretenders for dignity's crown:

> We simply cannot make sense of the kind of value dignity is outside of an interpersonal context. Unlike an ice cream cone, that might be relished were it and some person the only objects in existence, dignity requires mention of an 'other' person. At least, that is what a formal metaethics says of it. Dignity comes to life within the interpersonal, even if only imagined: in the café, classroom, clinic, court, combat zone, or closet.[31]

Feldman agrees that 'Giving weight to dignity adds a new value to the legal system which changes the way in which questions are asked and answered, *allowing a wider range of interests to be taken into account*'[32] (added emphasis).

So then, if one has a proper view of dignity, in analysing a proposed action or inaction, one conducts an audit of dignity in general rather than the dignity of a particular patient.

This might sound hopelessly insubstantial; as if I am simply saying: 'To do good bioethics you've got to take everything into account.' And it is of course true that you do. But this approach facilitates the proper consideration of all legitimate claims, giving conscientiously objecting doctors (for instance) a recognised place at the negotiating table, rather than having to clamour to be heard above objections that they have no *locus standi*. It also uses the same test (the dignity test) in evaluating the claims. It proposes a single philosophical currency, whereas many have been confusingly used before.

---

[28] Cited by Baroness Hale, 'Dignity' (2009) 31 *Journal of Social Welfare and Family Law* 101.

[29] R Dworkin, *Is Democracy Possible Here?* (Princeton, NJ, Princeton University Press, 2006) 16–17, cited by Baroness Hale, ibid. Dworkin has another helpful gloss of Kant's view in *Life's Dominion* (New York: Knopf, 1993) 236: 'Understanding that dignity means recognizing a person's critical interests ... provides a useful reading of the Kantian principle that people should be treated as ends and never merely as means'.

[30] Baroness Hale, 'Dignity'.

[31] Debes, 'Dignity's Gauntlet' 67.

[32] D Feldman, *Civil Liberties and Human Rights in England and Wales* (Oxford, OUP, 2002) 133. He does continue, pessimistically, that this does 'not thereby [make] intractable moral and legal issues easier.' Not easier, perhaps, but more satisfactory.

Whether or not it is workable, and whether or not it has anything real to add to existing methods of analysis, remains to be seen. It can only be seen by demonstration. Most of this book is concerned with that demonstration.

Four observations:

(i) My talk of dignity 'interests' might imply that my notion of dignity is akin to a legal right. It is not. Of course I will contend that the possession of dignity —or, perhaps better, participation in human dignity—has certain corollaries that are conveniently translated into law using the language of rights. But the corollaries are not the thing itself, and the convenience of the translation does not mean that dignity is reducible to a right. Rights are necessarily parasitic on something deeper. Whenever you see a right, ask: 'Why is that there?'; 'Because it is' is never a satisfactory answer. Any philosopher or lawyer who is happy simply to talk about rights (as many autonomy advocates are), is simply shallow. Burrow beneath the right and you will always find a deeper source. Burrow as far as one can go beneath any right worth defending and, I contend, you will hit dignity.

(ii) It may be objected that in defining dignity in the way I have done, I am not writing a book about dignity at all, and that the book should be entitled instead something like: 'Human thriving: some bioethical and legal reflections'. A defence to that charge must be primarily hermeneutic. I begin to mount that defence in Chapter 3, and continue it at various points throughout the book. I will contend not only that my version falls squarely within the ambit of the meanings of dignity suggested by commentators down the ages, but that it is a view that resolves the tension between the two broad understandings of dignity articulated in the literature—namely dignity as constraint and dignity as empowerment (a tension often expressed in terms of dignity as status and dignity as a quality). Accordingly it represents a usually unacknowledged consensus, and, as a broker of peace between the factions, has a good claim to the throne of the united nation.

(iii) It would of course be absurd to say that someone in PVS was in any subjective sense thriving. To read my thesis that way would be to misread it—That way lie madness and vitalism. It would also be wrong to say that someone in PVS was in any sense not human. The way to analyse the PVS case is suggested by the ear ashtray analysis. I accept entirely two important propositions. First, that there will be times when the transactional analysis equation indicates that the dignity interests of persons other than the PVS patient (for instance the relatives, the carers, and possibly those who would benefit from the allocation to them of the funds expended on maintaining the PVS patient) should trump any dignity interest that the patient might have. Second, that although one should not conclude as a general principle that a patient in PVS has no positive dignity interest that tends to suggest they should be kept alive, it may sometimes (and possibly often) be the case that their dignity interests tend to suggest that life-sustaining treatment be withdrawn.

17

The torture victim is flourishing in the sense of being as fully human as the circumstances allowed him to be. It doesn't follow that dignity necessarily demands that he remain alive. It may be that the net amount of dignity in the world would be increased by his biological death.

(iv) I asserted above that I was prepared to accept the possibility that things other than human beings might have dignity in the same sense as humans. It follows that I must concede that in doing the audit of the dignity interests in play in a particular transaction, non-human dignity should be in the balance.

In practice it may be difficult to identify what, other than mere survival, is entailed in non-human thriving. It may accordingly be difficult to quantify the dignity interest of a non-human with sufficient certainty to warrant them having a place in the equation at all. And even when they do have a place, surely the interest would carry relatively little weight beside competing human dignity interests. But that is not to dismiss non-human interests. In a competition between several thousand acres of virginal rain forest and the dignity interests of some potential fellers, the forest may well prevail. And that is not just because human dignity is outraged by the loss of the forest (although it certainly is).

(c) Looking Back at this Pair of Steps

This solution may seem trite. It may seem as if I am saying nothing more than 'look at the situation in the round', or 'consider all the available evidence'.

Two responses: first, it is actually quite unusual in ethics to look at things in the round, or to consider all the evidence. Indeed if one suggests that this should be done, one sometimes gets the feeling that you are regarded in the Academy as intellectually sloppy. Properly analytic people would never do such a thing. You don't need a PhD for that. Decent analysis, we're made to feel, involves squeezing the situation into one standard pigeonhole and then describing the situation by identifying the pigeonhole—preferably in Latin.

Second: the lens through which I suggest all things are examined is not the usual one. While there are many who would regard human thriving as the ultimate point of ethics, it is not usual to see thriving deployed *directly* as a tool for ascertaining correct action. Indeed, many would doubtless say that if one could ascertain directly what constituted or facilitated human thriving, there would be no need for ethical discourse at all. It is normally thought axiomatic that the big question—what facilitates human thriving?—can only be approached by deploying other concepts such as autonomy, beneficence and so on. I suggest that a direct path is not only possible but essential. The fewer conceptual middlemen, the better. The more middlemen, the more value we lose on the way.

I hinted above that the voice of dignity might be the concerted voice of all the classical ethical principles. That metaphor remains undisturbed by the notion of the direct path.

This step is likely to meet with the disapproval of many professional philosophers, on the grounds that it involves swallowing a cocktail made of many concepts that, according to the formal rules of their profession, simply don't mix. Debes, in his splendidly waspish essay *Dignity's Gauntlet,* can speak for them all. Denouncing the like of Simone Weil,[33] Richard Rorty[34] and Herbert Spigelberg,[35] his verdict is that 'the frank truth is that they make for a rather slapdash mix of normative, substantive, and formal metatheory, which we ironically seem compelled to treat both charitably and casually.'[36] This criticism doesn't worry me much. It seems to be another way of saying that dignity is elusive yet big, and that to get a proper view of it one has to look from a number of vantage points. Debes points out very impressively the failure of philosophers of impeccable pedigree to generate an adequate account of dignity, which might suggest that there is something inadequate about the existing methods of formal analysis. Perhaps those methods are simply too pure to deal with humans in all their contradiction and messiness?[37]

Step 5: Dignity is the Bioethical Theory of Everything

This sounds hysterically grandiose. Searches for a Theory of Everything ('TOE'), although they occupy many of the waking hours (and probably more of the dreaming hours) of physical scientists, have not been dramatically successful. The theory of evolution by natural selection is the best candidate for a TOE in biology, but rumours of its omnipotence may have been exaggerated. There are a few faithful ultra-Darwinians on the jackbooted extreme right wing of evolutionary biology who think that neo-Darwinism says it all, but there is a growing biological pluralism—an appreciation that we have to heap so many caveats onto neo-Darwinian orthodoxy that it no longer looks like the reassuring monolith it once was.

Outside the sciences, grand, all-explanatory notions are unfashionable. And for good reason. Archaeology, science, literary criticism, and the insufferable bigotry of its adherents, have robbed the Judaeo-Christian tradition (with the distinct emphasis on the Christian bit), of much of its authority and its explanatory power. Marxism failed. The free market is failing. There is more to both ethics and economics than autonomy.

So why not accept defeat? Why not accept that to get the right answer in bioethics and law, you have to do what the economists, the political scientists and the biologists have long accepted is necessary—to select from the well-stocked philosophical toolbox whatever principle is necessary for the job in

---

[33] S Weil, 'Human Personality' in S Miles (ed), *Simone Weil: An anthology* (New York, Weidenfeld & Nicolson, 1950).

[34] R Rorty, 'Postmodernist bourgeois liberalism' (1983) 80 *Journal of Philosophy* 583.

[35] H Spigelberg 'Human dignity: a Challenge to Contemporary Philosophy' (1971) 9 *Philosophy Forum* 39.

[36] Debes, 'Dignity's Gauntlet' 49.

[37] Debes' own account of human dignity, which purports to be free of the flaws that he sees in other people's efforts, seems to me to mix the normative and the empirical in a way for which I think he should be applauded, but which, if I am right, he would no doubt deplore.

hand? Isn't it dangerous fundamentalism to insist, despite the evidence from other fields, that one principle is enough? Isn't that insistence at root theological? Mustn't it rest on some dogmatic metaphysical assertions about the nature of man?

This is the sort of diatribe to which proponents of human dignity are treated. Since those diatribes tend, as that one did, to conflate many objections, they rarely get the answers they purport to seek.

The reason why we should not accept defeat is that acceptance is unnecessary and irrational. Dignity can only begin to stake a claim as the TOE if it works better than the alternatives. If a 5 mm Phillips screwdriver, and only a 5 mm Phillips screwdriver, fits perfectly all the screws necessary for a job, it is absurd, in the name of liberal pluralism, to insist on using a wide variety of tools. You'll botch the job and damage the tools. Remember Occam.

It is certainly fundamentalism to insist that one principle works, and it is certainly dangerous fundamentalism to insist that one principle works if it plainly doesn't. But the fact that there are dangerously misguided fundamentalists doesn't mean that there are no fundamentals. If there are fundamentals, it is rather more dangerous to fail to acknowledge them.

There are better grounds to be optimistic about a TOE in bioethics and bio-law than there are in biology, politics, economics or any of the other social sciences. The scope of bioethics and bio-law is far smaller than that of the other disciplines. Biology deals with life: with mind-bogglingly complex interrelationships of molecules, mitochondria, memes and moles. Politics and economics paint their pictures on huge canvases. Like biology, they are concerned with huge nexuses: they are ecological disciplines. But bioethics is primarily concerned with the way that one particular organism, *Homo sapiens*, deals with a small range of problems: birthing, consent, confidentiality, reproduction, dying, transplanting, ageing, suffering and so on. The problems affect every part of his life, true, but individual lives, *in the sense in which bioethics and law deal with them*, are little things. Or at least relatively little things.

I have contended and will contend further that human beings cannot be understood as atomistic entities: that they are quintessentially relational: that to describe a human being is necessarily to describe a nexus, and to describe a human nexus is necessarily to describe a human individual. But nonetheless, the numbers and complexities of the relationships concerned in bioethical problems are (with the exception of some problems concerned with healthcare resource allocation) much less than those involved in economic and political questions.

This forces me to acknowledge that dignity doesn't look very TOE-like in those areas of bioethics that are concerned with economic and political questions. It is not very obviously superior to other principles in the realm of resource allocation and distributive justice more generally. Its superiority is most dramatically on display when the focus of the ethical inquiry is on the status of an individual human.

Is dignity-talk incurably theological? Well, no: or not necessarily: or not if you don't choose to see it that way. But if it is, so what? The fact that it was the Psalmist who asked 'What is man?'[38] doesn't reduce the importance of the question for law, medicine, neuroscience, politics, child rearing or our choice of TV programme.

That said, it is not, in fact, this question that lies at the heart of the dignity-talk that I'm urging. I'm suggesting that we need to answer a different, but presumably related question: what is good for man? In approaching that lesser question, we will all, no doubt, have our own views about the answer to the greater. But those views need not and should not taint our answers to the lesser. They needn't, and shouldn't, rest on any metaphysical assertions at all. They can be derived from some basic anthropological and sociological observations. If those observations happen to coincide with the view of the authors of Genesis, the Bhagavad Gita, the *Rubaiyat of Omar Khayyam,* or *Das Kapital,* it is hard to see why that coincidence reduces their importance. Should one reject any observation simply because, in the view of some believers, it happens to have a metaphysical corollary?

Assume that it can be demonstrated that dignity works more satisfactorily in the humdrum world of clinical ethics than anything else, and that it is the only thing that works on the distant frontiers. It doesn't necessarily follow that it is the TOE, although the observations are suggestive. One can never have an algebraic proof of dignity's TOE status. The best one can do it is to note that, wherever one looks, it is philosophic top-dog, and then to show that its top-dog status is a consequence of its derivation from the most fundamental characteristics of humans. If the other principles competing with dignity in the marketplace cannot trace their roots as deeply, or originate from a smaller collection of basic characteristics, one is then well on the way to crowning dignity as the TOE.

Step 6: Being Reassured by our Intuitions

It isn't disreputable to ask whether the destination *feels* like the right one.

I partly share John Harris's suspicion of 'olfactory philosophy'—the notion that your ethical nose is a reliable guide to the correct answer.[39] But to neglect our intuitions entirely is foolish and unnecessary.[40] If we're trying to design ethical solutions for the human beings that we are, or to whom we are related, it is unscientific to excise from our consideration the intuitions that we as humans have. Those

---

[38] Psalm 8:4.

[39] J Harris 'Cloning and Human Dignity' (1998) 7 *Cambridge Quarterly of Healthcare Ethics* 163, 166. He traces it back to David Hume, who said that morality 'is more properly felt than judg'd of': cited in Harris, 'Cloning and human dignity' 166.

[40] Sandel has of course responded substantively and robustly to this allegation. With some reservations, which do not matter for present purposes, I adopt his response: see below in chs 9 and 10. Baroness Hale of Richmond, writing extra-judicially, has commented: 'Instinctively we know that these things are wrong and should not be allowed to happen in a civilised world. Why is that? The answer is that such treatment offends against basic human dignity'. B Hale 'Dignity' (2009) 31 *Journal of Social Welfare and Family Law* 2, 101, 103.

intuitions are vertiginously ancient, distributed surprisingly uniformly amongst humans of very varying cultures, and have presumably been selected for very rigorously by natural selection. They are likely to tell us something meaningful. If they are outraged, it is legitimate to wonder why. But of course we must be careful. Our intuitions are of such mysterious ancestry that often we cannot be sure that we fully understand the language in which they speak to us—lyrical and intoxicating though its cadences are. They are too close to us for us to be able to evaluate their contribution as critically as would be necessary for them to be allowed much of a voice at the table where decisions are made.

What place do they have? Their place is only here, in the final step. And it is only to provide some sort of corroborative reassurance that our other navigational aids (the only ones used to get us to our destination) haven't failed us. Once here, we can inhale philosophically, whatever John Harris says, and say: 'Yes, that smells right.' We can then go about our business in the destination more confidently and comfortably.

Assumptions about the Role of Law

Unless it is to be simply a game for academic bioethicists, bioethics needs teeth. The most nuanced bioethical proposition is pointless unless its nuances are palpable on the wards. There are various ways in which bioethics can be made to matter. They can transform the *zeitgeist*, and the *zeitgeist* itself can transform the healthcare professionals who have such awesome power over patients. But the *zeitgeist*, eventually and imperfectly, is translated into domestic and international declarations, into regulatory codes, authoritative and persuasive guidelines, and hence (often courtesy of *Bolam*)[41] into the substantive law. Although something is generally lost in the translation, something is often gained too. 'Bioethics in practice requires a healthy dose of old-fashioned *prudence*', observed Adam Schulman, 'and is not well served by a dogmatic adherence to the artificial division between an ethics of principles and an ethics of consequences.'[42] Quite right. And when bioethics is dosed with prudence, it turns into the raw material of law: it becomes juris*prudence*.

If I contend, as I do, for a sort of neo-Aristotelian virtue ethic, it should follow that I contend for a virtue jurisprudence. And so I do. I start by believing that any law is regrettable, and that the imposition of any law requires very explicit justification. What might amount to sufficient justification? Here I follow Colin Farrelly and Lawrence Solum in believing that virtue (not economics, or rights, or anything else) is the only legitimate legal draftsman:

---

[41] See n 16 above.
[42] A Schulman, 'Bioethics and the Question of Human Dignity' in Pellegrino et al (eds), *Human Dignity and Bioethics* 12.

the fundamental concepts of legal philosophy should not be welfare, efficiency, autonomy or equality; the fundamental notions of legal theory should be virtue and excellence ... [The goal of law is] not to maximise preference satisfaction or to protect some set of rights and privileges: the final end of law is to promote human flourishing to enable humans to lead excellent ones.[43]

I do not propose to argue this position here. Farrelly and Solum do not need my help. This book is about the main problem involved in making their position practically useful; namely the problem of saying in what 'human flourishing' consists. I have suggested that human dignity is objective flourishing. There is room in this argument for the consequentialist assertion that the role of law is to maximise the dignity of the greatest number to the greatest possible degree, but I do not in fact make that assertion. This is not because I believe it to be untrue, but because I am agnostic on the point. This book therefore focuses on whether, and if so, how, the law can maximise the dignity of individuals.

Law, importantly, has an expressivist function. It declares the values of its society. Declaration isn't just pomp and wind. It can change, enshrine and preserve. Even if my version of dignity is wholly misconceived, or isn't as fundamentally true as I argue, it has some value. A dignity analysis of legal problems will have the effect of saying that one should strive to make and construe laws in a way that will humanise. However many philosophical brickbats can be thrown at that proposition, and however many questions it begs, the proposition won't take you far off the right path. At least it won't take you anywhere nasty, as can (for instance) the unfettered rule of autonomy.

People and institutions tend to live up or down to the names that they are given or, more importantly, give themselves. When someone takes up running, one of the main benefits is that he immediately—long before he has any measurable increase in cardiac output, and while he is still wobbling ludicrously along—self-identifies himself as a 'runner'. It is because he is a 'runner' that he immediately gives up the deadly Big Mac and fries. And it is that abstention that makes him fit; makes him live up to the name; turns him, in fact, into a runner. It's the same with a dignity approach to law and ethics. If we say that law and ethics are really all about the maximisation of dignity, law and ethics will tend to generate full-blooded, thriving humans. Which is a Good Thing.

[43] C Farrelly and L Solum (eds), *Virtue Jurisprudence* (London, Palgrave Macmillan, 2008). See the discussion in C Cimino, 'Private Law, Public Consequence and Virtue Jurisprudence' (2010) 71 *University of Pittsburgh Law Review* 279.

2

A Short History of Dignity

Semantics dog many discussions of dignity. The discussants are often at angry cross-purposes, with X denouncing Y's endorsement of an understanding of dignity that Y has never held. Because the language of X's understanding is similar to that of Y's, Y will often never notice that she has been misunderstood. And so the accusations and counter-accusations multiply, generating heat but no light. Whole books and theses have been written on the basis of such misunderstandings. There are some epic gladiatorial disputes in the arena of dignity, but many of the casualties are straw men.

A look at the history can help to reduce these unfortunate casualties.[1] We owe it to the straw men.

The Emergence of Men

The first anatomically modern men we know of emerged about 100,000 years ago. So far as we can see from the fossil record (and that is quite a long way), they had all the neurological hardware that we have, and with more or less the same processing power. And yet they were not behaviourally modern. The museum shelves representing these early *Homo sapiens* are dull. They give no indication whatever of consciousness: of a sense of 'I' as distinct from the world: of subjectivity: of the ubiquitous human sensation of teetering always on the brink of ontological catastrophe.

And then (perhaps quite quickly, although the speed of the revolution is controversial), it all changed. Around 40–50,000 years ago, something happened to those pre-primed but relatively inert brains. There are many candidates for the trigger of the change: language, cooking, pharmacologically or physiologically induced altered states of consciousness, and so on.[2] Quite a lot of modern anthropology is concerned with arguments about the trigger. But everyone agrees about the result. There was a spectacular explosion of symbols. You can see them on the museum shelves. As soon as you get to the Upper Palaeolithic, you see representational art, including, poignantly, the first representations of the human form. For

---

[1] The most detailed exposition of the history of the notion of dignity is in D Kretzmer and K Eckart, *The Concept of Human Dignity in Human Rights Discourse* (The Hague, Kluwer, 2002).

[2] There is a good short summary of the claims of some of the candidates in C Pasternak, *What Makes Us Human?* (London, OneWorld, 2007).

the first time people were hovering outside themselves and saying: 'That is what I am.' Subjectivity oozes from the art. And beauty, pointless except for itself, was obviously cherished. Pots were stamped with prettifying patterns that said: 'Man is more than what he eats', and 'This is *my* pattern: nobody else's.' The symbolising revolution conferred an obvious selective advantage (although the birth of consciousness did not).[3] It conferred an ability to construct in one's head, and test in one's head, a multitude of different models of the world. Mental modelling of the possible vagaries of a mammoth hunt was far less thermodynamically costly and dangerous than facing the unforeseen charge of an enraged rogue.

Nobody knows precisely how symbolising and self-consciousness were causally related to each other, if indeed they were. But they seem to have arisen at around the same time, give or take a few thousand years. And one or the other, or both, produced in these newly modern apes a fear of extinction and, quite quickly, as a corollary, a belief that biological life is not all that there is. In some ways they had recognised that already, of course. That was the main message of the patterned pots. But the fear took archaeological shape as sophisticated burial.

There are some who contend that Neanderthals symbolised and buried their dead. Their case is not completely unarguable, but it is difficult. What is certain is that, if anything other than *Homo sapiens* symbolised or buried, they did it with a crudeness that makes it incomparable to truly human activity. If it is not actually true that only *Homo sapiens* symbolised or buried, it is so nearly true that it comfortably bears the weight of the thesis I am about to build on it.

If you can sit in your cave imagining all the possible permutations of a mammoth hunt, you can sit in your cave imagining where the essence of your dead grandfather has gone. If you can say: 'There is an entity that I call "I", which existed yesterday, exists today and will hopefully exist tomorrow', you can wonder too where the 'I' will go when a sabre-toothed tiger does to your thorax what it did to your grandfather. And those early behaviourally modern men did exactly that.

When bodies stopped breathing, they did not sling them to the hyenas: they laboriously dug pits, dressed the bodies in finery, draped them with jewellery, smeared them with red ochre, and lowered them reverently into the ground. They treated them, in other words, with what we today would call (accurately or sloppily we have yet to determine), *dignity*.

As consciousness and symbolism emerged, there were two over-arching and connected corollaries, which I suggest are central to any definition of human dignity. Humans saw themselves as *stories*, and as part of a bigger story—a metanarrative.

My consciousness takes the form of an unfashionably Cartesian conviction that there is an 'I'—a Charles Foster. The 'I' that is sitting in a library in Oxford and co-operating in some mysterious way with the pair of hands that is typing this paragraph is the same 'I' that went to London yesterday, that was educated

---

[3] C Foster, *Wired for God? The Biology of Spiritual Experience* (London, Hodder & Stoughton, 2010).

at the University of Cambridge many years ago, and which, all being well, will go to see *King Lear* tomorrow. Whether that conviction *is* the ultimately illusory 'I', or a consequence of a real 'I', is the business of the mind–body problem. And it need not bother us here. Daniel Dennett and Sue Blackmore can protest all they like that there is no 'I': that we are nothing but the experiences that we have. But they, like all of us, pepper everything they say with personal pronouns, and agree that, for some reason, we can't bear the thought that those experiences aren't linked. They contend that the 'I' is an illusion that we invent to join the experiences together—to make the story that we call ourselves. And that's fine for present purposes. Whether it's an illusion or not, it is ancient, ubiquitous and, if not unique to humans, probably particularly highly developed in us. So: we're stories.

It is perhaps not surprising that stories insist on placing themselves within stories. If stories are our essence, perhaps there is psychologically no alternative. But whether there is an alternative or not, we are, and have been since the Upper Palaeolithic, incurable myth-makers. We see ourselves as actors in a play. The play has many names: Hinduism, Judaism, Communism, the Grand Drama of Humankind, Our Place in the Evolving Cosmos, and so on.

We feel ontologically threatened if anything looms over our own sense of 'I'—whether the threat is a cancer or a diagnosis of dementia. And similarly we get upset if anything interferes or threatens to interfere with our understanding of the play in which we are performing. This sort of interference might be a challenge to the fundamentals of our religious or scientific faith (often dealt with by a relapse into cognitive dissonance), a breakdown of the marriage in which we assumed we would live and die, or a radical cultural or political shift.

We are protective of our myths. The protective language in which we speak of them looks similar to the language in which some commentators talk about human dignity. That, I suggest, is because the raw material of the personal myth and the metanarrative myth is the same as that of dignity.

So, then, when humans first became recognisable as such, they: (a) had a new sense of 'I', which involved seeing their own lives as distinct from those of others; (b) saw their own lives as stories; (c) saw those stories as having a place in a bigger story; and (d) thought that there was more to these lives and these stories than mere biological survival. In these observations lie the seeds of a definition of human dignity that is useful in the operating theatre and the enhancement laboratory.

It might be said that other traits, emerging at around this time, were quintessential, defining, human characteristics: certain ways of relating to one another, for instance, that are not obviously seen amongst social insects or wolves. But the contention would have to rest on some zoological assertions that might well be proven wrong tomorrow. And in any event, characteristics (a) to (d) will do for present purposes.

It is worth pointing out at this point that we are not trying to dissect out the characteristics that distinguish humans from other mammals. We have embarked on a quest to discover what principles we should apply in deciding how to treat humans. The characteristics of human beings are important in that process, but it does not matter at all if the crucial characteristics happen to be ones that we share with higher primates, rabbits or cockroaches. If, and to the extent that, they are shared, we should treat cockroaches as we treat humans. It may also be that we should treat cockroaches as we treat humans, not because cockroaches share human characteristics, but because a consequence of the essential human characteristics is that we presume humanity even when all the evidence suggests that it is absent. We will explore this possibility later.[4]

The Ancient World

Humans have remained essentially Upper Palaeolithic. There have been no paradigm-shattering new discoveries for the last 45,000 years.[5] Humans elaborated and systematised some of those early convictions and characteristics. Red-ochre pit burials became barrows and gorgeous mausolea. The geography of spirit-worlds was described in detail, and men plotted their eternal travels on detailed maps. Human conduct in this world was regulated by canons that at least arguably were based on the principle: 'Humans shouldn't do X/should do Y, because it is contrary to/concordant with their nature', although the perceived interest of supernatural beings in the affairs of men complicated the picture considerably. There were detailed codes of honour, enforced with gruesome draconianism. Men told stories about gods and great men, and the stories formed the templates for their own lives and dreams. The quintessential sounds of the ancient world were the murmur of the bard at the fireside, and the clash of flint, bronze and iron as the ideals articulated by the bards were violently translated into political and economic reality.

Homer spoke for many of the ancients: a dignified person was an unusually excellent one; a member of an ontological elite. The excellence would certainly be evidenced by particular characteristics (bravery, war-craft, generosity, and so on), but there is a clear sense that the characteristics themselves are secondary. A man is brave because he is dignified, not vice versa. The gods have wandered through the earth, bestowing dignity on the favoured few, and as a result the few do noble things that the hoi polloi would not and could not do.

The Stoics started a modest revolution. They asserted that all men had dignity because of their intrinsic rationality. This, of course, imposed a duty on men to act in accordance with this rational nature. In many ways Kant, despite his perceived importance, had little to add to this formulation. It was taken up

---

[4] It is relevant when considering the withdrawal of treatment from people (very often children) whose enjoyment of continued existence is doubtful: see ch11.

[5] Unless you agree, as I do not, with Julian Jaynes' bicameral mind theory: J Jaynes, *The Origin of Consciousness in the Breakdown of the Bicameral Mind* (New York, Houghton Mifflin, 1990). My own reasons for disagreeing are set out in detail in Foster, *Wired for God?*

by that master of philosophical PR, Cicero, and given an ascetic slant that was to have disastrous consequences for the development of dignity in the hands of the Christians.[6] Cicero's reasoning started from a conviction that humans and animals were radically different. But in what respect? Well, animals think only of 'bodily satisfactions'. Human minds, on the other hand, are 'developed by study and reflection ... From this we may learn that sensual pleasure is wholly unworthy of the dignity of the human race.'[7] The scene was set for an understanding of dignity that rendered it almost useless in any medical or bioethical context.

Made in the Image of God: Judaeo-Christian Understandings of Human Dignity

Man, in the Judaeo-Christian tradition, is made in the image of God.[8] That, it is said, confers a dignity on man. This has become a slogan—an immovable axiom in much religious-dominated ethical discourse. It merits a critical look. A look generates more questions than answers. Even for a believer, the *Imago Dei* is not the key that effortlessly unlocks all of bioethics' most heavily encoded problems.[9]

If it is true that man was made in the image of God, why should that give man dignity? Well, God is to be worshipped. There is presumably, therefore, something in creatures that bear his stamp that also should make knees bend. But what is it? Is it a quality or qualities of God? If so, what qualities are they? Can man lose or give up those qualities—so diminishing or losing the image of God in him? If he can, are we justified in treating him as an animal to the extent that his God-like characteristics are absent? If not, why not? If he cannot lose or surrender the qualities, does he have dignity by reason of his divine bloodline? Is dignity, then, an inalienable status? If it is, then what consequences does it have for the bearer of the status?

The Bible spells out some of the consequences for anyone who interferes with the status-bearer. The most famous is the *lex talionis*: 'Whoever sheds the blood of a human, by a human shall that person's blood be shed; for in his own image

---

[6] 'If we wish to reflect on the excellence and dignity [*dignitas*] of our nature', wrote Cicero, 'we shall realize how dishonourable it is to sink into luxury and to live a dainty and soft lifestyle, but how honourable to live thriftily, strictly, with self-restraint, and soberly.' *De Officilis*, cited in D Sulmasy, 'Dignity and bioethics: history, theory and selected applications', in E Pellegrino, A Schulman and T Merrill (eds), *Human Dignity and Bioethics* (Notre Dame, IN, University of Notre Dame Press, 2009) 471.

[7] Cicero, De Officilis I, 30, cited in C McCrudden, 'Human dignity and judicial interpretation of human rights' (2008) *European Journal of International Law* 655, 657.

[8] 'Then God said, "Let us make humankind in our image, according to our likeness; and let them have dominion over the fish of the sea, and over the birds of the air, and over the cattle, and over all the wild animals of the earth, and over every creeping thing that creeps upon the earth." So God created humankind in his image, in the image of God he created them; male and female he created them.' Genesis 1: 36–27, New Revised Standard Version.

[9] See, eg, G Fletcher, 'In God's image: the religious imperative of equality under law' (1999) 6 *Columbia Law Review* 1608.

God made humankind.'[10,11] But can we conclude anything about the nature of the status (other than that it to be taken seriously) from the magnitude and nature of this sanction?

Christianity has given no consistent answer to these questions.[12] Thomas Aquinas, talking about murder, and taking his cue almost verbatim from Cicero and Seneca, thought that: 'a man who sins deviates from the rational order, and so loses his human dignity ... To that extent, then, he lapses into the subjection of the beasts', whereas Pope John Paul II, whom one might have thought would have seen eye-to-eye with Aquinas, declared in his 1995 Encyclical *Evangelium Vitae*: 'Not even a murderer loses his personal dignity'.[13]

There is no greater consistency in the Protestant world. Conservative evangelicals use the *lex talionis* to demand the death penalty for murderers, and liberal Protestants use the *Imago Dei* to insist that the death penalty is a theological obscenity.

Judaism has proceeded more cautiously, and its insights are correspondingly more useful. Aramaic translations of the Pentateuch use a happily amorphous word, akin to 'similitude', instead of the more definite 'image', and there is a general rabbinic reluctance to say what is meant by 'the image of God'.[14] Kraynak believes that this is the result of a carefully considered policy. If the God-like attributes of humans were to be identified, the argument goes, it would result in a noxious spiritual apartheid.[15]

But cautious exegesis is not the same as no exegesis at all. Judaism has deployed the notion of the *Imago Dei*, and to great effect. Yes, the rabbis have been rather taciturn, but that is perhaps because the text of the Torah is actually quite explicit, if one looks closely.

---

[10] Genesis 9:6, New Revised Standard Version.

[11] The immediately preceding passage (Genesis 9:1–5), reads: 'God blessed Noah and his sons, and said to them, 'Be fruitful and multiply, and fill the earth. The fear and dread of you shall rest on every animal of the earth, and on every bird of the air, on everything that creeps on the ground, and on all the fish of the sea; into your hand they are delivered. Every moving thing that lives shall be food for you; and just as I gave you the green plants, I give you everything. Only, you shall not eat flesh with its life, that is, its blood. For your own lifeblood I will surely require a reckoning: from every animal I will require it and from human beings, each one for the blood of another, I will require a reckoning for human life.' New Revised Standard Version.

[12] See A Altmann, '*Homo Imago Dei* in Jewish and Christian theology' (1968) 48 *Journal of Religion* 235.

[13] A useful catalogue of quotations from Catholic social teaching on the theme of human dignity is at www.osjspm.org/human_dignity.aspx.

[14] See Altmann, '*Homo Imago Dei* in Jewish and Christian theology'.

[15] R Kraynak, 'Human Dignity and the Mystery of the Human Soul' in Pellegrino et al (eds), *Human Dignity and Bioethics* 75.

The starting point is the first of the two Biblical creation stories.[16] Here God shows us quite a lot of himself. He initiates,[17] makes,[18] speaks,[19] commands,[20] names (and endorses man's naming of things),[21] divides[22] and generally taxonomises, delegates,[23] creates beings in his own image,[24] provides for his creatures,[25] endorses other creative processes,[26] stands back and appreciates his handiwork,[27] and rests.[28] Although he is designated by masculine pronouns, 'he' plainly has both male and female characteristics: 'So God created man in his own image, in the image of God created he him; male and female created he them.'[29] He is apparently concerned about animal suffering, originally ordering universal vegetarianism[30] and only later, reluctantly, as a compromising dispensation, allowing meat-eating[31] (and even then expressing his distaste for blood[32] and his disapproval of predation).[33]

In the second of the stories, God states that humans are built for relationship, an observation that, if the notion of the *Imago Dei* is correct, indicates his own relational nature: 'Then the Lord God said, "It is not good that the man should be alone; I will make him a helper as his partner."'[34]

So: God acts freely; he speaks, contemplates, has compassion and a sense of continuing pastoral responsibility, has ethical and aesthetic concerns, embodies the quintessentially masculine and feminine qualities, and values relationship. The broad outlines of the *Imago Dei* are clear enough.

When the prototypical humans Adam and Eve start displaying the divine characteristic of freedom, they (disastrously, according to the story), acquire the knowledge of the distinction between good and evil. And this 'Fall' seems to be a fall *up*. They were made in God's image before, but after eating the forbidden fruit they are even more like him. God prohibited them from eating the fruit precisely because he knew that this would happen: 'Then the Lord God said, "See, the man

---

[16] Genesis 1:1–2:3.

[17] Genesis 1:1.

[18] Genesis 1:1.

[19] Genesis 1:3 et seq.

[20] Genesis 1:3 et seq.

[21] God himself names things in Genesis 1, 5, 8 and 10, and endorses man's names for things in Genesis 2:19, 23.

[22] Genesis 1:4.

[23] Genesis 1:11, 26–29.

[24] Genesis 1:27.

[25] Genesis 1:29–30.

[26] Genesis 1:11–12.

[27] 'And God saw everything that he had made, and behold it was very good': Genesis 1:31. Also 'good', although not 'very good', in Genesis 1:10, 12, 18, 21, 25.

[28] Genesis 2:2.

[29] Genesis 1:27.

[30] Genesis 1:30.

[31] Genesis 9:1–3.

[32] Genesis 9:4.

[33] For instance by the exclusion of predators and scavengers from the list of 'clean' (ie edible) animals.

[34] Genesis 2:18, New Revised Standard Version.

has become like one of us, knowing good and evil; and now, he might reach out his hand and take also from the tree of life, and eat, and live for ever.'"[35] Adam and Eve are evicted from the garden lest they take the next Promethean step of eating the fruit of immortality (they seem to be mortal at this point), and consequently becoming even more dangerous challengers of the divine prerogative.[36]

Moving away from the question of the *Imago Dei*, there is more to be had from Genesis. It comes from the stern text of the *lex talionis*. It is a gruesome but democratic edict. If a king kills a peasant, the king's life is forfeit. And the price of one life is one life; not more. Human lives seem to have equal worth.

The god-characteristics of the Genesis story are all the sorts of attributes that we would typically say are important in describing a thriving human being. Of course one can thrive without having many of these attributes, but their absence doesn't help. And if the *lex talionis* is right, the reason that the killing of humans is wrong is because they have the god-image status that is responsible for their possession of these qualities.

If one treats a human being with 'dignity', one will act in a way that maximises her ability to express these god-attributes. One also won't kill her. There is a practical and a theological reason for that. The theological reason is that sticking a knife into her heart would not be treating her with the respect due to a creature bearing the image of God: another dignity argument. The practical reason is that if her heart stops, her ability to manifest god-characteristics will be truncated. And that, if the exercise of god-characteristics is dignity-enhancing, is yet another dignity-argument.

We will leave these threads dangling for a moment. We pick them up again very shortly. It is perhaps necessary to say that to find these Genesis stories helpful, one doesn't have to be Jewish or Christian. Indeed they are probably more obviously helpful if they are not encrusted with the theological detritus of millennia. Put at its lowest, these are tales that embody very old and durable insights into the nature of humans. They seem to be anthropologically sound. It's not emancipated to reject them completely: it's putting yourself at an unnecessary expository disadvantage.

Christians and Jews agree about one thing: God is a spirit. In the light of that observation, how should we understand the *Imago Dei*? Does it mean that God-like attributes are necessarily and only relevant to our souls? This thought has obsessed and paralysed Christians. 'Who,' asked Augustine, 'would be so utterly out of his mind as to say that we are or shall be similar to God in the body? In the inner [person] therefore is this likeness.'[37] And mainstream Christianity followed him. I identify below some of the consequences for Christian bioethics in general, and dignity theory in particular, of following Augustine. Some of those consequences flow from his view of the *Imago Dei*. Judaism, by and large, except where it was contaminated by neo-Platonism, escaped the obsession and the paralysis.

---

[35] Genesis 3:22, New Revised Standard Version.
[36] Genesis 3:22.
[37] Augustine, *Letters*, XCII 3.

Subsequent Christian Understandings of Dignity

Christianity insists that God took flesh and walked around Palestine, eating, drinking and urinating. And that after his death, he returned physically and ate kippers on a beach. One might have thought that this would entail an endorsement of human bodies. And indeed if one reads histories of early Christianity, they all insist that Christianity fought tooth and nail against the Gnostics. The Gnostics denigrated the body, despised the material world, held that salvation involved breaking free from the dirty material humdrum, and accordingly believed that Jesus was not *really* human. Pure spirit wouldn't soil itself by being clothed in carrion.

The books all say that orthodox Christianity won the war against the Gnostics. It is true that Jesus' humanity is asserted in the historic creeds of the church, but the supposed victory was cosmetic. The subsequent history of Christianity is the history of Gnosticism's triumph. 'John Brown's body lies a mouldering in the grave, but his soul goes marching on', goes the old hymn, taking its theology from Platonic Athens, or from second-century Gnosticism, but certainly not from the canonical gospels. And that's been the general tone. Christianity is concerned with the salvation of souls, an enterprise best effected by subduing the turbulent flesh.

Some of the blame for this can be attributed to Christianity's mistaken belief that Jesus would return imminently. Why bother with things like marriage, child-rearing or politics, when the Universe was about to be rolled up? And some can be laid at the door of early Christianity's nervous accommodation with the Gnostics. In theory those Christians believed, as Jesus the Jew evidently believed, that humans were mind-body-spirit unities: metaphysical amphibians existing in several dimensions at once. But they often didn't behave or write that way. Their intrinsic Gnosticism was crystallised in body-hating doctrines such as sacerdotal celibacy and the perpetual virginity of Mary. So when Augustine burst into the North African Christian world, he found a ready audience for his soul-is-all pastiche of historic Christianity.

He had been a practising Manichean, and never really stopped.[38] For Augustine, sex (being a bodily thing) was necessarily a dirty business: sex was at war with the soul. Hence his doctrine of Original Sin. Humans were born as a result of a sexual act, and hence born contaminated by the bestial lust of their parents.

Augustine became canonical. He eclipsed the joking, wine-drinking man-god of Christianity. And Christianity was almost literally emasculated as a meaningful contributor to the philosophical debate about what it was legitimate to do with one's body. The history of Christianity became the history of celibate monasticism; of private piety, politics and pogroms. Of course some Christians did wonderful things to bodies: they built hospitals and washed lepers' sores. But rarely did

---

[38] Although he fulminated against them: see, for example, *On Genesis against the Manichees*.

they do this because they thought that the bodies themselves were important. Sometimes they did it to increase their own chance of redemption, and sometimes because they thought that the leper they loved was Jesus. Whatever one thinks of these motives, they were hardly likely to help to forge a notion of dignity that is useful in twenty-first-century wards. Authentically incarnational Christianity, interested in lepers' bodies because bodies themselves are theologically important, is more promising. Unfortunately the promise remains latent. Augustine's dead hand has strangled most well-meaning Christian attempts to persuade dignity to get its hands medically dirty.

The Middle Ages and the Renaissance

Mediaeval and Renaissance scholars, soused in the notion of the *Imago Dei* and continually, with shouts of 'Eureka', re-finding Greece and Rome, inserted a number of caveats (all of questionable significance), to Stoical understandings of dignity. The general trend is clear. The starting point is agreed. Man is different from the animals because (if you're in the Judaeo-Christian tradition), man is made in God's image, and animals are not. In what does the difference consist?

Initially, most scholars were content to *assert* the *Imago Dei,* rather than attempting to analyse its essence. In the light of the exegetical difficulties plaguing any would-be interpreter of Genesis 1, this caution is understandable. But the Church was not coy about identifying some of the *corollaries* of the *Imago Dei.*[39] Without an analysis of the essence, this was likely to lead to theological poverty and doctrinal petrification. And so it did. '*Imago Dei*' became, and to some still is, an unquestioned mantra justifying everything from human exploitation of the natural world to the expenditure of resources in maintaining patients in proven permanent vegetative state.

Natural law theorists such as Pufendorf saw dignity both as a consequence of man's possession of a 'soul', and as a characteristic of that soul. For him and others, man was above all other living beings because he possessed a soul that enabled him to recognise other people and other things as distinct from himself and from one another.[40] It was a crude identification of the soul with what we would now recognise as consciousness.

The relationship of reason and consciousness is mysterious and controversial, but from the early Middle Ages onwards there was a tendency to elide them. Aquinas had hinted at the essence of the divine-image-given human dignity, following the Stoics in identifying it with human reason. The Renaissance humanists enthusiastically agreed, and quickly took the next step—an equation

---

[39] For instance the right of decent burial, even of enemies: see Hugo Grotius, *De Jure Belli ac Pacis*, Book 2: ch19. Cited in McCrudden, 'Human Dignity and Judicial Interpretation of Human Rights' 658–59.

[40] See F Bohling (ed), S Pufendorf, *De Jure Naturae et GentiumLibriocto*, 1672, GesamelteWerke Vol 4, (Berlin 1998) 1, III, 1: 37, II: 1:5: 109.

of reason with autonomy, and therefore of dignity with autonomy. 'It is given to [man] to have that which he chooses, and to be that which he wills', wrote Pico della Mirandola in 1486, in his *On the Dignity of Man*.[41] The gift was the stamp of the divine: its status was dignity, its nature was reason, and its consequence was autonomy.

This is a pleasingly neat formulation. It pleased the Renaissance, it pleased Kant, and it continues to please many modern bioethicists. But neat formulations don't do well when confronted with the messiness of real humans.

More Footnotes on Stoicism: Kant and the Enlightenment

Many discussions of Kant's view of dignity proceed on the basis of a pastiche of his views. His writing is so difficult, at least to me, that it is unsurprising that most of us use executive summaries prepared by others.

The typical executive summary is based on a famous, and famously obscure, passage in the *Grundlegung—The Groundwork*. It has been so influential, and I am going to be so critical of it, that it must be quoted in full. Its ambition is vaulting: it is to discover 'the principle of morality':

> Looking back now on all previous attempts to discover the principle of morality, we need not wonder why they all failed. It was seen that man was bound to laws by duty, but it was not observed that the laws to which he is subject are only those of his own giving, though at the same time they are universal, and that he is only bound to act in conformity with his own will; a will, however, which is designed by nature to give universal laws. For when one has conceived man only as subject to a law (no matter what), then this law required some interest, either by way of attraction or constraint, since it did not originate as a law from his own will, but this will was according to a law obliged by something else to act in a certain manner. Now by this necessary consequence all the labour spent in finding a supreme principle of duty was irrevocably lost. For men never elicited duty, but only a necessity of acting from a certain interest. Whether this interest was private or otherwise, in any case the imperative must be conditional and could not by any means be capable of being a moral command. I will therefore call this the principle of autonomy of the will, in contrast with every other which I accordingly reckon as heteronomy.

> The conception of the will of every rational being as one which must consider itself as giving in all the maxims of its will universal laws, so as to judge itself and its actions from this point of view- this conception leads to another which depends on it and is very fruitful, namely that of a kingdom of ends.

> By a kingdom I understand the union of different rational beings in a system by common laws. Now since it is by laws that ends are determined as regards their universal validity, hence, if we abstract from the personal differences of rational beings and likewise from

---

[41] P della Mirandola, *On the Dignity of Man* (CG Wallis (tr) (Indianapolis, IN, Hackett Publishing, 1998). Cited in McCrudden, 'Human Dignity and Judicial Interpretation of Human Rights' 659. Della Mirandola saw the purpose of intellectual endeavour and the liberal arts as being the emulation of the 'dignity and glory' of the angels.

all the content of their private ends, we shall be able to conceive all ends combined in a systematic whole (including both rational beings as ends in themselves, and also the special ends which each may propose to himself), that is to say, we can conceive a kingdom of ends, which on the preceding principles is possible.

For all rational beings come under the law that each of them must treat itself and all others never merely as means, but in every case at the same time as ends in themselves. Hence results a systematic union of rational being by common objective laws, i.e., a kingdom which may be called a kingdom of ends, since what these laws have in view is just the relation of these beings to one another as ends and means. It is certainly only an ideal.

A rational being belongs as a member to the kingdom of ends when, although giving universal laws in it, he is also himself subject to these laws. He belongs to it as sovereign when, while giving laws, he is not subject to the will of any other.

A rational being must always regard himself as giving laws either as member or as sovereign in a kingdom of ends which is rendered possible by the freedom of will. He cannot, however, maintain the latter position merely by the maxims of his will, but only in case he is a completely independent being without wants and with unrestricted power adequate to his will.

Morality consists then in the reference of all action to the legislation which alone can render a kingdom of ends possible. This legislation must be capable of existing in every rational being and of emanating from his will, so that the principle of this will is never to act on any maxim which could not without contradiction be also a universal law and, accordingly, always so to act that the will could at the same time regard itself as giving in its maxims universal laws. If now the maxims of rational beings are not by their own nature coincident with this objective principle, then the necessity of acting on it is called practical necessitation, i.e., duty. Duty does not apply to the sovereign in the kingdom of ends, but it does to every member of it and to all in the same degree.

The practical necessity of acting on this principle, i.e., duty, does not rest at all on feelings, impulses, or inclinations, but solely on the relation of rational beings to one another, a relation in which the will of a rational being must always be regarded as legislative, since otherwise it could not be conceived as an end in itself. Reason then refers every maxim of the will, regarding it as legislating universally, to every other will and also to every action towards oneself; and this not on account of any other practical motive or any future advantage, but from the idea of the dignity of a rational being, obeying no law but that which he himself also gives.

In the kingdom of ends everything has either value or dignity. Whatever has a value can be replaced by something else which is equivalent; whatever, on the other hand, is above all value, and therefore admits of no equivalent, has a dignity.

Whatever has reference to the general inclinations and wants of mankind has a market value; whatever, without presupposing a want, corresponds to a certain taste, that is to a satisfaction in the mere purposeless play of our faculties, has a fancy value; but that which constitutes the condition under which alone anything can be an end in itself, this has not merely a relative worth, i.e., value, but an intrinsic worth, that is, dignity.

Now morality is the condition under which alone a rational being can be an end in himself, since by this alone is it possible that he should be a legislating member in the kingdom of ends. Thus morality, and humanity as capable of it, is that which alone has dignity. Skill and diligence in labour have a market value; wit, lively imagination, and humour, have fancy value; on the other hand, fidelity to promises, benevolence from principle (not from instinct), have an intrinsic worth. Neither nature nor art contains anything which in default of these it could put in their place, for their worth consists not in the effects which spring from them, not in the use and advantage which they secure, but in the disposition of mind, that is, the maxims of the will which are ready to manifest themselves in such actions, even though they should not have the desired effect. These actions also need no recommendation from any subjective taste or sentiment, that they may be looked on with immediate favour and satisfaction: they need no immediate propension or feeling for them; they exhibit the will that performs them as an object of an immediate respect, and nothing but reason is required to impose them on the will; not to flatter it into them, which, in the case of duties, would be a contradiction. This estimation therefore shows that the worth of such a disposition is dignity, and places it infinitely above all value, with which it cannot for a moment be brought into comparison or competition without as it were violating its sanctity.

What then is it which justifies virtue or the morally good disposition, in making such lofty claims? It is nothing less than the privilege it secures to the rational being of participating in the giving of universal laws, by which it qualifies him to be a member of a possible kingdom of ends, a privilege to which he was already destined by his own nature as being an end in himself and, on that account, legislating in the kingdom of ends; free as regards all laws of physical nature, and obeying those only which he himself gives, and by which his maxims can belong to a system of universal law, to which at the same time he submits himself. For nothing has any worth except what the law assigns it. Now the legislation itself which assigns the worth of everything must for that very reason possess dignity, that is an unconditional incomparable worth; and the word respect alone supplies a becoming expression for the esteem which a rational being must have for it. Autonomy then is the basis of the dignity of human and of every rational nature.[42]

Dietmar von der Pfordten, summarising these contentions, points out that dignity, here:

is not the ultimate reason for ethical obligation. The ultimate reason for ethical obligation rather lies in the capacity of the human being for self-legislation, in the 'fact of reason' or in the 'moral law within me'. Dignity as absolute 'inner worth' is an idealistic-analytic specification of this ultimate source of ethical obligation, namely, the idea of the legislating status of the human being in the Kingdom of Ends.[43]

Fourteen years later, though, in *The Doctrine of Virtue*, the second section of *The Metaphysics of Morals*, Kant says something that sounds rather different:

---

[42] This translation is by Thomas Kingsmill Abbott, available at www.gutenberg.org/cache/epub/5682/pg5682.html.

[43] D von der Pfordten, 'On the Dignity of Man in Kant'(2009) 84 *Philosophy* 371, 385. Citations are from M Gregor (tr and ed), I Kant, *Groundwork of the Metaphysics of Morals* (Cambridge, CUP, 1998).

Every human being has a legitimate claim to respect for his fellow human beings and is *in turn* bound to respect every other ... Humanity itself is a dignity; for a human being cannot be used merely as a means by any human being (either by others or even by himself), but must always be used at the same time as an end. It is just in this that his dignity (personality) consists, by which he raises himself above all other beings in the world that are not human beings and yet can be use, and so over all *things*.[44]

Are these two views divergent? Many have spent their careers saying so; others in saying not.[45] Unless one thinks of Kant's words in the way that Christian fundamentalists think of the Bible, it perhaps doesn't matter all that much. But if it is necessary to reconcile the passages, Oliver Sensen does the job. He notes that:

[Kant] conceives of dignity as sublimity (Erhabenheit) or the highest elevation of something over something else. 'Dignity' expresses that something is 'raised above' all else. What it is raised above, and in virtue of what, depends on the context in which Kant uses 'dignity'. For instance, he talks about the dignity of a monarch to refer to his rank as the ruler of his subjects. When Kant refers to the dignity of humanity, he expresses the view that human beings have a prerogative over the rest of nature in virtue of being free. What Kant is saying in the famous Grundlegung passage on dignity is that morality is raised above other determinations of will in that morality alone should be valued unconditionally.[46]

Where does this leave us? We're back to Stoicism.[47] In fact, throughout the Dark Ages, the Middle Ages, the Renaissance and the Enlightenment, we never really left it.

Kant is always cited whenever there is a discussion about dignity. He is interesting, and he is important. But he is really not very useful.[48] He seems to have

---

[44] M Gregor (tr and ed), I Kant, *The Metaphysics of Morals: Metaphysical First Principles of the Doctrine of Virtue* (Cambridge, CUP, 1996) 462: 1: 18.

[45] The issues are reviewed well and accessibly by Rachel Bayefsky in *The Concepts of Dignity and Honour in Kant* (2010), www.psa.ac.*United Kingdom*/spgrp/51/2010/Ppr/PGC2_BayefskyRachel_The %20Concepts%20of%20Dignity%20and%20Honour%20in%20Kant.pdf.

[46] O Sensen, 'Kant's Conception of Human Dignity' (2009) 100 *Kant-Studien* 309, 309.

[47] Sensen expressly argues that 'Kant's conception of dignity is a more Stoic one': Sensen, 'Kant's Conception of Human Dignity' 309.

[48] Suzy Killmister notes that: 'If the Kantian concept of dignity were to underpin bio-ethics, we would immediately encounter a significant problem: if dignity were inalienable, we would have nothing to fear from those acts that are sometimes said to threaten it. For example, it is often claimed that what is wrong with torture is that it strips the victim of her dignity. Similarly, it is often claimed that prolonging the life of a terminally ill patient in chronic pain and without control of her bodily functions strips her of her dignity. If the Kantian concept holds true, these claims must be false. As dignity is an inalienable property held by all rational creatures, being subject to such situations cannot strip an individual of her dignity. It thus provides little in the way of guidelines for action: at most, we could claim that the possession of dignity entitles its bearers to a certain standard of treatment—in Kantian terms, because of our dignity we must be treated as ends rather than means. Indeed, this is the approach taken by most human rights documents, whereby our dignity is held to be inviolable. Nonetheless, this approach leaves us with such a thin conception that its utility for medical practice is questionable'. In S Killmister, 'Dignity: Not Such a Useless Concept' (2010) 36 *Journal of Medical Ethics* 160, 162.

acknowledged this himself.[49] From our bioethical perspective there are four broad reasons why Kant is an academic curiosity rather than a *vade mecum* for the Emergency Room.

First, for Kant, having dignity involves being 'free', but freedom turns out to have a very restrictive meaning. It means acting in accordance with the 'Universal Law'—a code that, for Kant, was more or less co-extensive with Christian morality. If one truly possessed the reason which is the guarantor and hallmark of freedom and dignity, one's reason would ensure that one freely chose the Christian option. Any other choice would not be free, and accordingly there was nothing offensive— nothing freedom-truncating—about preventing the delinquent from making such a wrong, undignified, and inhuman choice. If one opted out of the human fold by choosing to make a choice that might be made by an animal that knew no better, one could hardly complain if one were treated like an animal. Suicide and extra-marital sexual intercourse were both beyond the Christian pale: suicide and forni-cation could both be penalised without interfering with any basic human dignity.

I have argued elsewhere that the ruling paradigm in medical law and ethics is still Kantian, and that we have merely got a new Universal law—a law that says that the only acceptable human behaviour is that which would be endorsed by an icily detached Millian autonomist; a drafter and dogmatic non-amender of a detailed life-plan.[50] But that's as maybe. The point for present purposes is simply that one's presumptions about what is ethically acceptable determine the nature of one's freedom and therefore the meaning of one's 'dignity'. If one is looking to dignity to determine what is ethically appropriate behaviour, one cannot at the same time allow a notion of ethically appropriate behaviour to determine the meaning of dignity. There is a dizzying circularity here, and there is no way out.

Second: if dignity is located only in rational autonomy, it cannot reach many of the important areas of bioethical discourse. It will have nothing to say, or will speak only haltingly, about infants and the mentally impaired, about human

---

[49] Von der Pfordten, 'On the Dignity of Man in Kant' 390–91, explains why Kant himself did not make much practical use of the idea of dignity. 'At the end, the question remains: Why does the con-cept of human dignity not appear at all in Kant's writings in legal and political philosophy? Otherwise put, why did Kant not attach any importance to human dignity within politics or law? This question can be answered in the following way: Politics and law are, according to Kant, necessarily restricted to external action, "external action" including all action beyond the immediate obligation by moral law. His legal and political philosophy rejects any form of obligation and coercion to morality. For Kant, the central category of law and politics rather is external freedom in the sense of the freedom to act, e.g. in his definition of the concept of law and the sole innate human right. The Dignity of Man in the sense of the absolute value of Self-Legislation and of the position in the Kingdom of Ends (the earlier understanding of the *Groundwork*), refers, just as the Dignity of Man in the sense of "End-in-Oneself-ness" (the later understanding of the *Doctrine of Virtue*), exclusively to the inner obligation by the moral law. This obligation only encompasses the core of the inner moral "acting" or obligation and is prior to all external freedom to act to which politics and law are restricted, according to Kant's liberal Enlightenment philosophy. This explains why neither of Kant's two ethical conceptions of the Dignity of Man could become significant for politics and law.' See further: M Meyer, 'Kant's concept of dignity and moral political thought' (1987) 8 *History of European Ideas* 319.

[50] See C Foster, *Choosing Life, Choosing Death: The Tyranny of Autonomy in Medical Ethics and Law* (Oxford, Hart, 2009).

enhancement or reproductive technological manipulation that does not affect cognitive function, and about the use of body parts. It will sit silently through much of any standard medical law course.

Third: a related point. Kant's analysis fails to take into account much of the evidence about ourselves that our instinct and our reason insist is likely to be pertinent. As Adam Schulman says: 'Kant denies any moral significance to other aspects of our humanity—including family life, loves, loyalties and other emotions—as well as the way we came into the world and all other merely biological facts about us.'[51] There are two important errors here. One is a general failure to consider all the evidence—preferring, irrationally, to rely only on one criterion only (a narrowly defined 'rationality'). The second is an essentially Gnostic error—a wholesale disregard of the body: a concentration on the supposedly 'higher' faculties while neglecting the bowels. Bodies are really quite important to people, and a system of bioethics that ignores them will be defective.

And fourth: Kantian anti-instrumentalism is simply too dogmatic. To be workable it has to be peppered with caveats. John Harris rightly observes that 'The Kantian principle, invoked without any qualification or gloss, is seldom helpful in medical or bioscientific contexts.'[52] He argues out that, applied strictly, it would outlaw blood transfusions, for instance. The donee normally neither knows nor cares about the donor, but uses the blood and the donor purely as a means to an end.

Since Kant, the idea of dignity has lain frozen in the icy matrix of his thought.[53] Only very recently have there been any signs of a thaw. The thaw is being caused by holism in medicine, political agitation by groups representing the incapacitated, and an increasingly fecund cross-fertilisation between medicine and philosophy.

The Popularisation of Dignity

After Kant, dignity joined the political mainstream. It was bound to be popular.[54] There were no votes or cheers in saying that dignity was unimportant. And so it became a slogan for the French Revolution and for those who carried its baton across the Atlantic; for those rallying against slavery; for the burgeoning Labour movements in many lands; for Communists and for anti-Communist Catholics.

---

[51] A Schulman, 'Bioethics and the Question of Human Dignity', in Pellegrino et al (eds), *Human Dignity and Bioethics* 12. But see too Susan Shell's defence of Kant. She thinks that the rigidity of his dualism and the inadequacy of his acknowledgment of the importance of the material have both been exaggerated, and that a more nuanced view of his thought allows him to be more helpful in bioethics than is often thought: in 'Kant's Concept of Human Dignity as a Resource for Bioethics', in Pellegrino et al (eds), *Human Dignity and Bioethics* 333 et seq.

[52] J Harris, 'Cloning and Human Dignity'(1998) 7 *Cambridge Quarterly of Healthcare Ethics* 163, 164.

[53] See C Dupre, 'Unlocking Human Dignity: Towards a Theory for the 21st Century' (2009) *European Human Rights Law Review* 190, 193–95.

[54] Its popularisation is discussed in detail by McCrudden, 'Human Dignity and Judicial Interpretation of Human Rights' 660–63.

But it was the Holocaust that secured dignity's place in the pantheon of ethical principles. The Nazi obscenities of World War II spawned many international declarations, many of which had 'dignity' at the core.

Popularity is not a friend of analysis. Nor, ultimately, is it a friend of reputation. Few stopped at the Paris barricades to think: 'Now what do we mean by the "dignities" for which we're fighting?' Thomas Paine, despite resting a whole political theory on the 'natural dignity of man', doesn't spend much time telling us what he means by that.[55] When Schiller wrote, gloriously, 'Give him food and shelter;/ When you have covered his nakedness, dignity will follow by itself', there was no definition clause.[56]

The association of dignity with Holocaust-inspired declarations and legislation was not likely to help clarify things, for whatever was meant by human dignity, it was certainly violated in Auschwitz and Sobibor. In the context of the declarations, this didn't matter: indeed dignity's potential breadth was undoubtedly an advantage. It was a highly appropriate place-holder; it covered a multitude of sins and described any human aspirations that might conceivably be regarded as good.[57]

But the promiscuous use of the word 'dignity' has led to a suspicion on the part of many that it is too vague to be useful—at least in a court or in a set of professional guidelines where substantive meaning is important. We look later at some of those suspicions, but I will conclude that while the suspicions are entirely appropriate, they should not lead to dignity being condemned as forensically useless.

Dignity Today: an Introduction

In the last half century, and increasingly, dignity has been discussed, reviled, praised, embodied into treaties and authoritative guidelines, and used, as it always was, as a counter in political gaming. Catherine Dupre comments that 'It is largely through bioethics that the concept of dignity emerged on the legal scene in the 1990s'.[58] So far as dignity in bioethics is concerned, Richard Ashcroft has identified four camps. Most modern scholars belong in one of them.[59]

First, there are those who say that talk about dignity is incoherent. This is the mainstream view in English-speaking bioethics. Second, there are those who accept that dignity-talk can be illuminating, but that essentially dignity amounts to autonomy. The high priests of this view are Brownsword and Beyleveld.[60] The third group are pluralists: they see dignity as just another tool in the bioethical toolbox. There are many concepts that deal with capabilities, functionings and

---

[55] T Paine, *Rights of Man: Part the First* (1791).

[56] Schiller, *Wurde des Menschen* (1798), cited in McCrudden, 'Human Dignity and Judicial Interpretation of Human Rights' 660.

[57] See D Luban, 'Human Dignity, Humiliation and Torture' (2009) 19 *Kennedy Institute of Ethics Journal* 211.

[58] Dupre, 'Unlocking Human Dignity', fn 36.

[59] R Ashcroft, 'Making Sense of Dignity'(2005) 31 *Journal of Medical Ethics* 679.

[60] D Beyleveld and R Brownsword, *Human Dignity in Bioethics and Biolaw* (Oxford, OUP, 2004).

social interactions. Dignity is one of them, and it is sometimes useful. Marmot[61] and Horton[62] are examples. And the final group are those who see dignity as a metaphysical property possessed by all human beings, and only by human beings. This, says Ashcroft, is the mainstream view in the still very Judaeo-Christian influenced world of European bioethics. Leon Kass, although an American, is the most prominent advocate of this view.[63]

While this system of classification is helpful, I do not adopt it in the chapters that follow. Instead I divide the scholarly world into two camps: those who think that dignity is useful, and those who think that it is not. In the 'useful' group I include the third and fourth classes in Ashcroft's taxonomy—the pluralists and the metaphysicians. Into the 'useless' group go the first two classes—the 'incoherent' group and the autonomists. The autonomists might resent their inclusion there. They will have their say in due course.

It may seem churlish, but I will be rejecting a good deal of the support offered to dignity by some of its supporters. I think that some seriously wrong turns have been taken, and that if dignity is to claim its rightful place at the bioethical coalface, we need to start more or less from scratch.

Before examining the stand-off between my two groups, it is worth considering the objection anticipated by Ashcroft. He says this:

> one methodological point is important. All of these [four] approaches take dignity to be a theoretical concept in that it plays a central role in moral theory and philosophical anthropology (the philosophical study of the nature of humanity and human agency). Even the dignity sceptics (the first group in my list above) mount their critique by attacking dignity based theories, rather than dignity as such. I am unaware of any radical critique of dignity that holds that the word itself is meaningless. Dignity sceptics want to tidy up the use of the word, and as far as possible 'reduce' it to some other moral or evaluative concept with better theoretical credentials... As well as using dignity in moral theories, all four groups offer theories of dignity (what it is or what it means). A major criticism of all four groups of theorists could be mounted on antitheoretical grounds. We could argue as follows. To understand the concept of dignity is nothing other than to understand the ways in which the word dignity is used in ordinary language, to study these usages carefully, and describe them clearly. The work of philosophy is then simply to disentangle verbal confusions involved in slipping between different, grammatically acceptable usages. It is quixotic to produce a theory of dignity, and equally so to try to dismiss it from the language, but it is not quixotic to try to grasp the linguistic usages of dignity in detail, and to try to gain some conceptual clarity in that way.[64]

Ashcroft identifies three broad types of response. First, he says, it is not at all clear that 'dignity' was ever part of ordinary language, as the anti-theorists claim, and even if it was, it could easily be exported beyond its workaday contexts to novel

---

[61] Eg M Marmot, 'Dignity and Inequality' (2004) 364 *Lancet* 1019.

[62] Eg R Horton, 'Rediscovering Human Dignity'(2004) 364 *Lancet* 1081.

[63] Kass's book *Life, Liberty and the Defense of Dignity* (San Francisco, CA, Encounter Books, 2002) is the *locus classicus*.

[64] Ibid 679–80.

situations.[65] Second, it can be credibly maintained that dignity is precisely a theoretical term, and accordingly demands and deserves the careful analysis due to a repercussive theory.[66] And third, it could be said that dignity is a 'thick' concept, combining both descriptive and evaluative meaning—both of which limbs have to be understood in order to understand the whole concept.[67]

I am sympathetic to each of these responses. They are not mutually exclusive. The first and the second are sufficiently convincing to make me think that the inquiry with which the rest of this book is concerned is not so obviously misconceived that it should be aborted. And as to the important question of whether dignity is a 'thick' concept—well, we shall have to wait and see.

We will turn soon to the contentions of the 'Dignity is useless' group. But first we need to say something about the various modern attempts to classify and define dignity.

---

[65] Ibid 680.
[66] Ibid 680.
[67] Ibid 680.

3

Defining and Dissecting Dignity

We will see in Chapter 4 that many have said that dignity is hopelessly nebulous. If that is so, it is certainly not because there have been no efforts to define it.

We have looked already at some historical understandings of the notion of dignity. Some of those will be revisited briefly here.

There are several taxonomic schemes,[1] but perhaps the nine most useful (which between them are representative of the various efforts that have been made) are those of David Feldman,[2] Doris Schroeder,[3] Suzy Killmister,[4] Andrew Clapham,[5] Nick Bostrom,[6] Luke Gormally[7] and Mette Lebech[8] (which I shall take together), Leon Kass,[9] and Deryck Beyleveld and Roger Brownsword.[10] Then there are the dogmatic non-definers. Ronald Dworkin can stand for them.

This chapter outlines the various schemes of classification. It serves as a short introduction to the views of some of those who contend that dignity is too vague to be useful, or that it is effectively reducible to autonomy (Dworkin, and Beyleveld and Brownsword respectively). Those views are not *evaluated* here. That is left to Chapter 4. The present chapter both outlines and evaluates the

---

[1] Others that I might have discussed include Matti Hayry's, in 'Another Look at Dignity' (2004) 13 *Cambridge Quarterly of Healthcare Ethics*, who identifies five meanings: the 'dignity of god' (p 222), the 'dignity of reason' (p 222), the 'dignity of genes' (p 223), the 'dignity of sentient beings' (p 224), and the 'dignity of important beings' (p 225).

[2] D Feldman, *Civil Liberties and Human Rights in England and Wales* (Oxford, OUP, 2002) 125–28.

[3] D Schroeder, 'Dignity: Two Riddles and Four Concepts' (2008) 17 *Cambridge Quarterly of Healthcare Ethics* 230.

[4] S Killmister, 'Dignity: Not Such a Useless Concept' (2010) 36 *Journal of Medical Ethics* 160.

[5] A Clapham, *Human Rights Obligations of Non-State Actors* (Oxford, OUP, 2006) 545–46, cited in C McCrudden, 'Human Dignity and Judicial Interpretation of Human Rights' (2008) *European Journal of International Law* 655, 686–87.

[6] N Bostrom, 'Dignity and Enhancement' in E Pellegrino, A Schulman and T Merrill (eds), *Human Dignity and Bioethics* (Notre Dame, IN, University of Notre Dame Press, 2009) 173 et seq.

[7] See, eg, L Gormally, 'Human Dignity and Respect for the Elderly', paper for II Jornadas Internacionales Bioetica, Granada, 25 September 1998, available at www.linacre.org/elderly.html.

[8] M Lebech, *On the Problem of Human Dignity. A Hermeneutical and Phenomenological Investigation* (Würzburg, Könighausen und Neumann, 2009).

[9] L Kass, 'Defending human dignity' in Pellegrino et al (eds), *Human Dignity and Bioethics* 297 et seq.

[10] D Beyleveld and R Brownsword, *Human Dignity in Bioethics and Biolaw* (Oxford, OUP, 2004).

views of dignity of those who think that dignity is useful (the other taxonomists mentioned). It begins with them.

Feldman

Feldman is a stratifier. He thinks that dignity operates on three levels: the dignity attaching to the whole human species; the dignity of groups within the species; and the dignity of human individuals.

To delineate the 'species' class you need rules that differentiate between humans and other species, and give special protection to the status of humans. When we deal with cloning we come to some expressions of this concern.

The second level, that of intra-specific groups, is characterised by rules that prohibit discrimination between groups on irrelevant grounds, and allows groups to pursue their own destiny.

At the third level, that of individuals, dignity demands the right to make one's own decisions and to contribute to decisions made by others that affect one's own life. Feldman notes, though, that 'we may be required to respect the dignity of people who lack freedom of choice' and comments, with commendable understatement, that 'Such cases present difficult questions about the relationship between dignity and autonomy, and between different kinds of dignity.'[11]

At the group and individual levels, Feldman comments, dignity has subjective and objective aspects. The subjective aspect 'is concerned with one's sense of self-worth, which is usually associated with forms of behaviour which communicate that sense to others',[12] whereas the objective aspect is about 'the state's and other people's attitudes to an individual or group, usually in the light of social norms or expectations. It is in this sense that people who lack the capacity to cultivate the subjective aspect of dignity can nonetheless be said to have a type of dignity which demands respect.'[13] He gives the example of very young people, and patients in PVS, who have 'intrinsic human dignity in this objective sense, in that responsible beings owe a moral, and often a legal, duty to have regard to their interests and rights when making decisions affecting their welfare.'[14]

Feldman acknowledges that this way of speaking about dignity implies a belief about human flourishing:

> A description of people as showing dignity relates to their behaviour and personalities in terms of social values which identity that sort of behaviour as good or worthwhile. In this way, ideas about descriptions of dignity are linked to beliefs about what is involved in living a good life, and to ideas of the Good more generally.[15]

---

[11] Feldman, *Civil Liberties and Human Rights* 126.
[12] Ibid 127.
[13] Ibid 127.
[14] Ibid 127.
[15] Ibid 127–28.

He believes, though, that such ideas are culturally specific, and accordingly that ideas of dignity will differ between cultures and societies.

He gently despairs of dignity as a problem-solver. For him it is a problem-setter: 'It seems ... that speaking of human dignity is a way of expressing a set of moral problems rather than a technique for resolving them (in hard cases at any rate).'[16]

Feldman's scheme is useful as a set of pigeonholes, but hardly as an analytic tool. To say that an undefined notion operates at various levels is not to propose a definition. His identification of 'group' dignity is presumably dependent in some way (that he does not identify) on individual dignity. His distinction between the subjective and objective meanings of individual and group dignity is the distinction that bedevils all serious discussion of dignity. It is not clear whether he contends that they are two sides of the same coin, and if so, how his argument to that effect would go. He seems to reject the most promising (and to my mind correct) argument—that based on how one lives a Good Life—in favour of despair.

Schroeder

Schroeder identifies four concepts of dignity. First, there is 'Kantian dignity', which we have examined already. But we are more interested now not in what Kant actually said, but in what he is taken to have said. Schroeder's gloss is fairly typical. She reads him as saying: 'Dignity is an inviolable property of all human beings, which gives the possessor the right never to be treated simply as a means, but always at the same time as an end.'[17]

Schroeder's second category is 'Aristocratic dignity'. This idea derives from the common use of the Latin term 'dignitas' in ancient societies, where it indicated that its possessor had a rank or quality that set them apart from the hoi polloi. Dignity, then, was necessarily something possessed by few. Schroeder's summary of this idea is: 'Dignity is the outwardly displayed quality of a human being who acts in accordance with her superior rank and position.'[18]

Third is 'comportment dignity', which connects dignity to outward displays. Dignity, here, is 'the outwardly displayed quality of a human being who acts in accordance with society's expectations of well-mannered demeanor and bearing.'[19]

And finally comes 'meritorious dignity'. This is, broadly speaking, an Aristotelian idea, and dignity, so understood, consists in *deserving* honours, not in displaying them—in being honourable. A person who has dignity in this sense will possess the four cardinal virtues of temperance, courage, justice and wisdom, and will make the best of the circumstances in which he finds himself: his essentially

---

[16] Ibid 128.
[17] Schroeder, 'Dignity: Two Riddles and Four Concepts' 233.
[18] Ibid 233.
[19] Ibid 234.

virtuous nature will not give way to the vicissitudes of life. Schroeder summarises: 'Dignity is a virtue, which subsumes the four cardinal virtues and one's sense of self-worth.'[20]

Schroeder paints with a brush that will be too broad for many philosophical tastes, but her scheme has the virtue of simplicity and some historical perspective.

Schroeder is a classic pluralist. Her defence of dignity consists essentially of saying: 'There are four possible meanings of the word. One or other of them is bound to be helpful in answering your bioethical conundrum. Choose whichever is most helpful.' That approach does not help the reputation of dignity itself. In relation to the physician-assisted suicide debate, for instance, she observes that the embarrassment to dignity caused by both the pro-PAS and anti-PAS lobbies enlisting dignity on their side can be relieved by noting that the anti-PAS lobby mean intrinsic, inalienable dignity, and the pro-PAS lobby mean the meritorious and comportment concepts.[21] This is of course true, but it is a *problem* for those who want dignity to have a prominent place in the bioethical debate, not a solution.

Schroeder's own claim for her analysis is modest: 'I hope to have shown ... that dignity is more than respect for autonomy and that an analysis of dignity concepts has the potential to illuminate debates as long as one does not expect dignity to have only one, clearly delineated meaning'.[22]

Killmister

Killmister is altogether more ambitious. She sees dignity as playing two roles. First, it is 'a (near) universal capacity that grounds the value of human life', and, second, it is a vehicle for articulating which actions are required for that capacity to be realised.[23]

Killmister castigates Macklin[24] for her tunnel vision, saying that Macklin wrongly focuses on the first to the exclusion of the second, so, perhaps unsurprisingly, undervaluing the concept of dignity as a whole.

Killmister criticises Schroeder more gently, acknowledging that her identification of the four strands is useful, but contending that Schroder stops too soon, and fails to see the important relationships between them. Only if one appreciates

---

[20] Ibid 235.

[21] Because 'What one might have tried all one's life, to fit into society's standards of decent behaviour, one might not [absent PAS] be able to achieve in death. And to have this witnessed by others on whom one is dependent leads to one's perception of lost comportment dignity. At the same time, unbearable pain and extreme anxiety may undermine the cardinal virtue of wisdom and thereby the associated cardinal virtues of courage, justice and temperance.' Ibid 236.

[22] Ibid 236–37.

[23] Killmister, 'Dignity: Not Such a Useless Concept' 164.

[24] See R Macklin 'Dignity is a Useless Concept' (2003) 327 *British Medical Journal* 1419, referred to in chs 1 and 4.

those relationships, says Killmister, can one see that dignity is big enough and complex enough to deal with whatever bioethics throws at it.

Killmister purports to take up where Schroeder left off. It is possible, she says, to find 'an underlying common thread uniting the four concepts identified by Schroeder.'[25] To do this, she begins by simplifying Schroeder's scheme. She reduces the four key concepts to two. These are the 'universal Kantian sense', identified by Schroeder, and the 'aspirational sense'. She takes the aspirational sense

> to contain both comportment dignity and meritorious dignity ... Both the comportment and the meritorious concepts of dignity stand in opposition to the Kantian sense, in that they are states to which individuals aspire, rather than a status that they hold simply by virtue of being human. This means that aspirational dignity can be lost, or we can be stripped of it, either through our own actions, the actions of others, or the circumstances in which we find ourselves.[26]

This opposition between aspirational and universal 'dignity' is a slightly rephrased version of the classic stand-off between dignity as empowerment, on the one hand, and constraint on the other—a conflict to which we will return. Killmister cleverly seeks to bring them together:

> The two concepts of comportment and meritorious dignity can be brought into alliance through seeing comportment dignity less as an upholding of external standards and norms, and more as the upholding of one's own standards and norms. This understanding of comportment dignity is more closely in line with how the term is utilised in the discourse of medical ethics—for example, when advocates of euthanasia argue that one should be entitled to die with dignity, or when patients in overcrowded wards complain that their dignity is being violated. It is not merely an inability to conform to social norms that may be experienced in situations of medical dependency, but also an inability to realise one's values of, perhaps, self-reliance, grace, courage, or even basic personal hygiene. Situations that constrain the individual to act in ways they find abhorrent or demeaning will undermine that individual's ability to live according to their own standards.[27]

Thus for Killmister, aspirational dignity is the quality held by individuals who are living in accordance with their principles. She notes that this understanding chimes well with reports from the wards. Many of the outraged rapid responses to Macklin's paper (which essentially said that dignity had nothing to add to autonomy), were from medical practitioners who felt that autonomy failed signally to capture one of the important ideas for which dignity gave an eloquent language—that of shame and humiliation.[28] We will see in Chapter 6 that this is a prominent strand in patients' own thinking about dignity, and that the relevant shame and humiliation is usually associated with an inability to maintain personal standards.

---

[25] Ibid 161.
[26] Ibid 161.
[27] Ibid 161.
[28] Ibid 161.

But this is still hard to understand. How can dignity be both inalienable *and* aspirational? Only, she acknowledges, by seeing dignity as a *capacity*. Seen thus, the inalienability of dignity stems from the fact that 'the potential for principled action grounds at least in part the moral worth of all persons'.[29] This, as Killmister expressly acknowledges, is more or less pure Kant, and therefore more or less pure Macklinite autonomy.[30] The aspirational element comes, says Killmister, from the fact that the realisation of these principles can be thwarted. Sometimes it will be almost impossible for someone to act in accordance with their values. If you can lose something, the argument seems to go, that something must be real.

Kant is a dangerous bedfellow, and Killmister knows it.[31] So she leaps adroitly out of bed. That leap is the most novel piece of intellectual gymnastics in her thesis. She argues that one has to distinguish between capacity and ability. A capacity is a 'latent potential'. If one has an ability, one can act immediately. An infant has the capacity for language, but not yet the ability to speak. An injured athlete does not have a present ability to run, but in Killmister's terms he has the capacity to run, since he can recover.

Having defined capacity this way, Killmister can conclude:

> To see dignity as the capacity for principled action, therefore, is to recognise that there is a latent potential in all persons so to act. Even if events make an instance of virtue impossible—an individual does not have the ability to remain courageous under conditions of torture, for example, or to uphold their standards of personal hygiene in substandard hospital care—their capacity remains intact.[32]

Dignity, then, is 'the inherent capacity for upholding one's principles'.[33]

This is cunning, but ultimately unconvincing. The analogy of the injured athlete exposes the weakness. What if the athlete has severed his lumbar spinal cord? He will never compete again. He has neither ability nor potential. And many of the most troubling conundrums in medical ethics are analogous. Children born with profound birth asphyxia may never have the neural hardware necessary to hold, let alone uphold, any principles. Intractable incontinence, pain, or an unsympathetic palliative care nurse, may ablate capacity in the terms defined by Killmister.

---

[29] Ibid 162.

[30] Ibid 162.

[31] She puts the problem herself very neatly: 'If the Kantian concept of dignity were to underpin bioethics, we would immediately encounter a significant problem: if dignity were inalienable, we would have nothing to fear from those acts that are sometimes said to threaten it. For example, it is often claimed that what is wrong with torture is that it strips the victim of her dignity. Similarly, it is often claimed that prolonging the life of a terminally ill patient in chronic pain and without control of her bodily functions strips her of her dignity. If the Kantian concept holds true, these claims must be false. As dignity is an inalienable property held by all rational creatures, being subject to such situations cannot strip an individual of her dignity.' Ibid 162.

[32] Ibid 162.

[33] Ibid 162.

Clapham

Clapham is concerned with the *corollaries* of respect for dignity. He does not attempt to give dignity a substantive meaning. This can be criticised. How can one say what follows from a proposition unless one identifies the proposition? Nevertheless one can glean something of the substantive meaning assumed by the adopter of a particular corollary, and his scheme is useful because it permits that gleaning. It is also useful because it is a good example of the approach adopted by many dignity-respecters—including almost all would-be wielders of the idea of dignity in the international human rights arena. They tend to be pragmatists, content to say: 'Well, whatever dignity is, it must have such and such an effect, and we should be legislating and litigating as if it does.' I do not denounce that approach. It may well be that politically and/or practically it is the only approach that can work in that context. But in the bioethical context I suggest that it is necessary to give a more fine-grained description of dignity.

Clapham identifies at least four aspects of concern for human dignity. These are: (a) the prohibition of inhuman treatment, degradation and humiliation; (b) a guarantee of the possibility of individual choice and the conditions necessary for the exercise of autonomy; (c) an acknowledgement that groups and their culture may be essential for the protection of personal dignity, and accordingly that groups and culture themselves require protection; and (d) the creation and protection of the conditions necessary for individuals' essential needs to be met.

The substantive meanings implicit in each of these concerns are clear enough. We see the usual mixture of status and attribute/constraint and empowerment in (a) and (d); empowerment (whose claim is arguably but not explicitly justified by status, in (b)); and a nod in (d) to the relational context in which any meaning of dignity one chooses to adopt has to be expressed.

Bostrom

Perhaps a more workmanlike distinction (and certainly a distinction around which recent academic conflicts have crystallised), is Nick Bostrom's. There are two main ways in which dignity has been understood, he says.[34] First, it has been thought of as a *quality*. Typically it has been a kind of excellence. To possess dignity is to be worthy, noble or honourable. There is no reason in principle why non-humans cannot possess this quality of dignity, and in humans the quality can be fostered or cultivated. There is no philosophical need to identify the quality with moral virtue or excellence in general.[35]

---

[34] Citing L Nordenfelt, 'The Varieties of Dignity' (2004) 12 *Health Care Analysis* 69. Bostrom identifies too the possibility of considering dignity as social status, but appears to reject that category on the ground that it is not particularly interesting in a bioethical context: see Bostrom, 'Dignity and Enhancement' 176. I agree with him that it is not very interesting.

[35] Ibid 175.

And second, there is what Bostrom calls 'human dignity'. This is the ground upon which, say some philosophers, rests the full moral status of humans beings, and of course there is loud disagreement about in what human dignity consists. We have seen some of those disagreements in the discussion of the *Imago Dei*, and indeed suspicion that all 'dignity' in this sense is at bottom theological has caused some to dismiss this whole category—throwing out, I suggest, the ontological baby with the perceived or actual theological bath water.[36]

Bostrom's distinction is broadly, but only broadly, adopted by both Gormally and Kass. They need to explain themselves in detail.

Bostrom's own attitude to the deployment of dignity is strange, fascinating and illuminating. It may come as a surprise to many, but he is broadly friendly to dignity. We see the curious colour of that friendship when we deal with the specific issue of human enhancement technologies.

Gormally and Lebech

Although, as we have seen,[37] the Catholic Church has not spoken consistently about dignity, it is now possible to identify a modern Catholic position. It is characterised by Luke Gormally and Mette Lebech.

Gormally distinguishes between existential and ontological dignity. His argument for this distinction is worth quoting in full:

> It is true that the distinctive dignity and value of human lives are **manifested** in those specific exercises of developed rational abilities in which we achieve some share in such humanly significant goods as truth, beauty, justice, friendship, integrity and the love of God. But the necessary rational abilities are acquired in virtue of an underlying or radical capacity, **given with our nature as human beings**, for developing precisely such abilities. It should be clear, however, that the dynamic of this radical natural capacity is not directed to the acquisition of rational abilities in order for them to be exercised in just any fashion. Our abilities to know and choose are not properly exercised by, for example, believing falsehood or choosing to act unjustly. The nature in virtue of which we come to acquire rational abilities has its proper fulfilment, then, in exercises of rational abilities in which we recognise worth and dignity. But if it is characteristic of the nature of human beings to acquire abilities which are properly exercised in ways which are inherently valuable, then it is reasonable to hold that there is an inherent value or dignity in the nature we share in common, and seriously unreasonable to judge that the lives of some human beings lack inherent value because those human beings lack developed and presently exercisable abilities of understanding and choice.

---

[36] A good example is Patricia Churchland, in her chapter 'Human Dignity from a Neurophilosophical Perspective' in E Pellegrino, A Schulman and T Merrill (eds) *Human Dignity and Bioethics* (Notre Dame, IN, University of Notre Dame Press, 2009) 99–121—a contribution which, as Gilbert Meilaender points out ('Commentary on Churchland' in Pellegrino et al (eds) *Human Dignity and Bioethics*112 et seq), is not about dignity at all, but is a diatribe against religion. Another is R Macklin, 'Dignity is a Useless Concept' 1419.

[37] Ch 2.

There is a second way in which one can show the ideological character of the philosophical radical's understanding of human dignity, i.e. its character as rationalization made plausible by its consonance with pervasive cultural assumptions rather than by reason. The radical's claim is that autonomy creates value, in the sense that it is a person's preferences and choices which determine what it is for his life to have value.

The exercise of autonomy as the capacity for self-determination through choice cannot as such determine what is valuable. It is clear that our preferences and choices can be self-destructive—can leave us viciously addicted, for example, or disposed to lies, hatred, or sexual perversions. If our choices are valuable they are **derivatively** valuable, because in our choosing we have been open to and respectful of an order of human goods: truth, friendship, marriage, justice, the love of God, and so on. We live our lives with dignity—with what one might call an **existential dignity**—in so far as our choices are consistent with an objective order of values. But part of this objective order of values is the prior ineradicable dignity which belongs to our nature—what we might call our **ontological dignity**.[38] (Original emphasis.)

If one is proposing dignity as the sole candidate for the post of bioethical governing principle (as I take Gormally to be doing, since he locates dignity in the *Imago Dei*—the most fundamental of all conceivable statements about human beings), it will not do to elide the very elements between which he is so careful to distinguish—ontological and existential dignity—saying that the second is simply a corollary of the first. Yet elide he does. And must, if he is to present dignity as a unified, universally applicable whole. As we observed when looking at Suzy Killmister's thesis, such a view founders when faced with (for instance) the congenitally incapacitated child. Such a child, on Gormally's view, can have no existential dignity at all. The old war between dignity as constraint and dignity as empowerment remains unresolved by his analysis. Only a definition of dignity that brings those two to terms can be taken seriously.

Mette Lebech provides a prolonged, highly sophisticated, yet traditional account of dignity, which she sees as the principle that humans have fundamental value entitling them to respect. Inspired by the *Imago Dei*, her apologetic is principally phenomenological. Dignity can function as a basis for law and ethics, she contends, 'because the value is indispensable to our experiences as human beings.'[39] Unlike many Catholic commentators, she expressly and resonantly acknowledges how important it is to see humans as embodied creatures:[40] she eschews the pathologically fastidious Gnostic Augustinianism that has often emasculated Catholic bioethics.

Lebech argues that there are three broad reasons why it is rational (in the sense endorsed by Habermas[41]) to affirm human dignity. First, it 'belongs to the essence of human dignity that it is a fundamental value, higher than other values and accounting for them by founding them. Such value is indispensable for any value to be experienced, and as we do experience value, it is rational to affirm human

---

[38] Gormally, 'Human Dignity and Respect for the Elderly'.
[39] M Lebech, *On the Problem of Human Dignity. A Hermeneutical and Phenomenological Investigation* (Würzburg, Könighausen und Neumann, 2009) 18.
[40] Ibid 282–83.
[41] See the discussion in ch 9 below.

dignity.[42] Surely, though, the fact that we experience value tells us nothing about its roots? It doesn't make Lebech's first statement (that dignity is higher than, and grounds, other values) any less bald an assertion.

Second: valuing dignity above other values facilitates reciprocity, thus enabling community: 'As [dignity] is valued equally in my own pole of human experience it institutes a sense of justice without which prolonged communication becomes impossible. The valuing of human dignity hence provides a factor of social integration that enables a society to function well, and to last'.[43] All true enough; but even wholly misconceived ideas, if generally believed, can act as social adhesives, causing societies to work efficiently together.

And third, 'Valuing human dignity above other values finally recognises it to be among the most resourceful of values, one that can motivate when all else fails. It structures the personality so that self-esteem relies securely on what is essential to the person (his or her humanity), thus confirming the value of the individual person, while favouring community'.[44]

I have difficulty understanding some of this. I cannot see, for instance, why one has to value human dignity above all values to see that it is resourceful. While I agree that its capacity to motivate when all else fails may be a reason to rate it above other values, that is not a necessary consequence of that capacity.

Overall, Lebech's work recruits phenomenology to prop up the corollaries of the *Imago Dei*. If you think that the *Imago Dei* is helpful, you will approve. If you do not, you will comment that pressed men seldom do a good job.

For obvious reasons, the *Imago Dei* is unfashionable in modern philosophical discourse. But it may have more to teach us about dignity than is popularly presumed. It does, after all, force one to confront more squarely than many other paradigms the question: 'What is human?' That it is not usually thought of as much of a guide to that question may be a consequence of its shallow treatment in the hands of its proponents.

In its analysis of the notion, the Church has often been blinded by some of the splendid things said about man in the Judaeo-Christian scriptures. 'What are human beings that you are mindful of them? Mortals that you care for them?', asks Psalm 8. '[Y]ou have made them a little lower than God, and crowned them with glory and honour. You have given them dominion over the works of your hands; you have put all things under their feet'.[45] It is a dazzling reply, and it has dazzled. It has often caused commentators to fail to see that the *Imago Dei* might illuminate the geriatric ward as well as the sports stadium or the Nobel Prize podium. Winifred Wing Han Lamb comments:

> These texts seem to assume adults in the prime of their lives, confident masters and mistresses of their domain. Being in the image of God and having dominion are associ-

[42] Ibid 288.
[43] Ibid 289.
[44] Ibid 289.
[45] Psalm 8:4–7, New Revised Standard Version.

ated with glory, honour and power. But what of the person who has lost dominion over his or her own body, let alone the power to care for the earth and all that is in it? Where is the glory and honour in one who is wheelchair-bound, who has nothing under their feet except a pair of old slippers? To include the frail aged in the notion of the image of God is to re-think glory, honour and power, as well as the way in which the image is applied to humanity.[46]

If the *Imago Dei* is to make a serious bid to re-enter bioethical discourse, glory, honour and power need to be re-thought. Doris Schroeder, writing in the context of assisted dying, hints dramatically at a way in which it might be rethought. She cites Mathewes-Green:

> We want our deaths to be free from pain, mess, embarrassment. But there is a long Christian tradition of 'holy death', that is, of allowing even a hard death to be a witness to God's grace. We're nowhere invited to bring down the curtain early to preserve our pride. How dignified did Jesus look on the way to the cross? Spattered with blood and spit, despised and rejected, he carried his own instrument of torture up a hill. Was this a death with dignity? Ironically, it was.[47]

Kass

A more convincing attempt at making peace between 'constraint' and 'empowerment' comes from Leon Kass. He distinguishes between the '*basic* dignity of human *being*', and the '*full* dignity of being (actively) human—of human *flourishing*.'[48] (Original emphasis.)

'Basic dignity' is commonly relied upon by religious commentators. Even when it is not in their hands, it often smells theological. Whatever its roots in any particular case, its proponents all share a *conviction* that it is morally wrong to say that any human being lives a more worthy life than any other, and purport to derive this conviction from the *fact* that each human being, good or bad, black or white, Jew or Gentile, possesses and enjoys human dignity in this sense simply because they are human.

The conviction is undoubtedly right. Any political or legal system that does not share it is obscene. Even if there is no reason to ground the conviction in dignity, we should certainly live, love, legislate and litigate on the basis of the conviction.

But what about the alleged 'fact'? Dignity cannot be demonstrated under a microscope or at a post mortem. It is elusive. Such quintessential human experiences as vulnerability, suffering and death are not in themselves particularly dignified, suggests Kass,[49] who then goes on to suggest that a 'deeper ground for equal

---

[46] W Wing Han Lamb and H Thomson H (2002), 'Wholeness, Dignity and the Aging Self: A Conversation between Philosophy and Theology' (2002) 12 *Journal of Religious Gerontology* 57, 59.

[47] F Matthewes-Green, 'Dignity, Always Dignity', *World Magazine*, 18 February 1995, cited in Schroeder, 'Dignity: Two Riddles and Four Concepts' 231.

[48] Kass, 'Defending Human Dignity' 299.

[49] Ibid 318.

human dignity may arguably be found in our equal membership of the human species.'[50] He then sidesteps the *Imago Dei*, acknowledging how tongue-tied the non-religious necessarily become if pressed to say just what it is about our membership of our species that justifies a special 'species pride', or a claim to inviolability of life and being. Unless you take your ontological bearings from the book of Genesis, it is hard to say coherently why I may kill and eat a Blue Whale, but not inject a terminally ill cancer patient with a heart-stopping dose of potassium chloride. Hard, Kass thinks, but not impossible. He assumes that humans do have a special status (and many of his critics depart from him there), and concludes that that status must turn on 'our special capacities and powers that, amongst the creatures, are ours and ours alone'.[51] He observes that, if one adopts such an analysis, one must return to examine the questions—some of the most pressing in medical ethics, of course—about humans who have lost or have never had the 'special capacities and powers'. And indeed he does return to them, but not, to my eye, convincingly.

In the marketplace of bioethical ideas, Kass's 'basic dignity' and 'full dignity' often seem to be competitors. Vitalists (who are typically Catholic), and the disability rights lobby, are in a curious coalition. They rest their contentions on the basic dignity of the human being. For them, the fact that a particular human lacks a particular faculty is neither here nor there. It does not impinge on her dignity, her worth, or her value in society. To note the lack is impermissible because it is to note an irrelevance.

It is difficult for these lobbyists consistently to acknowledge that anything akin to Kass's 'full dignity' is legitimately in play in any bioethical debate. For them, if you have basic dignity, you have everything that a human being can expect, and what you have is glorious, and don't you forget it. The polemical terms in which the contentions are often framed does not help analysis. The child with Down's syndrome says to Kass: 'Do you say I'm not flourishing? If you do, surely you're saying that there's an important sense in which I'm less human than you?'

Kass hears the objection, and is unfazed by it. The first part of his answer is a gentle retort, along the lines of: 'Do you seriously say that an inability to do things is as good as being able to do them? Does a cripple really not wish that he could walk?' The answers, to most minds, must be no. And so Kass moves on to look at the real relationship between 'basic' and 'full' dignity. This analysis is his most vaulting contribution to the dignity debate. Instead of being competitors, or being entirely unrelated concepts, he sees 'basic' and 'full' dignity as being crucially interdependent.

> The flourishing of human possibility [represented by 'full dignity'] depends absolutely on active human vitality [represented by 'basic dignity']—ie on the good and worth of life as such. The basic dignity of human being (sometimes expressed as the sanctity of

---

[50] Ibid 319.
[51] Ibid 320.

life or the respect owed to human life) in fact depends on the higher dignity of being human.[52]

Kass derives this conclusion (or perhaps only illustrates it—it is not completely clear which) from the insights in Genesis 1. This is not necessarily to say that he has smuggled back in the *Imago Dei*, although, as we will see, he resorts to its language. He would say that the Genesis text encapsulates truths about the nature of what it means to be human that are valuable whether or not one subscribes to the theological background against which the text is usually read.

Kass notes the respects in which man is said (being made in God's image) to be God-like. Amongst those divine characteristics are (a) being able to distinguish between good and evil, and (b) having speech and freedom.

What does man do with this pair of characteristics? If he lives life as he should, the architecture of his life is determined by the distinction between good and evil, and he will, as God in the Judaeo-Christian tradition does, promulgate and abide by moral rules that reflect the distinction.

Then comes Kass's crucial step. The primary moral rule made by God, and to be emulated and enacted by men, is that homicide is wrong. Thus, says Kass, 'the inviolability of human life rests absolutely on the higher dignity—the god-like-ness of human beings.'[53] Because we are embodied creatures, respecting human bodies is a necessary consequence of respecting every other bit of humanness. And vice versa.

> Respect for anything human requires respecting everything human—requires respecting human beings *as such*. The wanton spilling of human blood is a violation and a desecration, not only of our laws and wills, but of being itself. Thus there is, in the end, no opposition between the dignity of human being (or the sanctity of life) and the dignity of being human.[54]

Humans, for Kass, are metaphysical amphibians, existing simultaneously in at least two worlds. And this has some important consequences.

> Human aspiration depends absolutely on our being creatures of need and finitude, and hence of longings and attachments. Pure reason and pure mind have no aspiration; the rational animal aspires in large part because he is an animal.

> This discovery gives rise to what might seem to be a paradox: human dignity is ours in part because of our 'animality', because we are not incorporeal minds, angels or gods. Indeed, once again it is our in-between status, at once god-like and animal—that is the deep truth about our nature, the ground of our special standing, and the wherewithal of our flourishing. Yet, at the same time, human dignity is not on all fours with the dignity of the other animals, even if it is linked to theirs and belongs to us only because we, like they, are embodied creatures.[55]

[52] Ibid 321.
[53] Ibid 325.
[54] Ibid 325–26.
[55] Ibid 326–27.

Lawler makes the same point, but focusing importantly and enlighteningly on the transience of our embodiment:

> We grasp our true dignity—the dignity of our minds—only by seeing that the mind necessarily depends on a body that exists for a moment nowhere in particular and then is gone. So my being at home as a mind depends on my radical homelessness or insignificance as a whole, embodied being. Any being that is genuinely eternal—such as a star—couldn't possibly know anything at all.[56]

For me, Kass hints seductively at the way that a reconciliation between his notions of basic and full dignity must be brokered, but although he purports to demonstrate that they are really two sides of the same coin, he does not convince. If we strip away his powerful metaphors, and chip off the theology, what is left that can be used in the bioethical front line? Simply the observation that what we do to our bodies affects every other part of us—including what, if it pleases you, you might choose to call your soul. But we can surely derive that from observing that if we miss lunch, we will be grumpy in the afternoon, and that our attitude to the present is coloured by our knowledge that we are poised always on the brink of oblivion. To delineate the relationship between two concepts is not to identify either one of them, to establish the usefulness of either of them, to demonstrate necessarily their dependence on one another, or to call a halt to a war between them. And so, while my instinctual sympathies lie with Kass, he doesn't help me much.

Beyleveld and Brownsword

Beyleveld and Brownsword see three main meanings of 'dignity' in bioethics.[57] First, it is a vehicle for and an expression of empowerment, and so is prominent in the promulgation of the notion of informed consent. Informed consent is essentially a positive doctrine. Dignity, as a positive attribute of the person, allows a person to choose her own destiny. Beyleveld and Brownsword note that those who use dignity in this sense are often unclear about just *why* humans should be thought to have this dignity. As Beyleveld and Brownsword understand the notion, it is hard to see how it differs in nature from autonomy.

Second, dignity acts as a form of constraint. The most obvious example is, again, informed consent. But this time, it is informed consent expressed negatively. One should not do something to a person unless she autonomously permits you to do it. To act without her consent is an affront to her dignity. Although dignity so understood is plainly in tension with dignity as empowerment[58] (since the

---

[56] P Lawler (2009), 'Modern and American Dignity' in Pellegrino et al (eds), *Human Dignity and Bioethics* 231. Stars, of course, aren't eternal, but his point is clear.

[57] Beyleveld and Brownsword, *Human Dignity in Bioethics and Biolaw*.

[58] See the comment on this by Kass in Pellegrino et al (eds), *Human Dignity and Bioethics* 273–74. See too S Wheatley, 'Human Rights and Human Dignity in the Resolution of Certain Ethical Questions in Biomedicine'(2001) 3 *European Human Rights Law Review* 312, where he suggests that for any

relevant constraints are on the use of autonomy rights), tension is not necessarily fundamental contradiction.

Third, observe Beyleveld and Brownsword, dignity can describe conduct deemed to be dignified. This begs a blindingly obvious question.

We return to Beyleveld and Brownsword in more detail in Chapter 4.

Ronald Dworkin

Dworkin is happy to say in broad terms what he means by dignity: it is 'respecting the inherent value of our own lives.'[59] But he is not prepared to be more explicit. Given the tentativeness of his formulation the tentativeness of his defence is understandable. In fact he offers no defence of the substance at all. He 'does not want to defend or elaborate these ideas [the notions of equality and dignity], but only to insist that anyone who claims that citizens have rights must accept ideas *very close* to these.'[60] This is music to the ear of the cynics, some of whom we meet shortly.[61] There are, of course, many who claim that citizens have no rights, and even those who do may say that rights do not rest on dignity, however it is defined. Also, more formally: to accept X, where X is a corollary of Y, is not an argument for Y having any particular nature.

Although there is a respectable place for vagueness about the meaning of dignity, it is not here, at the level of definition. Here it is an admission of defeat. But one can well understand the draftsman of an international declaration using dignity as a placeholder, saying to himself: 'There is not yet sufficient consensus about the meaning of dignity for me to put a definition clause at the end of this document. But no other word will convey sufficiently the high aspiration that needs to be embodied in the declaration. Whatever dignity is ultimately held to mean, it will encapsulate the sense that I want.'

---

limitations on individual self-determination to be justified, the limitations must be based in the protection of human dignity.

[59] R Dworkin, *Taking Rights Seriously* (Cambridge, MA, Harvard University Press, 1977) 238.

[60] Ibid 199.

[61] See particularly M Bagaric and J Allan, 'The vacuous concept of dignity'(2006) 5 *Journal of Human Rights* 257, discussed in ch4 below. They seize particularly eagerly on this statement from Dworkin.

4

'Dignity is Useless'

Opponents of the deployment of dignity in bioethics fall into two overlapping camps. First there is the 'dignity is nice but hopeless', brigade. They think that dignity is well-meaning but terminally vague, and lends itself too wantonly to slogan. They rarely have a bad word to say about dignity itself. Indeed part of their criticism is that dignity is too alluring for its own good, intoxicating its disciples and making them abandon their critical faculties. Their ire is usually spared for those disciples, and about them they can be very rude indeed.

And then there are those who discriminate against dignity because of its actual or presumed origins. Religion-haters will often take it out on dignity because they think that it is a creature of the church.

We will look briefly at each of these camps.

'Dignity is too Amorphous to be Useful'

'Appeals to human dignity populate the landscape of medical ethics', rightly observes Ruth Macklin:

Claims that some feature of medical research or practice violates or threatens human dignity abound, often in connection with developments in genetics or reproductive technology. But are such claims coherent? Is dignity a useful concept for an ethical analysis of medical activities? A close inspection of leading examples shows that appeals to dignity are either vague restatements of other, more precise, notions, or mere slogans that add nothing to an understanding of the topic.[1]

She is in august company; but the allegation of sloganism is often met by slogan. Three examples make the point. In Schopenhauer's 1837 broadside against Kant, he thundered that the whole notion of dignity was vacuous:

This expression 'Human Dignity', once it was uttered by Kant, became the shibboleth of all perplexed and empty-headed moralists. For behind that imposing formula they concealed their lack, not to say, of a real ethical basis, but of any basis at all which was possessed of an intelligible meaning; supposing cleverly enough that their readers would

---

[1] R Macklin, 'Dignity is a Useless Concept' (2003) 327 *British Medical Journal* 1419.

be so pleased to see themselves invested with such a 'dignity' that they would be quite satisfied.[2]

And a 1983 US Presidential Commission agreed: 'Phrases like ... "death with dignity" ...have been used in such conflicting ways that their meanings, if they ever were clear, have become hopelessly blurred.'[3] For Peter Singer, as for many, dignity is an alternative to proper analysis: 'Philosophers frequently introduce ideas of dignity, respect, and worth at the point at which reasons appear to be lacking, but this is hardly good enough. Fine phrases are the last resort of those who have run out of arguments.'[4] John Harris believes that 'Appeals to human dignity are, of course, universally attractive; they are also comprehensively vague.'[5]

Although cursory dismissiveness is the more common manifestation of scholarly cynicism about dignity, some scholars have worked hard to justify their cynicism. Bagaric and Allan are the best examples.[6] Their position is fairly traditional:

> We argue that the concept of dignity is itself vacuous. As a legal or philosophical concept it is without bounds and ultimately is one incapable of explaining or justifying any narrower interests; it cannot do the work non-consequentialist rights adherents demand of it. Instead, it is a notion that is used by academics, judges, and legislators when rational justifications have been exhausted.[7]

Having sketched the history of the concept of dignity and surveyed some of the efforts that have been made to say what dignity means, they observe that there is still a good deal of disagreement about its nature and philosophical origins. They acknowledge that 'Lack of convergence regarding the meaning of, and foundations for, a normative concept is not a knock down argument against the existence of the concept, of course. It might simply indicate, for example, that we are still working toward establishing some widely accepted meaning.' Quite right. They go on, however, to say that 'the diversity in the range of meanings that can credibly be assigned to the concept of dignity at least raises a presumption that something is amiss. Meanwhile, amid all this indeterminacy, the concept of dignity is being asked by many to carry an ever more onerous burden.'[8]

All this is fair. The burden of proving the usefulness of dignity must rest on the shoulders of those who assert that it is useful.

---

[2] AB Bullock (tr and intro), A Schopenhauer, *The Basis of Morality* (London, S Sonnenschein, 1903) Pt II, Critique of Kant's Basis of Ethics. Cited in C McCrudden, 'Human Dignity and Judicial Interpretation of Human Rights' (2008) 194 *European Journal of International Law* 655, 661.

[3] President's Commission for the Study of Ethical Problems in Medicine and Biomedical and Behavioral Research, *Deciding to Forego Life-sustaining Treatment* (Washington DC, US Government Printing Office, 1983) 24, cited in Macklin, 'Dignity is a Useless Concept' 1419.

[4] P Singer, *Applied Ethics* (Oxford, OUP, 1986)228.

[5] J Harris, 'Cloning and Human Dignity' (1998) 7 *Cambridge Quarterly of Healthcare Ethics* 163.

[6] M Bagaric and J Allan, 'The Vacuous Concept of Dignity' (2006) 5 *Journal of Human Rights* 257.

[7] Ibid 260.

[8] Ibid 265.

One of the main grounds of Bagaric and Allan's scepticism is that dignity can, as we have noted, be used on both sides of the same argument—both as a restraining and an empowering concept. A house so divided, they say, must fall philosophically:

> What is clear, at least to us, is that the concept of human dignity is easily able to be used as some sort of empowering notion, one that confers rights and entitlements and protects interests. Here is the world of Dworkin and Beyleveld and Brownsword. Yet the same concept of dignity is equally easily able to be used as a sort of constraint on action, in the Kantian and Linacre Centre sense. Worse, nothing within the concept of dignity itself provides any obvious criteria for adjudicating between these two conceptions even though they lead to polar opposite results. The dispute appears insoluble because of the amorphous nature of the concept being used to try to resolve it. Hence, it is tempting to agree that 'an argumentative device capable of justifying anything is capable of justifying nothing'.[9]

Despairing of making sense of any idea that can be pressed into such mercenary service, and complaining that dignity cannot be 'demonstrated',[10] Bagaric and Allan throw up their hands: 'Against such a background, the victor in any debate involving dignity may simply be the side that yells the loudest or uses the most skilled polemicists.'[11]

Bagaric and Allan are unusual in attempting a serious analytic challenge. Macklin's strategy is typical. She follows the usual template in citing a number of examples in support of her thesis that dignity has been deployed inconsistently and vaguely.[12] And then comes the peroration. She congratulates the Nuffield Council on Bioethics for attempting, in its report *Genetics, Freedom and Human Dignity*, to indicate more precisely than other users of the concept just what they mean by 'dignity'. That report says that the sense of responsibility is 'an essential ingredient in the conception of human dignity, in the presumption that one is a person whose actions, thoughts and concerns are worthy of intrinsic respect, because they have been chosen, organised and guided in a way which makes sense from a distinctively individual point of view.'[13] What does this amount to?, she asks. Nothing more than 'a capacity for rational thought and action, the central features conveyed in the principle of respect for autonomy.'[14] She has an interesting further comment, however, which is contained both in her subtitle '[Dignity] means no more than respect *for persons* or their autonomy',[15] and in the substance of the text: 'Why, then, do so many articles and reports appeal to human dignity, as if it means something over and above respect *for persons* or for their autonomy'[16] (added emphasis).

---

[9] Ibid 265.

[10] Ibid 265–66.

[11] Ibid 267.

[12] Macklin, 'Dignity is a Useless Concept' 1419–20.

[13] Nuffield Council on Bioethics, Genetics and Human Behaviour, www.nuffieldbioethics.org/publications/pp_0000000015.asp, cited in Macklin, 'Dignity is a Useless Concept' 1420.

[14] Macklin, 'Dignity is a Useless Concept' 1420.

[15] Ibid 1419.

[16] Ibid 1420.

We come in a moment to look at those who think that dignity boils down to autonomy, but the point for the moment is not what Macklin thinks various dignity-formulas amount to, but that she, along with others in her camp, thinks that all contenders for a definition of dignity are reducible to something else; something less exotic; something more familiar. Her contention, then, is precisely the opposite of mine. I contend that if you dig deep enough through the other principles, you eventually hit dignity. She sees those other principles as lower denominators of dignity.

Yet implicit in her invocation of 'respect for persons' is an acknowledgment, which she disavows, of a deeper principle at work. Her analysis does not go to the root of things. Why should one have any respect for persons at all? Or, for that matter, respect for their autonomy? To give an account of that respect one has to go to a level below the respect itself, and whatever that level is, it is at the metaphysical altitude of dignity.

What follows from Macklin's diagnosis? She is in no doubt: 'Dignity is a useless concept in medical ethics and can be eliminated without any loss of content.'[17]

How fair are the substantive criticisms? Several points can be made.

All the criticisms are either of the vague way that dignity has been *used*, or of one particular definition. So far as I can see, none bites on the definition I suggest. In many of the criticisms there is more than an element of shooting the messenger. The criticism that dignity can be and has been recruited on two sides of an argument sounds like a fundamental objection, but again is a criticism of the manner of use and/or of a definition. But even if it were an objection to the correct definition of dignity, it would scarcely be a killer point. The critics are demanding much more of dignity than they demand of any other concept. Sonja Grover rightly observes:

> In this regard, the concept of 'human dignity' can be analogised to the notion of 'justice'. We would not disavow the notion of justice because two courts reached different conclusions on the same case. Each individual court may have its own particular interpretation of the facts and the law, leading to different conclusions of what constitutes justice on the fact pattern of the case as that court constructed it in its final judgment. There is no absolute way to determine which of the two lower courts or indeed whether the ultimate high court has it right.[18]

But if, after this observation, the tension between constraint and empowerment is troubling, Kass can broker some sort of peace.[19]

There is, then, a double standard at work. The other principles upon which the Macklin-ites rely are no more precise, and dictate answers to ethical problems with no more precision or predictability, than some models of dignity.[20]

---

[17] Ibid 1420.

[18] S Grover, 'A Response to Bagaric and Allan's "The Vacuous Concept of Dignity"'(2009) 13 *International Journal of Human Rights* 615, 619.

[19] See ch 3.

[20] See R Dresser, 'Human Dignity and the Seriously Ill Patient', in E Pellegrino, A Schulman and T Merrill (eds) *Human Dignity and Bioethics* (Notre Dame, IN, University of Notre Dame Press, 2009) 507. Jean McHale comments that 'Dignity is indeed a nebulous concept, but then so are many ethical

And, what's more, they tend to need help from other principles. Autonomy, unqualified by other principles, is the philosophy of the snivelling, selfish, atomistic brat. Beneficence needs other principles to tell it what the good is upon which it insists. And so on. Can one 'demonstrate' non-maleficence or justice in the sense that Bagaric and Allan demand that dignity is demonstrated before they will take dignity seriously? Of course not.[21]

Rebecca Dresser trenchantly observes that many common criticisms of dignity (and particularly Macklin's) are rather premature. One shouldn't criticise a child for not being an adult. Defining dignity is work in progress. It needs support, not bile. Its embryonic status is a reason to give it more support, not less.[22] Dresser seems rather over-defensive. If dignity claims a part in the bioethical debate (as it does), and still more if it claims the principal voice in the debate (as it does), it can hardly complain if it is treated the same as the others. But it can complain if it is discriminated against. And it often is, and sometimes on the grounds of its presumed religious origins.

'Dignity is Intrinsically Religious, and Hence Suspect'

For many, religion is a synonym for the utterly irrational, and accordingly if dignity has sprung from the loins of the Judaeo-Christian tradition, it can be dismissed without a further look.[23]

The Autonomists

Beyleveld and Brownsword have written one of the most influential books ever written on the notion of dignity in bioethics.[24] But, in common with some other commentators, I question whether it is really about dignity at all.[25]

---

principles with which healthcare lawyers engage': J McHale, 'Human Dignity in Bioethics and Biolaw' (2003) 119 *Law Quarterly Report* 343, 347.

[21] Sonja Grover suggests that dignity can be demonstrated. She says that 'human dignity is *demonstrated* in all wilful resistance to oppression; that resistance being an affirmation of one's human dignity as an individual and/or as part of a collective. Of course, individuals and populations can be misled as to who the real oppressor is, but, accurate perception or not, resistance is often at its very root born of the perceived need to preserve one's dignity. Thus, resistance to tyrants comes often from the meek and not just opposing powerful parties. It is to be emphasised also that while resistance can be an *expression or demonstration* of dignity, the lack of resistance, while frequently demoralising, does not in any way diminish one's humanity or the dignity associated with that humanity'. Grover, 'A Response to Bagaric and Allan's "The Vacuous Concept of Dignity"' 617. While sympathetic to these observations, I feel that she and Bagaric and Allan are probably at cross-purposes. I take Bagaric and Allan to mean that there can be no formal philosophical proof of the quality of dignity.

[22] Dresser, 'Human Dignity and the Seriously Ill Patient'.

[23] Eg P Churchland, 'Human Dignity from a Neurophilosophical Perspective' in Pellegrino et al (eds), *Human Dignity and Bioethics* 99–121.

[24] D Beyleveld and R Brownsword, *Human Dignity in Bioethics and Biolaw* (Oxford, OUP, 2004).

[25] Eg Isabel Karpin comments: 'it is not about human dignity so much as agency'. I Karpin, 'Human Dignity in Bioethics and Biolaw (Review)' (2004) *Medical Law Review* 323, 326.

I have already outlined the three meanings of dignity with which Beyleveld and Brownsword deal. Their argument is neatly summarised by Deirdre Dwyer: '(1) that we possess rights by virtue of our rationality, and must similarly respect the rights of other rational agents; (2) that human dignity is the basis of these agency rights; (3) that legal reasoning increasingly recognises this agency-derived concept of dignity; (4) that biolaw decisions are best informed by bioethical decisions made in this paradigm.'[26]

Rejecting membership of the species *Homo sapiens* as a good ground for a claim of dignity, they ground the claim on Alan Gewirth's neo-Kantian Principle of Generic Consistency (PGC). PGC, they assert, is 'the supreme principle of bioethics and biolaw (indeed all ethics and law) in so far as these are concerned with prescription.'[27] The PGC is an agency-facilitating concept. It deems as rights whatever is needed to ensure true agency. There is an important reciprocity: unless X accepts the PGC's proposition that all agents have generic rights enforceable against X, X himself will not be entitled to eat the fruits of the PGC: one cannot have rights (the corollary of the PGC), without signing up to the PGC. When one talks coherently about dignity, one is talking about the dignity not of a human, but of an agent.

Dignity, for Brownsword and Beyleveld, is the response of fearful, finite, creatures who look fearfully at the eventual certainty of their own extinction, but respond appropriately to that certainty. Our vulnerability is a precondition of our dignity. If we acknowledge our own vulnerability, and stare manfully at it with Kantian rationality, we are dignified.[28]

Their understanding of dignity, as one would expect from analysts who have imported *rights* into the discussion at such an early stage, is much more an empowerment than a constraint model.[29] They are right to highlight (as they do by quoting at length from David Feldman's famous paper) that dignity, read one way, can be tyrannous.[30] But why bring in dignity at all? It seems unnecessary. Their theory of rights, and all the ethical results they derive from their model, can be derived directly from the PGC. No interposing principle is needed.

---

[26] D Dwyer, 'Beyond Autonomy: The Role of Dignity in "Biolaw"' (2003) *Oxford Journal of Legal Studies* 319, 320.

[27] Beyleveld and Brownsword, *Human Dignity in Bioethics and Biolaw* 69.

[28] They say that 'being subject to existential anxiety is central to what constitutes possessing dignity as the basis for generic rights' (Ibid 134). Kant then helps them to the conclusion that 'Dignified conduct may be said to reflect a dignified character, which may be viewed as the personality to which reason requires human agents to aspire. With this in mind, we might view a dignified character simply as a personality disposed to respect the moral law. Relative to this, dignified conduct is action in accordance with the moral law performed out of commitment to obey the moral law' (Ibid 138). A corollary is that 'displaying fortitude in the face of adversity is to be considered virtuous in Gewirthian theory' (Ibid 141).

[29] They insist, though, that dignity is a precursor to rights, and that rights are dependent on their notion of dignity: Ibid 134.

[30] The relevant quote from Feldman is at p 14 above. It is cited in Beyleveld and Brownsword, *Human Dignity in Bioethics and Biolaw* 26.

They purport to import a hard-edged notion of dignity in order to answer the most obvious of indictments levelled against Kantians—that a philosophy based purely on rational agency cannot protect those beings who are biologically human but who are not rational and not capable of being Gewirthian agents. But their definition of dignity is so tainted with agency that, like all autonomy-based theories, it ultimately fails to provide a defence to, or even mitigate the offence of, the indictment.

If their model is the right one, one would expect it to deliver consistently satisfactory results throughout bioethics. Theirs does not. It fails where autonomy *simpliciter* (which is really their bedrock) fails. Karpin exposes the weakness well. The Bevleveld and Brownsword model works comprehensibly enough in analytically easy cases, she points out. Is it wrong, for instance, to deploy pre-implantation genetic diagnosis to select against an anencephalic child? No, they say, because human dignity as the PGC understands it is not affronted where the being selected against is not capable of being an agent at all.[31] Fair enough, but one does not need dignity to reach this conclusion.

What about the sort of case where Kant very obviously fails? Take a patient in PVS. Suppose that it is conclusively demonstrated that the patient has not and never will have any capacity for agency.[32] Can the withdrawal of treatment be justified, and if so, how? They identify three possible justifications: '(1) as the fulfilment of an obligation undertaken to the previously ostensible agent [the patient]; or (2) as a permissible fulfilment of a preference that one assumes the previously ostensible agent would have had; or (3) as a reallocation of scarce resources in order to protect the generic interests of ostensible agents.'[33] Each of these options is familiar to medical lawyers:(1) is the situation where there is an advanced directive;(2) is the notion of substituted judgment; and(3) is, as Jean McHale describes it, 'the honest and uncomfortable justification that bioethicists and lawyers alike tend to steer away from.'[34] It is surely less strained to say, as is conventional, that autonomy is the author of (1) and (2), and autonomy and justice the co-authors of (3). My point at the moment is not to say that there is anything wrong with these analyses (I have said that before, and in detail),[35] but simply to suggest that when one pares down Beyleveld and Brownsword, there is no new, radically transformative idea of dignity beneath.

If there were, one would expect to see it in dignity's natural habitat—the transhumanism debate. Where Beyleveld and Brownsword are tested there, they are found wanting. That is because autonomy is found wanting. Here, just when faith is needed, they become agnostic. Talking about a chimera formed from totipotent

---

[31] Karpin, 'Human Dignity in Bioethics and Biolaw (Review)' 326.

[32] They are rightly cautious about permitting any agency-ablating treatment or withdrawal of treatment, and accordingly endorse Gewirth's 'precautionary principle'.

[33] Beyleveld and Brownsword, *Human Dignity in Bioethics and Biolaw* 253.

[34] McHale, 'Human Dignity in Bioethics and Biolaw' 345.

[35] C Foster, *Choosing Life, Choosing Death: The Tyranny of Autonomy in Medical Ethics and Law* (Oxford, Hart, 2009).

cells of human and non-human animals, 'precautionary reasoning requires us to consider (no more or less) that these might possibly be sentient/agents and thus possibly have dignity'.[36]

This is an enlightening expression of doubt. Karpin comments: 'If the use of agency or sentience is the critical factor for the authors in determining moral treatment, it is surprising that the concept of the human retains a critical presence at all. The idea of the human starts to seem redundant in the face of this analysis and the future of biotechnology'.[37] There has in fact been no real notion of the quintessential human at any stage of Beyleveld and Brownsword's thesis. Here, the introduction of such a notion is essential to avoid absurdity or immorality, but it is too late. The authors' queasy and reluctant half-acknowledgment that agency/sentience might fail to give an acceptable result reflects back and reflects badly on those simpler instances where their notion of dignity seemed at first blush to make sense. Diana Schaub wisely observes that 'human dignity lies in acknowledging the way in which aging and dying very often involve becoming more and more a patient (and needing to learn patience) and less and less an agent.'[38]

Other conflaters of dignity and autonomy are more forthright about the effects of that conflation. Martha Nussbaum, for instance, writing in the context of the debate about allowing dangerous sports, believes that 'respecting human dignity requires informing people about their choices, restricting dangerous choices for children, but permitting adults to make a full range of choices, including unhealthy ones—with the proviso that competitive sports need to set reasonable safety conditions so that unwilling participants are not dragooned into taking a health risk that they don't want to take'.[39] For her, dignity is autonomy. And when it comes to medical ethics, she grasps the Kantian nettle boldly but chillingly: 'We would not accord equal dignity to a person in a persistent vegetative state, or an anencephalic child, since it would appear that there is no striving there, no reaching out for functioning.'[40]

Sometimes, though, forthright though she is, one wonders if she really means everything she says. She thinks that some rights are necessary in order to safeguard dignity. All citizens, she says, are entitled to a threshold level of 10 core capabilities or opportunities to function, all of which are 'necessary conditions of a life worthy of human dignity'.[41] They are: life, bodily health, bodily integrity, senses/imagination/thought, emotions, practical reason (being able to form a

[36] Beyleveld and Brownsword, *Human Dignity in Bioethics and Biolaw*165; cited and discussed in Karpin, 'Human Dignity in Bioethics and Biolaw (Review)' 326–27.

[37] Karpin, 'Human Dignity in Bioethics and Biolaw (Review)' 326–27.

[38] D Schaub, 'Commentary on Meilaender and Lawler' in Pellegrino et al (eds), *Human Dignity and Bioethics* 285.

[39] M Nussbaum, 'Human Dignity and Political Entitlements' in Pellegrino et al (eds), *Human Dignity and Bioethics* 372.

[40] Ibid 374.

[41] Ibid 351.

conception of the good and to engage in critical reflection about the planning of one's life), affiliation, concern for and relation to other species, play, control over one's environment (political and material).[42] How many would follow her here? Is sight a necessary condition of human dignity? The ability to walk? One cannot fault Nussbaum's consistency as an autonomist, but one can and must doubt the ability of simple autonomy to deliver an acceptable account of human dignity.

Can Rights do the Job of Dignity?

Another way of nudging dignity out of bioethical or legal discourse is to say that rights can do its job. Diana Schaub, for instance, thinks that the language of equal rights is preferable to the language of equal dignity.[43] She illustrates her position by reference to the question of incarceration. A rights analysis, she says, has no problem with locking up or otherwise punishing a criminal in a way that, prima facie, compromises his human dignity. The rights analysis is straightforward: Rights are inalienable, but also imply reciprocity and responsibility. Those who violate the rights of others have rendered some of their own rights forfeit.[44] But dignity, she says, struggles to speak coherently in a penological setting.

Schaub gives up on dignity too easily. She fails to ask and answer two crucial questions:

(a) Why should any human be accorded any rights? Rights are not free-standing: they are parasitic on other, more fundamental principles. Rights can stand on dignity (and also other things), but not vice versa.
(b) If you conclude that dignity is unsatisfactory as a basis for determining right behaviour, what do you do with the universal conviction that dignity (whatever that is) is real and has some ethical consequences? Can dignity simply be ignored?

When these questions are not ignored, one inevitably agrees that a rights analysis begs a dignity analysis. In the Supreme Court of Israel case of *Jerusalem Community Burial Society v Kestenbaum*, a case that many other jurisdictions would have been happy to treat as one of conflicting rights, Justice Barak said: 'Human dignity in Israel is not a metaphor. It is the reality, and we draw operative conclusions from it.'[45] It is, in other words, what lies beneath rights, and one can and should draw one's forensic water direct from the wellspring.

There are many other examples.[46] Here is my paraphrase of the examples cited, and of the general position in jurisdictions that take dignity seriously: dignity

---

[42] Ibid 377–78.
[43] Schaub, 'Commentary on Meilaender and Lawler' 284 et seq.
[44] Ibid 288.
[45] *Jerusalem Community Burial Society v Kestenbaum* CA 294/91, 46(2) 464.
[46] A good example is in Beyleveld and Brownsword, *Human Dignity in Bioethics and Biolaw* 22–25. See too: (a) the judgment of the Constitutional Court of South Africa in *Dawood v Minister of Justice*:

is at the bottom of all we do. Sometimes it will be practicable to use dignity ı its own name. When that is so, it is a good thing: using dignity's name itself has an ethically antiseptic effect. But sometimes, in order to translate dignity more effectively into legislation and judicial reasoning, it makes sense to refer to mechanisms which are derived from dignity and dependent on it. One of those mechanisms is 'rights'. The change of name does not amount to denial of parentage. Far from it. We must not forget that rights are mere mechanisms: executors of another's will.

'The value of dignity in our Constitutional framework cannot therefore be doubted. The Constitution asserts dignity to contradict our past in which human dignity for black South Africans was routinely and cruelly denied. It asserts it too to inform the future, to invest in our democracy respect for the intrinsic worth of all human beings. Human dignity therefore informs constitutional adjudication and interpretation at a range of levels. It is a value that informs the interpretation of many, possibly all, other rights. This Court has already acknowledged the importance of the constitutional value of dignity in interpreting rights such as the right to equality, the right not to be punished in a cruel, inhuman or degrading way, and the right to life. Human dignity is also a constitutional value that is of central significance in the limitations analysis. Section 10, however, makes it plain that dignity is not only a *value* fundamental to our Constitution, it is a justiciable and enforceable *right* that must be respected and protected. In many cases, however, where the value of human dignity is offended, the primary constitutional breach occasioned may be of a more specific right such as the right to bodily integrity,the right to equality or the right not to be subjected to slavery, servitude or forced labour.' (b) In the Supreme Court of Canada case *Re B. Motor Vehicle Act* [1985] 2 SCR 486, Lamer J, as he then was, said, to similar effect, at 512: 'Sections 8 to 14 address specific deprivations of the "right"to life, liberty and security of the person in breach of the principles of fundamental justice, and as such, violations of s. 7. They are therefore illustrative of the meaning, in criminal or penal law, of "principles of fundamental justice"; they represent principles which have been recognized by the common law, the international conventions and by the very fact of entrenchment in the *Charter*, as essential elements of a system for the administration of justice which is founded upon the belief in the dignity and worth of the human person and the rule of law.' (c) In the first German Constitutional Court abortion case, the Court said: 'the Basic Law of the Federal Republic of Germany has erected an order bound together by values which places the individual human being and his dignity at the focal point of all of its ordinances. At its basis lies the concept, as the Federal Constitutional Court previously pronounced (Decisions of the Federal Constitutional Court, 2, i 12), that human beings possess an inherent worth as individuals in order of creation which uncompromisingly demands unconditional respect for the life of every individual human being, even for the apparently socially "worthless," and which therefore excludes the destruction of such life without legally justifiable grounds. This fundamental constitutional decision determines the structure and the interpretation of the entire legal order.' Abortion Case, 39 BverfGE R 1 (1975): http://groups.csail.mit.edu/mac/users/rauch/nvp/german/german_abortion_decision2.html.

5

What do Non-philosophers and Non-lawyers Mean by Dignity?

The debate about the definition and utility of dignity has raged in academic journals. It has even affected some lawyers' speeches. But rarely has anyone who has engaged in these debates stopped to ask, when discussing what is meant by a patient's dignity, what patients themselves think.

Probably this is in the main due to the academic paternalism with which many in the world of medical ethics are familiar. Patients are often valued only because they present the problems that clever theories can solve.

This is slowly changing. Empirical ethics is now a recognised sub-discipline. The profundity of the old-fashioned philosophers' disapproval of empirical ethics ought to be encouraging to empirical ethicists. The philosophers have hardly covered themselves in glory. Part of empirical ethics is of course concerned with determining what should be done by reference to what the people potentially affected by a proposed intervention think should be done. In that sense its philosophical roots are utilitarian: in deciding on the greatest good of the greatest number, it thinks it sensible to ask the greatest number where they think the good might lie.

But if we are examining bioethical problems through the lens of dignity, and suggesting that at the root of dignity is a notion of what a human being is, it might be at least interesting to ask patients or potential patients what they think they are: what they mean by dignity. Reluctance by the philosophical professionals to do this is akin to the old colonial anthropologists' assumption that there was no need to ask the indigenous subjects of their research what a particular practice signified: the natives hadn't read Levi-Strauss and therefore couldn't possibly be expected to have anything useful to say.

Since I posit an account of dignity founded on the idea of objective human thriving, and although I, perhaps patronisingly, italicise the word 'objective' in that formulation, my account demands that we listen to humans on the subject of what they think makes them thrive. The reassuring surprise is that there is so much overlap between my idea of what is necessary for objective thriving, and people's subjective perception of what is necessary.

'What is the meaning of "losing dignity"?' asked 'Lilbubbleangel7', on a Yahoo forum. 'I've been hearing this a lot but don't know what it actually means. Please explain it clearly on what it really means [sic] with good examples.' The answer voted by forum readers to be the most helpful came from 'Bopeep'. She (I suppose it is a she) wrote:

> An easy way to describe this is to think of an elderly person. For all of their life they have been independent, able to go where they want and do what they want, and then perhaps they become ill and have to go into hospital or a home, and suddenly they can no longer dress themselves, or have to call someone when they need to go to the toilet ... they might feel that they have lost their dignity and have to put up with all sorts of things that are embarrassing or uncomfortable.

> Another example might be a woman who falls over in the street. If her skirt goes flying up over her head, she might quickly cover herself to restore her dignity—meaning that she is embarrassed and needs to fix her skirt.

> Final example—a true one! An elderly lady had to call the fire brigade to help her when whilst having a bath she accidentally got her toe stuck inside the bath tap! The firemen came into the bathroom with their eyes covered and handed her a towel so that she could cover herself and keep her dignity. Had they not been sensitive to her situation she could have felt that she had lost all dignity.[1]

'Hope that helps', wrote Bopeep. Well, yes it does. We will return later to what it helps with.

Egonsson argued that people generally equated dignity with 'being human'. This was his so-called 'Standard Attitude'.[2] Wertheimer agreed. This was the 'Standard Belief'.[3] But both agreed that mere membership of the species was not enough to make a holder of the Standard Attitude or Belief ascribe dignity to an individual. The empirical basis of Egonsson and Wertheimer's assertion about popular understandings is uncertain. In any event, their work is now quite old. There is some more recent work. We come to it in a moment.

But first it is worth looking at the way in which dignity is deployed in some professional codes within the healthcare professions. While legal eyes have no doubt been cast over the codes, there are few traces of significant lawyerly contamination. Indeed, as we will see, the courts have been so agnostic about the meaning of dignity that they are more likely to take their cue from the professional codes than vice versa.

What follows is simply a sample: dignity appears in some form or other in most of the relevant codes, and the formulations are similar. There is no doubt at all that dignity (whatever that is) is regarded as crucially important in healthcare. In the UK the Health Act 2009 requires all NHS organisations to take account of the rights and pledges in the NHS Constitution. That Constitution (which itself is a creature of the Act) tells each patient that 'You have the right to be treated

---

[1] http://answers.yahoo.com/question/index?qid=20080719001056AAYeLQb.

[2] D Egonsson, *Dimensions of Dignity: The Moral Importance of Being Human* (Dordrecht, Kluwer Academic, 1998) 132.

[3] R Wertheimer, 'Philosophy on Humanity' in R Perkins (ed), *Abortion: Pro and Con* (Cambridge, MA, Schenkman, 1974) 107–28.

with dignity and respect, in accordance with your human rights.'[4] The UK Royal College of Nursing (RCN), for instance, says that 'Dignity is at the heart of everything we do.'[5] The cynic might say that this is simply a feel-good slogan, but that is not borne out by the evidence. The RCN conducted a very diligent survey which indicated precisely that.[6] There are many other government and other initiatives directed towards maximising dignity in the healthcare setting.[7] There is no reason to suppose that they are motivated simply by some banal political correctness.

But what do they understand by 'dignity'? In a few sample cases of organisations who have decided to promulgate a definition of dignity, I set down the definition.

Some major professional organisations choose to assume that their readers know what is meant by dignity.[8] The General Medical Council is a good example. Its core guidance, 'Good Medical Practice', tells doctors that 'You must treat your patients with dignity,'[9] but, although it gives some practical guidance as to how that might be done in specific instances, wisely or cowardly does not attempt a definition. By its injunction to 'Treat patients as individuals and respect their dignity', it merely specifies that doctors should 'Treat patients politely and considerately' and 'Respect patients' right to confidentiality.'[10]

The UK Care Quality Commission (CQC) similarly notes that 'dignity is a core issue for CQC and is at the heart of its rights-based approach to regulation. Promoting dignity is key to the CQC corporate priority of 'Making sure that care is centred on people's needs and protects their rights',[11] but stops short of defining what is meant by dignity.

We see a similar pattern in other jurisdictions.[12] The American Medical Association states that 'A physician shall be dedicated to providing competent

---

[4] NHS Constitution s 2a. The official commentary on the Constitution states that 'The right to be treated with dignity and respect is derived from the rights conferred by the European Convention on Human Rights, as given effect in UKlaw by the Human Rights Act 1998. The relevant rights under the ECHR are the right to life (Article 2), the right not to be subject to inhuman or degrading treatment (Article 3), and the right to respect for private and family life (Article 8)'. *The Handbook to the NHS Constitution*, 8 March 2010 p 121: www.dh.gov.uk/en/Publicationsandstatistics/Publications/PublicationsPolicyAndGuidance/DH_113614.

[5] Royal College of Nursing, *Defending Dignity: Challenges and Opportunities for Nursing*, June 2008: www.rcn.org.*United Kingdom/__data/assets/pdf_file/0011/166655/003257.pdf.

[6] Ibid.

[7] See the list at www.rcn.org.United Kingdom/__data/assets/pdf_file/0011/166655/003257.pdf at p 10, and the Report of the UK Parliament's Joint Committee on Human Rights (2007) at www.publications.parliament.uk/pa/jt200607/jtselect/jtrights/156/15602.htm.

[8] Other examples, in addition to those listed here, include the Nursing and Midwifery Council: see 'Standards of Conduct, Performance and Ethics for Nurses and Midwives', May 2008, www.nmc-United Kingdom.org/Nurses-and-midwives/The-code/The-code-in-full/#dignity.

[9] Para 21b.

[10] The duties of a doctor registered with the General Medical Council: www.gmc-United Kingdom.org/guidance/good_medical_practice/duties_of_a_doctor.asp.

[11] www.cqc.org.United Kingdom/newsandevents/newsstories.cfm?widCall1=customWidgets.content_view_1&cit_id=35914.

[12] The Australian Medical Association is unusual in not referring to dignity in its primary ethical guidance. Dignity is mentioned, but only in the context of the dying patient: 'try to ensure that death

medical care, with compassion and respect for human dignity and rights'.[13] The New Zealand Medical Association urges practitioners to 'practise the science and art of medicine to the best of your ability, with moral integrity, compassion and respect for human dignity.'[14] The Health Professions Council of South Africa states that 'health care practitioners should respect patients as persons, and acknowledge their intrinsic worth, dignity and sense of value'—distinguishing, interestingly, between this value and non-maleficence, beneficence, human rights, autonomy, professional integrity, compassion, confidentiality, justice and tolerance.[15]

The UK General Dental Council regards 'Respecting patients' dignity and choices' as a core value,[16] but, like many of the organisations mentioned above, chooses to illustrate rather than define what it means by this. Its illustrations are concise but fairly typical of the non-defining illustrating school. Respecting dignity and choices will involve an obligation to:

> Treat patients politely and with respect, in recognition of their dignity and rights as individuals.[17]

> Recognise and promote patients' responsibility for making decisions about their bodies, their principles and their care, making sure you do not take any steps without patients' consent (permission) …[18]

> Treat patients fairly and in line with the law. Promote equal opportunities for all patients. Do not discriminate against patients or groups of patients because of their sex, age, race, ethnic origin, nationality, special needs or disability, sexuality, health, lifestyle, belief or any other irrelevant consideration.[19]

> Listen to patients and give them the information they need, in a way they can use, so that they can make decisions.[20]

occurs with dignity and comfort': Code of Ethics, 2004, revised 2006: http://ama.com.au/codeofethics. Nor is there any mention of dignity in the Indian Medical Council (Professional Conduct, Etiquette and Ethics) Regulations 2002.

[13] 'Principles of Medical Ethics', revised June 2001: www.ama-assn.org/ama/pub/physician-resources/medical-ethics/code-medical-ethics/principles-medical-ethics.shtml; cp the Code of Ethics of the American Association of Facial, Plastic and Reconstructive Surgery, September 2001, which provide that 'The patient has the right to courtesy, respect, dignity, responsiveness, and timely attention to his or her needs': www.ama-assn.org/ama/pub/physician-resources/medical-ethics/about-ethics-group/ethics-resource-center/educational-resources/federation-repository-ethics-documents-online/facial-plastic-reconstructive.shtml. Most of the other specialist groups within the American medical profession have comparable provisions.

[14] NZMA Code of Ethics, May 2008: www.nzma.org.nz/about/Code%20of%20Ethics%20-%20for%20the%20NZ%20medical%20profession.pdf.

[15] HPCSA, General Ethical Guidelines for Healthcare professionals, May 2008: www.hpcsa.co.za/downloads/conduct_ethics/rules/generic_ethical_rules/booklet_1_guidelines_good_prac.pdf.

[16] Cp the General Dental Council, Standards for Dental Professionals.

[17] Ibid cl 2.1.

[18] Ibid cl 2.2.

[19] Ibid cl 2.3.

[20] Ibid cl 2.4.

Maintain appropriate boundaries in the relationships you have with patients. Do not abuse these relationships.[21]

One might compare and contrast what the GDC and the GMC (for instance) say about dignity. One might note, for instance, that the GMC, in its very terse list of dignity's demands, chose to include confidentiality and to exclude a specific mention of inappropriate relationships with patients, whereas the GDC bracketed abusive relationships as a dignity issue, but has a completely separate category for confidentiality in which dignity is not specifically invoked. But this is not a very enlightening comparison. To build any thesis on such a comparison would be to assume an improbable degree of philosophical forethought on the part of the draftsmen of these codes. It is unlikely that, if pressed, the GMC's draftsman would say: 'Dignity has nothing to say about a doctor sleeping with a vulnerable patient', or that the GDC's draftsman would maintain that confidentiality raises no issues that are appropriately discussed in the language of dignity.

We now turn to three sample *definers*, initially without comment.

The Royal College of Nursing (UK)

Dignity is concerned with how people feel, think and behave in relation to the worth or value of themselves and others. To treat people with dignity is to treat them as being of worth, in a way that is respectful of them as valued individuals.

In care situations, dignity may be promoted or diminished by: the physical environment; organisational culture; by the attitudes and behaviour of nurses and others and by the way in which care activities are carried out. When dignity is present people feel in control, valued, confident, comfortable and able to make decisions for themselves.

When dignity is absent people feel devalued, lacking control and comfort. They may lack confidence and be unable to make decisions for themselves. They may feel humiliated, embarrassed and ashamed.

Dignity applies equally to those who have capacity and to those who lack it. Everyone has equal worth as human beings and must be treated as if they are able to feel, think and behave in relation to their own worth or value.

Nurses should, therefore, treat all people in all settings and of any health status with dignity, and dignified care should continue after death.[22]

The Social Care Institute for Excellence (UK)

Despite being widely used and discussed, dignity has seemed a difficult term to pin down. It is often linked with respect from others and with privacy, autonomy and control, with self-respect and with a sense of who you are. Threats to dignity have been identified with a very wide range of issues: how you are addressed having to sell your house to pay for long-term care; the kind of care patients receive at the end of life; or

---

[21] Ibid cl 2.5.
[22] Royal College of Nursing, *Defending Dignity: Challenges and Opportunities for Nursing*.

inadequate help to clean or maintain your home. And the impact of factors linked to disadvantage and discrimination of all kinds further complicate the picture.

The provisional meaning of dignity used for this guide is based on a standard dictionary definition:

'A state, quality or manner worthy of esteem or respect; and (by extension) self-respect.' Dignity in care, therefore, means the kind of care, in any setting, which supports and promotes, and does not undermine, a person's self-respect regardless of any difference.

Or, as one person receiving care put it more briefly, 'Being treated like I was somebody' (Policy Research Institute on Ageing and Ethnicity/Help the Aged, 2001).[23]

The American Association of Colleges of Nursing (USA)

Human Dignity is respect for the inherent worth and uniqueness of individuals and populations. In professional practice, human dignity is reflected when the [Clinical Nurse Leader] values and respects all clients and colleagues. Sample professional behaviors include:

– provides culturally competent and sensitive care;
– protects the client's privacy;
– preserves the confidentiality of clients and health care providers; and
– designs care with sensitivity to individual client needs.[24]

We can now compare the definers and the non-definers. It is notable and significant that those organisations that purport to articulate a *definition* of dignity tend to conclude that dignity has a wider and deeper reach than those organisations who pay it only lip service. The more you think about dignity, the more fundamental it seems to be. There is little in the GMC and GDC corollaries of dignity (for instance) that cannot be adequately described in terms of simple autonomy interests.

I do not propose to make again the case that there is more to medical ethics than autonomy,[25] but would merely comment here that however great one's respect for autonomy (and it should be great), and however heavy one's emphasis on the importance of upholding autonomy interests (and it should be heavy), it is plain enough that to assert respect for autonomy begs a number of questions about the origins of or justification for that respect. Whatever one says about the definitions of autonomy enshrined in the purported definitions above, they purport to address an ontological depth to which autonomy, even at its most ambitious, never begins to aspire.

---

[23] SCIE, Dignity in Care, June 2010, www.scie.org.United Kingdom/publications/guides/guide15/ backgroundresearch/selectedresearch/whatdignitymeans.asp.

[24] White Paper on the role of the Clinical Nurse Leader, July 2007, www.aacn.nche.edu/Publications/ WhitePapers/ClinicalNurseLeader.htm.

[25] I have set out the case for this proposition in detail in C Foster, *Choosing Life, Choosing Death: The Tyranny of Autonomy in Medical Law and Ethics* (Oxford, Hart, 2009).

Any professional philosopher would have a field day with the definitions. Yes, they mix the normative and the not-even-trying-to-be-normative, and they seem unembarrassed to describe dignity both as a status and as an attribute. They embody, in short, all the problems which the previous few chapters (dealing with the history and hermeneutic of dignity) have acknowledged. But surely, even at their worst, they side-step the criticism of Ruth Macklin. They are talking about more than autonomy, and if they are talking about respect for persons, the respect in which they invoke that idea is something that implies a grander view of the reason for respect than Kant ever dreamed of.

The View from the Ward

There is a good deal of interest, particularly in the nursing and palliative care literature, in promoting and conserving dignity. Most of the studies exhort health professionals to take dignity seriously, and instruct them how to do so. Perhaps the best known work in this genre is that of Chochinov et al, which noted, without much empirical justification, that concerns about illness and social matters can impact on dignity, and proposed a 'dignity conserving repertoire'.[26,27] There is little written about what patients themselves understand by dignity.[28] Many studies specifically asking patients about dignity do not seek to ascertain what the patients think dignity is.[29]

Pleschberger conducted a qualitative study with 20 old people in nursing homes in western Germany.[30] Dignity was very important to all of them.

---

[26] H Chochinov et al, 'Dignity in the Terminally Ill: A Developing Empirical Model'(2002) 54 *Social Science & Medicine* 433; H Chochinov et al, 'Dignity in the Terminally Ill: A Cross-sectional Cohort Study' (2002) 360 *Lancet* (North American edn) 2026; H Chochinov, 'Dignity and the Essence of Medicine: the A, B, C and D of Dignity Conserving Care'(2007) 335*British Medical Journal (BMJ)* 184; see too I Higginson,'Rediscovering Dignity at the Bedside'(2007) 335 *British Medical Journal* 167; and K Lothian and I Philp,'Maintaining the Dignity and Autonomy of Older People in the Healthcare Setting' (2001) 322 *British Medical Journal* 668.

[27] Cp L De Raeve, 'Dignity and Integrity at the End of Life' (1996) 2 *International Journal of Palliative Nursing* 71; W Tadd et al, 'Dignity in Health Care: Reality or Rhetoric' (2002) 12 *Review of Clinical Gerontology* 1.

[28] Some examples of work in this area other than this specifically discussed here include K Walsh and I Kowanko, 'Nurses' and Patients' Perceptions of Dignity' (2002) 8 *International Journal of Nursing Practice* 143; I Randers and A Mattiasson, 'The Experiences of Elderly People in Geriatric Care with Special Reference to Integrity' (2000) 7 *Nursing Ethics* 503; L Franklin, B Ternestedt and L Nordenfelt, 'Views on Dignity of Elderly Nursing Home Residents (2006) 13*Nursing Ethics* 130.

[29] A good example is F Simonstein and M Maschiach-Eizenberg, 'The Artificial Womb: A Pilot Study Considering People's Views on the Artificial Womb and Ectogenesis in Israel' (2009) 18 *Cambridge Quarterly of Healthcare Ethics* 87. It was a fascinating study, flawed by the failure to ask the simple question: 'What is dignity?' There was one particularly tantalising pair of results: 47.2% of all respondents agreed that the development of a foetus in an artificial wombs is against human nature, but 57.9% disagreed with the proposition that the development of a foetus in an artificial womb is against human dignity: see ibid 90–91. There is a whole thesis in the 10% gap.

[30] S Pleschberger, 'Dignity and the challenge of dying in nursing homes: the residents' view' (2007) 36 *Age and Ageing* 197. Her methods, aims and conclusions are similar to those of Hall et al, 'Living and Dying with Dignity: A Qualitative Study of the Views of Older People in Nursing Homes' (2009)

Pleschberger concluded that the subjects' understanding of dignity fell into two classes.[31] First, there was dignity as an interpersonal concept ('those elements that are grounded in personal beliefs and aspects of the body'). Of this element, Pleschberger commented that 'Dignity seems to be a personal refuge; one cannot be deprived of the core of dignity even under the worst of circumstances.'[32] Around this core is the second element, 'relational dignity'. By this she means that part of dignity that is 'socially constructed by the act of recognition, and therefore requires recognition.'[33] Residents saw their social relationships and encounters as 'dignifying'. Pleschberger constructed, and expressed in graphic form, the typical nursing home resident's concept of dignity. It is reproduced below.

Figure 5.1: Typical nursing home resident's concept of dignity (Pleschberger)[34]

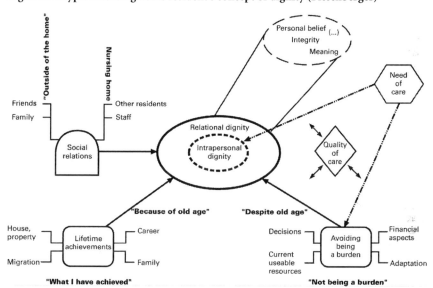

In another age, and perhaps outside the Western world (which increasingly sees dignity in terms of one's attributes, and—although it would never put it to itself like this—particularly in terms of economic usefulness), dignity might seem to

38 *Age and Ageing* 411; and Woolhead et al, 'Dignity in Older Age: What Do Older People in the United Kingdom Think?' (2004) 33 *Age and Ageing* 165.

[31] Broadly following the categories identified by L Nordenfelt, 'The Varieties of Dignity' (2004) 12 *Health Care Annals* 69.

[32] Pleschberger, 'Dignity and the Challenge of Dying in Nursing Homes' 199.

[33] Ibid 199.

[34] Ibid 199 © OUP: Oxford Journals.

increase with age. But that was not how Pleschberger's respondents saw it. They saw themselves as struggling to retain dignity *despite* their old age.[35]

Illness was seen as threatening both the interpersonal and relational components of dignity: the interpersonal because illness and the consequent need for care affect the body and therefore one's identity,[36] and the relational primarily because of a concern about 'being a burden'.[37]

Dementia was seen as posing a particular risk to dignity: 'If you lose your mind you will soon lose in value', said one resident.[38] And yet, if the view expressed by another can be taken as a comment on the same fear, the loss in value was not an absolute loss, but a loss in the eyes of the beholder. Dignity could be maintained, even in dementia, if sympathetic relationships were maintained. The resident was asked: 'Can one have a dignified old age, despite dementia?' The answer seems to be: 'Yes, if you are seen as dignified and treated with dignity.' The words actually were: 'I think that, when you become bed-ridden, you should above all be kept clean, and that they should nevertheless try to talk with you, and that you shouldn't be left alone so much if you become bed-ridden, that's basically what I understand about that.'[39]

What did these people, teetering on the edge of death, mean by a dignified death? Pleschberger highlighted two particularly important components.[40] These were: saying goodbye, and dying 'at the right time'. As to saying goodbye, it seemed clear that being alone or accompanied at the time of death was not in itself of such importance: what mattered crucially was *who* was there at the bedside.

It may be more obviously convenient to my thesis if, by 'dying at the right time', the residents meant something like the writer of Ecclesiastes presumably meant when he insisted that there was a 'time to die'[41]—that a particular time was the proper time to make the person's story literarily, as well as literally, complete. But it does not seem that that was their meaning. They meant: 'before something that is considered undignified happened'.[42] We return in a moment to the significance of this comment.

---

[35] Pleschberger, 'Dignity and the Challenge of Dying in Nursing Homes' 199.

[36] The identity component is illustrated well by Jack, a resident in a nursing home, and one of the respondents cited by Hall et al, 'Living and Dying with Dignity' 413: 'Christian, military, dignity ... I am fond of speaking about these things. It's a pleasure for me, this is my dignity ... I value my dignity. I display my dignity wherever I am'.

[37] Pleschberger, 'Dignity and the Challenge of Dying in Nursing Homes' 200; cp Pearlman et al, 'Insights Pertaining to Patient Assessments of Status Worse than Death'(1993) 4 *Journal of Clinical Ethics* 33.

[38] Pleschberger, 'Dignity and the Challenge of Dying in Nursing Homes' 200.

[39] Ibid 200.

[40] Three interrelated components were identified (Pleschberger, 'Dignity and the Challenge of Dying in Nursing Homes' 200): being active to the last, having one's will respected and being allowed to die, and being among persons close to one.

[41] Ecclesiastes 3:1–2, states: 'For everything there is a season, and a time for every matter under heaven: a time to be born, and a time to die.' New Revised Standard Version.

[42] Pleschberger, 'Dignity and the Challenge of Dying in Nursing Homes' 200. In the study by Woolhead et al, 'Dignity in Older Age', euthanasia was seen as a corollary of the (dignity-based) right to live (and die) in the way the patient chose. One respondent was quoted (ibid 168) as saying: 'Having

Pleschberger noted that most of the respondents' thoughts about interpersonal dignity were 'grounded in religious beliefs', and then went on to say 'and thus they established no basis for a secular human dignity'[43]—arguably a non-sequitur. The residents did not frame their observations in terms of human rights, and, again questionably, Pleschberger assumed that this will be differently for future generations.[44]

Pleschberger's data are valuable. Patients untutored in philosophy except by a lifetime of being human and by the imminence of death, draw the same distinction between dignity as status and dignity as a quality as the literature overwhelmingly does.

To dismiss their insistence on status dignity as an artefact of religious belief is naive, for three reasons. First, amongst many academic adherents of the notion that there is status dignity, there are many dyed-in-the-wool atheists. Second (a point that I am conscious seems to contradict the first), very few people are purely non-religious, even at the most stress-free of times: even those who aggressively disclaim established religion often have some non-materialistic beliefs, at least about themselves and their loved ones. And third, there is some truth in the cliché that there are no atheists in foxholes, and more truth in the observation that there are few atheists on the palliative care ward. This is not an evangelistic, or even a theistic point. I simply observe that most people have dignity-as-status beliefs. The origin of those beliefs is, for present purposes, neither here nor there. Vagueness will do: those beliefs seem to be either a consequence, or the source, or both, of something that is of the inalienable essence of human beings.

It is significant, too, that Pleschberger's patients regarded their relationships as crucially self-defining. They rejected emphatically the atomistic parody to which many philosophers expect their subjects to conform. They did not see their own skins as representing the boundaries of themselves. At the intimate moment of their own death they did not regard themselves as whole—as wholly themselves—unless they were accompanied by the people who, in life, had been an essential part of them.

---

my dignity maintained by still being able to make those choices about how I should die. I had no choice about being brought into the world, but I hope and want a choice about how I should depart from it'. Another, for similar reasons, sang the praises of advance directives (ibid 168): 'I think this living will thing is a very good thing. As long as you have done it when you are in your right mind and it is written on your card that you don't want any resuscitation.'

[43] Pleschberger, 'Dignity and the Challenge of Dying in Nursing Homes' 200–01.

[44] Note, however, that in Woolhead et al's study ('Dignity in Older Age'), human rights were included as a category of concern. Some of the relevant passages from the interviews have been cited: see n 44. But these concerns are not really human rights concerns: they are concerns about the preservation of dignity and autonomy interests. Indeed the authors seem to acknowledge this, beginning the section entitled 'Human Rights', with: 'This category included the themes of human dignity, human rights and equality. Being human involves possessing an intrinsic dignity that is inalienable. Statements such as "every human being has dignity", and "everyone should be treated as an individual" were used to describe human dignity. Being treated as an equal, regardless of age, was also important.' (Ibid 167–68.)

What about 'dying at the right time'—before something undignified happened? It is not too romantic to see this as an affirmation that the rightness of the whole life—the nature of the whole life—is conditioned by the quality identified as dignity. The residents were worried that the whole story of their lives, characterised by life's quintessence—dignity—might get an ending that jarred with what had gone before. So to have a 'dignified' end was to affirm the principles that had governed the rest of life. It was to be consistent, and thus to have, in the literal sense, integrity.[45]

This last paragraph sounds very like the sort of rhetoric so popular with the pro-euthanasia lobby—rhetoric drafted by the Millian autonomists whom I contend have lost the plot (or, more accurately, have failed to consider much of the plot). I am not changing sides. If Pleschberger's residents thought that their dignity would be compromised if they soiled their bedsheets in the terminal phase, they were wrong. They were wrong because, like most academic commentators, they failed to recognise the complex but vitally interdependent relationship between dignity as a status and dignity as a quality. There is an illuminating irony here: the sort of dignity that they are honouring in wanting not to be seen with an unwiped bottom is the sort of dignity that can never be bruised by a nurse's failure to give a bed bath.

The fact that the residents did not find it useful to talk in terms of human rights is unlikely to be a consequence of their generation. When everything you have is inevitably and imminently going to be ripped from you, even the most sullen, rights-marinated teenager knows better than to stand on his rights. Imminent death forces one to fundamentals. The residents intuited what many well-schooled jurisprudential thinkers miss—that beneath rights, there is something much deeper, which gives rise, no doubt to rights, but has many other intellectual and experiential offspring. This is dignity.

Similar conclusions result from studies in areas of medicine and nursing far from the care home and the palliative care ward. Matthews and Callister, writing about the experiences of childbearing women, cited a respondent to their study as saying: 'You are so used to being a private person, and your body is your body. And then all of a sudden your body is being stared at by twenty other people.'[46]

Why should that be a problem? It is a problem hard to describe in terms of the lawyers' conventional categories of damage. In one sense it is an affirmation of the relational nature of self-definition. What we are is at least in part defined by the people to whom we choose to reveal ourselves. If you have no choice about who sees you physically or emotionally naked, something about your identity is

---

[45] Dworkin's view is helpful here. He said that 'Integrity is closely connected to dignity ... we think that someone who acts out of character, for gain or to avoid trouble, has insufficient respect for himself.' R Dworkin *Life's Dominion* (New York, Knopf, 1993) 205. See too Gentzler's discussion of this notion in J Gentzler 'What is a Death with Dignity?' (2003) 28 *Journal of Medicine and Philosophy* 461, 483.

[46] R Matthews and LC Callister, 'Childbearing Women's Perceptions of Nursing Care that Promotes Dignity' (2006) 33 *Journal of Obstetric, Gynecologic and Neonatal Nursing* 501.

affronted. To describe this as affronted autonomy isn't exactly inaccurate; it just doesn't say anything like enough.

Another of Matthews' and Callister's women said: 'Lack of dignity doesn't even come down to lack of modesty. It's just an issue of remembering that the mother having the baby usually wants it to be a private experience because it's so significant and special.'[47]

What is going on here? 'Significant'? 'Special'? This is the language of reverence, and it is not spoken by any bioethical principle other than dignity. And yet, say these women, it is a crucial factor in determining what is and is not appropriate nursing care. It is saying that the process of childbirth needs to be consecrated, and that this consecration needs somehow to be written into the ward protocols.

Participants in the Matthews and Callister study wanted nurses to demonstrate reverence for the birth experience by, inter alia, 'sharing the joy'.[48]

Here, too, is the relational element. The sharing is part of the whole experience. If the experience is not shared, it is diminished.

There are other ways in which the experience can be profaned. A woman interviewed by Callister reflected on her experience of delivery with the help of an epidural:

> I had my first [child] in a way I view as traditional, where the doctor was in control and he encouraged me to have an epidural. It was such a frightening experience. Afterwards I thought: 'This isn't childbirth. There's got to be more to it than just lying there with a numb body.'[49]

For this woman in childbirth, and I suggest for humans in general, there is a 'right' way to do things (a way consistent with our dignity; with our thriving), and a multitude of not so right ways. Again, the more traditional principles of bioethics have no way to describe, explain or justify this conclusion.

---

[47] Ibid 501.

[48] Ibid 503. The paper is written as if this were a conclusion in V Waldenstrom, 'Women's Memory of Childbirth at Two Months and One Year After Birth' (2003) 30 *Birth* 248, but in fact it is Matthews' and Callister's own.

[49] L Callister, 'Beliefs and Perceptions of Childbearing Women Choosing Different Primary Care Providers' (1995) 4 *Clinical Nursing Research* 168, 175 (cited in Matthews and Callister, 'Childbearing Women's Perceptions of Nursing Care that Promotes Dignity').

6

Taking Stock of the View from the Academy and the Ward

W^e have now surveyed what dignity has meant to professional thinkers over the millennia and means now, and what it means to those who have no professional training, but are simply humans trying to make sense of the curious business of being human. It is now time to step back and wonder where all this takes us.

For as long as humans have been recognisably human, they have asked themselves what they are, and what distinguishes them as individuals from other individuals, and what distinguishes humans from non-humans. Often that debate has crystallised around, or been (rightly or wrongly) conflated with the question of so-called human dignity.

The antiquity of the debate, and the fact that precisely the same themes occur from millennium to millennium, evoking in each generation almost identical nods and head-shakes, should suggest that the questions come from somewhere fairly deep within humans. Ruth Macklin can protest all she likes about the slipperiness of dignity, but it is not going to slip away. Wherever there is a human, schooled or unschooled in Seneca, Aquinas or Kant, there is a conviction that dignity means something—at least when that person moves from the lecture theatre to the real world of the labour ward, the geriatric ward or the crematorium.

The questions asked in the dignity debate are truly perennial, and so are the answers. There has been little real philosophical progress since the Stoics. The contribution of the philosophical professionals has been to provide different taxonomic schemes. They have simply sliced dignity in slightly different ways, and stuck the pieces in their albums under new or rediscovered labels. Sometimes they have sprinkled some theological stardust over the album, and said that they had finally seen what dignity was all about. And sometimes they have blown away all the theological stardust, and said precisely the same thing.

Dignity's opponents, by and large, have not said that there is no such thing as dignity, but said either that it is too elusive to be useful, or that when you boil it down it looks much like autonomy, or respect for persons, or something similarly comfortable, familiar and non-metaphysical. But when the reductionists are pressed about the reason *why* we should respect (for instance) an autonomy right, they become tongue-tied. Their silence over the last three thousand years or so is itself good reason to suggest that there's something lurking beneath their principles, on which the principles are dependent.

The taxonomists in all cultures and all ages have consistently identified two strands within dignity. The taxonomists describe dignity as a quality that persons can possess, and they describe it as a status. Each strand has its proponents, and, at least in modern popular bioethical discourse, the proponents of each have tended to see their strand as providing the only legitimate colour for the banner of real dignity. So they have woven their banners exclusively from either status or quality. This is best and most tragically seen in the euthanasia debate. The anti-euthanasists have insisted that killing even the most compromised human is illegitimate and inconsistent with the inalienable status of humans. The pro-euthanasists counter that if someone no longer has the dignity associated with faecal and urinary continence, and accordingly can't bear to be seen or smelt by her relatives, the dignified thing to give would be a mercifully fatal cocktail of drugs. This sort of unseemly barracking, resting as it does on an over-simplified parody of dignity by each side, has done nothing to increase the reputation of dignity in academic eyes. But still its grasp on us is so tight that even the sceptics continue to write papers about dignity. They can't leave it alone.

Some have tried to weave the two strands together. Perhaps the most successful is Leon Kass, but as I have observed, his attempt, based on the *Imago Dei*, is unconvincing. That is not because there is anything necessarily wrong with the idea of *Imago Dei* (although it will have to work on its PR if it wants to get tenure in most modern universities).

Other proponents of the *Imago Dei* have drained from the doctrine much of its power to bring peace between the two bickering dignity-factions because of their Gnostic obsession with souls, and their Gnostic contempt for the body.

When we listen to BoPeep from the Yahoo chat forum, and to the residents in Pleschberger's nursing homes, we might wonder whether there is any point in reading philosophy at university. They artlessly intuit everything that the dignity-sages have said. The fact that lay and academic versions of dignity agree so completely might suggest that we can trust our intuitions in this area more confidently than we might in other areas of ethical analysis. People *in extremis* are particularly eloquent when articulating their ideas of dignity, and particularly certain that they have dignity interests. That may suggest what a look at the deficiencies of (eg) autonomy as a principle for explaining human conduct has already suggested—namely that dignity (whatever it is) lies as deep within people as one can drill, and therefore within all correct philosophy about people. The fact that dignity is seen to be engaged when bedpans are being changed or bedsores dressed may suggest, too, that it is more likely to be useful as a bioethical principle than other candidates who are less happy to get their hands dirty.

BoPeep can tell us something that it is easy to miss when we read Kant. It's there in him, and in all the other great thinkers, but sometimes their sheer cleverness covers it up. It is, very simply, that the business of dignity is about being human, and being human well. Humans being what they are, being and doing are generally related. But this is not a necessary connection. When we are asleep, or anaesthetised, or in PVS, we are still going about the business of being human, and things done to us when we are in those states affect the way in which our human being is manifested.

The language in which we constantly express ourselves gives away our beliefs about dignity: 'It's unworthy of him'; 'He's let himself down'. In this simple but enigmatic language lies the reconciliation between quality and status. Why will a particular form of (undignified) behaviour 'let someone down'? Because they have failed to live in accordance with the status being referred to—which is often a status that is no more and no less than human. What is the consequence of 'letting oneself down'? We can generalise, and it is important to do so. The consequence is that the person's ability to manifest his human being—to thrive in all the ways that full human being entails—will be compromised.

Both BoPeep and the philosophers whom we have examined, therefore, were talking about the same thing: thriving as a human being, being as a thriving human; spin it how you choose. The version of dignity I advocated in Chapter 1 emerges clearly as the main theme of the dignity debate down the ages. It is hermeneutically justifiable to call this a book about dignity.

I suggested in Chapter 1 that the question: 'What makes humans thrive?' is essentially an empirical one—but that at the levels we are talking about (the most fundamental levels possible), the empirical, as you'd expect, *becomes* the normative. It follows that to make correct ethical (and, by extension, legal) decisions, one has to inquire scientifically into what's good for us. You need a bioethical and bio-legal anthropology.

'In the end' writes Edward Pellegrino, 'the edifices of bioethical systems are grounded in some idea of the purposes and destiny of human life. This is, of course, the anthropological question: "What are human beings?" Our answers provide the templates for decisions we make about which technologies we believe contribute to, or detract from, our flourishing as the kind of being we are.'[1]

I suggested in Chapter 1 a few of the characteristics that I would expect to find in such an anthropology. On the evidence presently available, I can go no further than I went there.

George Kateb notes that 'It would be foolish to attempt a comprehensive philosophical anthropology. Even more, it would be foolish to try to present a view of human nature, if by that phrase we mean a detailed description of everything a human being or the human species is capable of, together with a complete repertory of their characteristic behaviours.'[2]

Well, perhaps. But even he gives a 'selective list of traits and attributes common to all human beings'.[3] He uses these to 'help provide a basis for the idea of

---

[1] E Pellegrino, 'The Lived Experience of Human Dignity' in E Pellegrino, A Schulman and T Merrill (eds), *Human Dignity and Bioethics* (Notre Dame, IN, University of Notre Dame Press, 2009) 514.

[2] G Kateb, *Human Dignity* (Cambridge, MA, Harvard University Press, 2011) 131.

[3] Ibid 131.

human dignity'.[4] His attributes are: the use of spoken language; the use of written language and other notational systems; the ability to think, including memory, which he describes as 'the glue of thinking'; the ability to accumulate knowledge and become self-conscious; from all these, the capacity for agency; from agency what Rousseau calls 'perfectability', and what Kateb prefers to call 'potentiality'; from potentiality, unpredictability and creativity (of which imagination is a crucial element).[5]

Other writers, notably Martha Nussbaum[6], have produced similar lists. They are useful if one wants to sing wondering hymns of praise to humans, which is a worthwhile and important thing to do (although I wonder if philosophers have the best voices for it), they are useful if one wants to use the idea of dignity simply to exhort, and they are useful in much purely political discourse.

But they are as useless as Kant ever was when it comes to dealing with the incapacitate or the truncated. Their obvious uselessness there, combined with our rightful reluctance to abandon wholly the idea of dignity, might cause one to hold tightly, but unfortunately, to the idea of dignity only as status.[7] Kateb comes as close as one can get to an acknowledgment that his notion of dignity is no help to us in bioethics. He says: 'I leave aside possible efforts to enhance human capacities by genetic manipulation. How such efforts would affect the idea of human dignity I do not know'.[8] Such humble agnosticism is unacceptable. It is like a motor mechanic saying: 'I've mended your car, but it won't go further than the end of your drive.' The whole point of thinking about dignity is that (to change the metaphor again), it illuminates where other principles do not.

In the light of my observations of very young children and the severely disabled I differ significantly from Kateb about what should be on the list. I am not particularly interested in whether a characteristic is *uniquely* human, which seems to be the focus of Kateb's inquiry. It does not seem to me that a characteristic crucially important to humans is less important simply because that characteristic is shared with guinea pigs or walnut trees.

The crucial question for me is very different from that for Kateb. It is: what does the evidence suggest about how human thriving can be maximised? If my formulation of dignity is right, the search for this second type of evidence is an ethically and legally urgent one.

The fact that I can go no further in speculating about what will ultimately be found to be the quintessential human-being-thriving characteristics makes necessarily tentative many of my suggestions about the way that the law should go. Indeed I rarely make such suggestions. In the legal discussion that follows, I

---

[4] Ibid 173.

[5] Ibid 131.

[6] See M Nussbaum, 'Human Dignity and Political Entitlements' in E Pellegrino, A Schulman and T Merrill (eds), *Human Dignity and Bioethics* (Notre Dame, IN, University of Notre Dame Press, 2009) 377–78.

[7] As Kateb himself seems to recognise in the context of political philosophy: see ibid 173.

[8] Ibid 132.

generally confine myself to an attempt to demonstrate that a dignity analysis does a better bio-legal job than its competitors.

Before we look at the way in which dignity might work in the areas important to medical and bio-lawyers, we need to look at how dignity has been wielded in the law in general.

7

Dignity in the Courtroom: General Overview

The Advocate General in the *Omega* case complained that 'there is hardly any legal principle more difficult to fathom in law that that of human dignity'.[1] And by and large, with some honourable exceptions, the courts have not tried to fathom it, being content instead to assume that it is a good thing, that their audience have a fair idea what it means, and that it needs to be protected.

This chapter notes:

(a) that dignity appears very commonly in national and international instruments;
(b) that some of those instruments deal specifically with healthcare and bioethics;
(c) that dignity has sometimes been used by national and international courts to deal with hard cases, and more commonly to lend gravitas to decisions made on other grounds;
(d) that the notion of dignity has not been given any very hard-edged substantive meaning in the national or international courts where it has been deployed;
(e) that accordingly there is no substantive understanding of dignity that has been rendered unusable by the courts. All interpretations remain available as forensic tools.

Dignity in National and International Instruments

The word 'dignity' appears in many national constitutions, international declarations and international conventions. Christopher McCrudden has catalogued their appearances,[2] and I see no point in duplicating his labour. The points necessary to my thesis can be made with a few examples.

Lawyers were, as lawyers often are, several centuries or even millennia behind other thinkers. As we have seen, philosophers and politicians have long been fluent, if ambiguous, in the language of dignity, but it was not until the first

---

[1] Case C-36/02 *Omega Spielhallen-und Automatenaufstellung GmbH v Oberbürgermeisterin der Bundesstadt Bonn* [2005] 1 CMLR 5 Opinion of Advocate-General Stix-Hacklpara 74.

[2] C McCrudden, 'Human Dignity and Judicial Interpretation of Human Rights' (2008) 19 *European Journal of International Law* 655.

few decades of the twentieth century that lawyers stammered out their first few phrases.[3] The horrors of the Second World War increased dramatically the perceived importance of dignity. Japan,[4] Italy[5] and West Germany[6] repentantly grafted dignity into their constitutions.

The Preamble of the Universal Declaration of Human Rights provides that 'recognition of the inherent dignity and of the equal and inalienable rights of all members of the human family is the foundation of freedom and peace in the world', and 'the peoples of the United Nations have in this Charter reaffirmed their faith in fundamental human rights, in the dignity and worth of the human person and in the equal rights of men and women'. Article 1 provides that 'All human beings are born free and equal in dignity and rights. They are endowed with reason and conscience and should act towards one another in a spirit of brotherhood'. In relation to social security, Article 22 provides that 'Everyone, as a member of society, has the right to social security and is entitled to realization ...of the economic, social and cultural rights indispensable for his dignity and the free development of his personality.' Article 23 deals with the right to work for remuneration that ensures for the worker 'and his family an existence worthy of human dignity.'[7]

Dignity features prominently in the Geneva Conventions—for instance in Common Article 3, which prohibits 'outrages upon personal dignity, in particular humiliating and degrading treatment', and in Additional Protocol 1, which outlaws 'outrages upon personal dignity, in particular degrading and humiliating treatment, enforced prostitution and any form of indecent assault.'

There are few significant international, regional or national human rights charters that do not rely explicitly on dignity.[8] One that does not is the European Convention on Human Rights. Of that, more later.

---

[3] See McCrudden, 'Human Dignity and Judicial Interpretation of Human Rights' 664. The following countries used the idea of dignity in their national constitutions: Mexico (1917); Germany (1919); Finland (1919); Portugal (1933); Ireland (1937); Cuba (1940).

[4] 1946.

[5] 1948.

[6] 1949.

[7] For a discussion of the meaning of dignity in the Universal Declaration, see H Schmidt, 'Whose Dignity? Resolving Ambiguities in the Scope of "Human Dignity" in the Universal Declaration on Bioethics and Human Rights' (2007) *Journal of Medical Ethics* 578.

[8] Examples of those that do include, apart from the national instruments already mentioned, the Slavery Conventions, the International Covenant on Civil and Political Rights, the International Covenant on Economic, Social and Cultural Rights, the International Convention on the Elimination of Racial Discrimination, the International Convention on Discrimination against Women, the Convention on the Prevention of Torture, the Convention on the Rights of Children, the Convention on the Rights of Migrant Workers, the Convention on the Protection against Forced Disappearance, the Convention on the Rights of Disabled Persons, the European Union Charter of Fundamental Rights, the constitution of South Africa and Israel's Basic Law on Human Dignity: see McCrudden, 'Human Dignity and Judicial Interpretation of Human Rights' 664–75.

International Instruments Dealing Specifically with Healthcare and Bioethics

This is far from an exhaustive list, but it does contain some of the more important instruments. The provisions get very repetitive. The purpose of the list and the accompanying text of the relevant articles is simply to give an indication of the way in which dignity is used in a bioethical way. I will comment later on this usage.

In addition to these provisions, there are of course many pieces of national legislation, reports of commissions and so on, which refer to dignity in a bioethical context. I do not include examples here, because they are of limited interest outside the jurisdiction concerned, and the general comments that I would make about them apply equally and more interestingly to the international material.

(a) *The Convention for the Protection of Human Rights and Dignity of the Human Being with Regard to the Application of Biology and Medicine: Convention on Human Rights and Biomedicine (the Oviedo Convention)*

The Preamble to the Oviedo Convention[9] refers, inter alia, to 'the need to respect the human being both as an individual and as a member of the human species and recognising the importance of ensuring the dignity of the human being', notes that it is 'Conscious that the misuse of biology and medicine may lead to acts endangering human dignity', and resolves 'to take such measures as are necessary to safeguard human dignity and the fundamental rights and freedoms of the individual with regard to the application of biology and medicine.'

Article 1 provides that:

> Parties to this Convention shall protect the dignity and identity of all human beings and guarantee everyone, without discrimination, respect for their integrity and other rights and fundamental freedoms with regard to the application of biology and medicine. Each Party shall take in its internal law the necessary measures to give effect to the provisions of this Convention.

(b) *The Additional Protocol to the Oviedo Convention, concerning Biomedical Research*

This protocol[10] notes in the Preamble that 'biomedical research that is contrary to human dignity and human rights should never be carried out', and resolves 'to take such measures as are necessary to safeguard human dignity and the fundamental rights and freedoms of the individual with regard to biomedical research.'

Article 1 of the Protocol provides that 'Parties to this Protocol shall protect the dignity and identity of all human beings and guarantee everyone, without

---

[9] 1997: http://conventions.coe.int/Treaty/en/Treaties/html/164.htm.
[10] 2005: http://conventions.coe.int/Treaty/en/Treaties/html/195.htm.

discrimination, respect for their integrity and other rights and fundamental freedoms with regard to any research involving interventions on human beings in the field of biomedicine.'[11]

(c) The Additional Protocol to the Oviedo Convention, on the Prohibition of Cloning Human Beings

This protocol[12] notes in the Preamble that 'the instrumentalisation of human beings through the deliberate creation of genetically identical human beings is contrary to human dignity and thus constitutes a misuse of biology and medicine.'

(d) The Additional Protocol to the Oviedo Convention, on Transplantation of Organs and Tissues of Human Origin

In this protocol[13] the Preamble notes that 'the misuse of organ and tissue transplantation may lead to acts endangering human life, well being or dignity' and resolves 'to take such measures as are necessary to safeguard human dignity and the rights and fundamental freedoms of the individual with regard to organ and tissue transplantation.'[14]

(e) The Additional Protocol to the Oviedo Convention, on Genetic Testing for Health Purposes.

This protocol[15] contains a resolve similar to that in the Additional Protocol on Transplantation.

(f) The UNESCO Universal Declaration on Bioethics and Human Rights

The Preamble to the Universal Declaration on Bioethics and Human Rights[16] recognises that 'ethical issues raised by the rapid advances in science and their technological applications should be examined with due respect to the dignity of the human person and universal respect for, and observance of, human rights and fundamental freedoms' and

> that, based on the freedom of science and research, scientific and technological developments have been, and can be, of great benefit to humankind in increasing, inter alia, life expectancy and improving the quality of life, and emphasizing that such developments should always seek to promote the welfare of individuals, families, groups or communities and humankind as a whole in the recognition of the dignity of the human

---

[11] There is a further reference to dignity in Art 9(2) of the Protocol: 'The purpose of the multidisciplinary examination of the ethical acceptability of the research project shall be to protect the dignity, rights, safety and well-being of research participants.'

[12] 1998: http://conventions.coe.int/Treaty/en/Treaties/html/168.htm.

[13] 2002: http://conventions.coe.int/Treaty/en/Treaties/Html/186.htm.

[14] A resolution embodied in Art 1 of the Protocol.

[15] 2008: http://conventions.coe.int/Treaty/EN/Treaties/Html/203.htm.

[16] 2005: http://portal.unesco.org/en/ev.php-url_id=31058&url_do=do_topic&url_section=201.html.

person and universal respect for, and observance of, human rights and fundamental freedoms.

Article 2(c) states that one of the aims of the Declaration is 'to promote respect for human dignity and protect human rights, by ensuring respect for the life of human beings, and fundamental freedoms, consistent with international human rights law', and Article 2(d) emphasises that human dignity should not be a casualty of scientific progress.

Article 3 provides: '(1) Human dignity, human rights and fundamental freedoms are to be fully respected. (2) The interests and welfare of the individual should have priority over the sole interest of science or society.'

Article 10 provides that 'the fundamental equality of all human beings in dignity and rights is to be respected so that they are treated justly and equitably.' Article 11 states that 'No individual or group should be discriminated against or stigmatized on any grounds, in violation of human dignity, human rights and fundamental freedoms', and Article 12 that 'The importance of cultural diversity and pluralism should be given due regard. However, such considerations are not to be invoked to infringe upon human dignity, human rights and fundamental freedoms, nor upon the principles set out in this Declaration, nor to limit their scope.'

(g) The UNESCO *Universal Declaration on the Human Genome and Human Rights*

The Preamble of the UNESCO Constitution refers to 'the democratic principles of the dignity, equality and mutual respect of men' and stipulates that 'that the wide diffusion of culture, and the education of humanity for justice and liberty and peace are indispensable to the dignity of men and constitute a sacred duty which all the nations must fulfil in a spirit of mutual assistance and concern'.

The Declaration on the Human Genome[17] builds on this, recognising in the Preamble that 'research on the human genome and the resulting applications open up vast prospects for progress in improving the health of individuals and of humankind as a whole, but emphasizing that such research should fully respect human dignity, freedom and human rights, as well as the prohibition of all forms of discrimination based on genetic characteristics.' Its Articles make frequent and explicit reference to dignity, as follows:

Article 1

The human genome underlies the fundamental unity of all members of the human family, as well as the recognition of their inherent dignity and diversity. In a symbolic sense, it is the heritage of humanity.

[17] 1997: http://portal.unesco.org/en/ev.php-url_id=13177&url_do=do_topic&url_section=201.html.

Article 2

(a) Everyone has a right to respect for their dignity and for their rights regardless of their genetic characteristics.
(b) That dignity makes it imperative not to reduce individuals to their genetic characteristics and to respect their uniqueness and diversity.

Article 6

No one shall be subjected to discrimination based on genetic characteristics that is intended to infringe or has the effect of infringing human rights, fundamental freedoms and human dignity.

Article 10

No research or research applications concerning the human genome, in particular in the fields of biology, genetics and medicine, should prevail over respect for the human rights, fundamental freedoms and human dignity of individuals or, where applicable, of groups of people.

Article 11

Practices which are contrary to human dignity, such as reproductive cloning of human beings, shall not be permitted. States and competent international organizations are invited to co-operate in identifying such practices and in taking, at national or international level, the measures necessary to ensure that the principles set out in this Declaration are respected.

Article 12

(a) Benefits from advances in biology, genetics and medicine, concerning the human genome, shall be made available to all, with due regard for the dignity and human rights of each individual.

Article 15

States should take appropriate steps to provide the framework for the free exercise of Research on the human genome with due regard for the principles set out in this Declaration, in order to safeguard respect for human rights, fundamental freedoms and human dignity and to protect public health. They should seek to ensure that research results are not used for non-peaceful purposes.

Article 21

States should take appropriate measures to encourage other forms of research, training and information dissemination conducive to raising the awareness of society and all of its members of their responsibilities regarding the fundamental issues relating to the defence of human dignity which may be raised by research in biology, in genetics and in medicine, and its applications. They should also undertake to facilitate on this subject an open international discussion, ensuring the free expression of various sociocultural, religious and philosophical opinions.

Article 24

The International Bioethics Committee of UNESCO should .... make recommendations, in accordance with UNESCO's statutory procedures, addressed to the General Conference and give advice concerning the follow-up of this Declaration, in particular regarding the identification of practices that could be contrary to human dignity, such as germ-line interventions.

(h) UNESCO International Declaration on Human Genetic Data

The Preamble of this Declaration[18] states, inter alia, 'that the collection, processing, use and storage of human genetic data have potential risks for the exercise and observance of human rights and fundamental freedoms and respect for human dignity ... that the interests and welfare of the individual should have priority over the rights and interests of society and research.' It reaffirmed that:

> the principles established in the Universal Declaration on the Human Genome and Human Rights and the principles of equality, justice, solidarity and responsibility as well as respect for human dignity, human rights and fundamental freedoms, particularly freedom of thought and expression, including freedom of research, and privacy and security of the person, which must underlie the collection, processing, use and storage of human genetic data.

Article 1(a) provides that:

> The aims of this Declaration are: to ensure the respect of human dignity and protection of human rights and fundamental freedoms in the collection, processing, use and storage of human genetic data, human proteomic data and of the biological samples from which they are derived, referred to hereinafter as 'biological samples', in keeping with the requirements of equality, justice and solidarity, while giving due consideration to freedom of thought and expression, including freedom of research; to set out the principles which should guide States in the formulation of their legislation and their policies on these issues; and to form the basis for guidelines of good practices in these areas for the institutions and individuals concerned,

and Article 7(a) that:

> Every effort should be made to ensure that human genetic data and human proteomic data are not used for purposes that discriminate in a way that is intended to infringe, or has the effect of infringing human rights, fundamental freedoms or human dignity of an individual or for purposes that lead to the stigmatization of an individual, a family, a group or communities.

(i) The World Medical Association Declaration of Helsinki: Ethical Principles for Medical Research involving Human Subjects

Article 11 of the Declaration of Helsinki[19] provides: 'It is the duty of physicians who participate in medical research to protect the life, health, dignity, integrity, right to self-determination, privacy, and confidentiality of personal information of research subjects.'

---

[18] 2003: http://portal.unesco.org/en/ev.php-url_id=17720&url_do=do_topic&url_section=201.html.
[19] 1964; repeatedly readopted, most recently in 2008: see www.wma.net/en/30publications/10policies/b3/index.html.

What is Meant by 'Dignity' in these and other Instruments?

McCrudden, surveying the way that 'dignity' has been interpreted in regional and international instruments, notes a 'more pluralistic, more culturally relative approach to the meaning of human dignity.'[20] What emerges from these differences, he says,

> is that some jurisdictions use dignity as the basis for (or another way of expressing) a comprehensive moral viewpoint, a 'whole moral world view', which seems distinctly different from region to region. In this sense, to speak of human dignity is a shorthand way of summing up how a complex, multi-faceted set of relationships involving Man is, or should be, governed: relationships between man and man, man and God, man and animals, man and the natural environment, man and the universe.[21]

Interestingly, McCrudden, having started by observing that 'some jurisdictions' use dignity this way, does not go on to state that other jurisdictions use dignity in another identified way. I think he is wise. I can identify no other significant understanding of dignity in any relevant instrument that is not covered by McCrudden's summary.

He does go on to observe that there are 'significant differences' in the way that the notion of dignity is incorporated into substantive law. 'In many of the instruments', he observes, 'dignity is to be found in the preamble, whereas in others it is used to explicate particular rights. In some it is referred to as foundational in some sense; in others not. In some, human dignity is a right in itself (and in some systems, a particularly privileged right), whilst in other jurisdictions, it is not a right but a general principle.'[22]

All these observations are correct, but in relation to those instruments that touch on medicine and bioethics, they do not seem to me to indicate anything very significant. There are many ways for legal draftsmen to skin their forensic cats. It is significant that in all the major healthcare instruments detailed above, except the Declaration of Helsinki, dignity appears in the Preamble and is unquestionably foundational. It is true that in the Introduction to the Declaration of Helsinki (the section akin to a Preamble, which sets out general principles), dignity is not mentioned as such. Article 11, therefore, is an example of dignity being used to explicate a particular obligation and, by extension, a particular right. But if healthcare professionals abide by their Article 11 obligations, nothing whatever that is contemplated by the Declaration would be unsuffused by dignity.

A more significant observation by McCrudden is that when talking about dignity, judges seem to be more ready than usual to draw on the jurisprudence of other jurisdictions, perhaps because they recognise, at some level, that they are talking about the universal experience of humans.[23]

---

[20] McCrudden, 'Human Dignity and Judicial Interpretation of Human Rights' 673.
[21] Ibid 674.
[22] Ibid 675.
[23] Ibid 151–52.

Whenever lawyers are pressed to identify their philosophical fundamentals, they tend to name dignity. A good example is in the European Convention on Human Rights. As noted, this, unusually amongst statements of fundamental principles of human rights, makes no explicit mention of dignity. But the Convention cannot do without it.[24] There was never much real doubt about it, but that which there was has been removed by a rare piece of non-ambiguity: 'the very essence of the Convention is respect for human dignity and human freedom', said the Strasbourg Court in *Pretty v United Kingdom*.[25]

Catherine Dupre summarises: 'There is general agreement that dignity is both the foundation and the ultimate aim of human rights systems.'[26]

In the arena of healthcare law, then, dignity, wherever it is explicitly mentioned, seems foundational, and its meaning is encompassed by McCrudden's definition.

But McCrudden, rightly, is not happy with so broad a formulation. He tries to spell out of the various instruments a firmer meaning. As we will see, he succeeds. But one of the obstacles in his way is the objection that dignity is simply a placeholder. We have touched on this idea already. Any possible defence to the charge of 'placeholder' has to be historical. One would have to show that the draftsmen of the various instruments in which 'dignity' appears had an identifiable meaning in mind. But defence is hopeless. McCrudden summarises the position thus:

> Those drafting the [UN] Charter and the Universal Declaration [of Human Rights] largely adopted this strategy. A theory of human rights was a necessary starting point for the enterprise that was being embarked upon. Dignity was included in that part of any discussion or text where the absence of a theory of human rights would have been embarrassing. Its utility was to enable those participating in the debate to insert their own theory. Everyone could agree that human dignity was central, but not why or how. As Doron Shultziner puts it, '[t]here is a major advantage to this approach, for the abstention from a philosophical decision regarding the source and cause for rights and duties paves the way for a political consent concerning the specific rights and duties that ought to be legislated and enforced in practice without waiving or compromising basic principles of belief. Thus, the different parties that take part in a constitutive act can conceive human dignity as representing their particular set of values and worldview. In other words, human dignity is used as a linguistic-symbol that can represent different outlooks, thereby justifying a concrete political agreement on a seemingly shared ground.' This is not to imply that dignity has no content at all. Unlike in linguistics, where a placeholder carries no semantic information, dignity carried an enormous amount of content, but different content for different people.[27]

---

[24] McCrudden summarises the use made by the Strasbourg Court of dignity: ibid 683.

[25] (1997) 35 EHRR 423 para 65. See too *SW v United Kingdom* (1996) 21 EHRR 363.

[26] C Dupre, 'Unlocking Human Dignity: Towards a Theory for the 21st Century' (2009) 2 *European Human Rights Law Review* 190, 201. See further: D Kretzmer and E Klein (eds), *The Concept of Human Dignity in Human Rights Discourse* (Alphen aan den Rijn, Kluwer Law International, 2002), and J Feinberg *Rights, Justice, and the Bounds of Liberty* (Princeton, NJ, Princeton University Press, 1980) esp p 151.

[27] McCrudden, 'Human Dignity and Judicial Interpretation of Human Rights' 678. Cp D Beyleveld and R Brownsword *Human Dignity in Bioethics and Biolaw* (Oxford, OUP, 2004) 30–33. See particularly their consideration of the significance of the Explanatory Report that accompanies the Convention on

The post-war maelstrom was not the right environment for considered definitions. Emotional temperatures were running too high. It was urgently necessary to say in a formal, imposing way that dignity mattered. It may well have been disastrous had an over-zealous draftsman attempted a definition clause.

But now, well over half a century later, there has been debate enough. The originally very significant advantages of being uncommitted to a substantive account of dignity are now outweighed, at least in healthcare ethics and law, by the urgent need to press dignity into frontline, courtroom service.

McCrudden thinks that one can exegetically extract from the various usages of dignity in the human rights instruments a common core. He says that, amongst the various uses, there are some discernable family resemblances, and that from those:

> we can, perhaps, see the outlines of a basic minimum content of 'human dignity' that all who use the term historically and all those who include it in human rights texts appear to agree is the core, whether they approve of it or disapprove of it. This basic minimum content seems to have at least three elements. The first is that every human being possesses an intrinsic worth, merely by being human. The second is that this intrinsic worth should be recognized and respected by others, and some forms of treatment by others are inconsistent with, or required by, respect for this intrinsic worth. The first element is what might be called the 'ontological' claim; the second might be called the 'relational' claim. This minimum core of the meaning of human dignity seems to be confirmed both by our discussion of the historical roots of dignity, and by the ways in which it has been incorporated into the human rights texts we have considered. The human rights texts have gone further and supplemented the relational element of the minimum core by supplying a third element regarding the relationship between the state and the individual. This is the claim that recognizing the intrinsic worth of the individual requires that the state should be seen to exist for the sake of the individual human being, and not vice versa (the limited-state claim).[28]

I agree, and think that this summary would be uncontroversial amongst readers of the dignity literature. But it is unsatisfactory. McCrudden does not pretend otherwise. He acknowledges that dignity is stated here 'at a very high level of generality'[29] and does not exclude the possibility that dignity may legitimately and usefully be given a more specific meaning.[30]

Human Rights and Biomedicine, at p 30. For their look at the notion of dignity that lies behind the Universal Declaration on the Human Genome and Human Rights, see pp 38–41.

[28] McCrudden, 'Human Dignity and Judicial Interpretation of Human Rights' 679.

[29] Ibid 679.

[30] He thinks that the problem is not that there is no coherent extra-legal idea of dignity that could be pressed into service in the courts, but rather that there are two many competing and inconsistent ideas. 'Dignity appears to become other than impossibly vague', he says, 'only when it is tethered to a coherent community of interpretation.' Ibid 723. And he is rightly pessimistic of wide agreement about what the framework of interpretation might be. For McCrudden, the foreseeable use of dignity is to give judges a 'language in which [they] can appear to justify how they deal with issues such as the weight of rights, the domestication and contextualization of rights, and the generation of new or more extensive rights' (ibid 724). (See too ibid 712–13, where he makes the case for the utility of dignity in

But the more fundamental problem with this as a definition is the one that we have repeatedly noted in looking at the philosophical literature: that it seeks to bear within itself two sometimes competing notions—those of dignity as status (with constraint as its corollary) and dignity as a quality (with empowerment as its corollary). Tension in itself is bearable, and indeed a sign of life, but we have seen that those tensions produce war when proponents of these two notions of dignity seek to wield them against each other in the bioethical colosseum. If dignity is a concept worthy of respect—let alone worthy of being designated bioethical-principle-in-chief—it needs to be free of the dangers of such civil war.

All this said, though, dignity has already done sterling service as a rallying call for basic decency and as a shot across the bows of would-be tyrants. But this might seem to be damning with faint praise, and to play into the hands of the Macklinite scoffers. And indeed there are few examples in the law books of decisions that could not have been reached or problems that could not have been unlocked satisfactorily without the help of dignity. Dignity has often been invoked by the judges—but often as a makeweight or a rhetorical flourish.[31] Rarely has it been wholly determinative of a decision.[32] Many of the decisions where it has featured prominently have been in medical cases. We look at those when we come to individual subjects such as the rights of the foetus, or end of life decision-making. Perhaps most of the future decisions in which dignity and nothing but dignity will do will be medical cases—and particularly those involving genetic modification and other transhumanist-type cases. We come to those too. But even so far there have been a few cases which *needed* dignity. The best known is the dwarf-throwing case.

Throwing Dwarfs in France

'Nobody tosses a dwarf', the outraged Gimli tells Aragorn in the film of 'The Lord of the Rings'. But he was wrong. They do, and commonly. It is popular in some parts of France. Dwarfs, paid for their pains, and wrapped in padded costumes,

process). I would observe that the notion of dignity embedded in the Basic Law of Israel (Basic Law: Human Dignity and Liberty: 17 March 1992, amended 9 March 1994) has been used by the judges there in precisely this way. Dignity, there, has been a very important and creative legal craftsman: see the discussion in D Kretzmer, 'Human Dignity in Israeli Jurisprudence' in D Kretzmer and E Klein (eds), *The Concept of Human Dignity in Human Rights Discourse* (Alphen aan den Rijn, Kluwer Law International, 2002).

[31] For a denunciation of the use of dignity as a flourish, see A Fagan, 'Dignity and Unfair Discrimination: A Value Misplaced and a Right Misunderstood' (1998) 14 *South African Journal of Human Rights* 220, and the discussion in Beyleveld and Brownsword, *Human Dignity in Bioethics and Biolaw* 20–21.

[32] Eg *Planned Parenthood of Southeastern Pennsylvania v Casey* 505 US 833 (1992) (re abortion in the US); *Pretty v United Kingdom* (2002) 35 EHRR 1 (re physician-assisted suicide in the United Kingdom); *National Coalition for Gay and Lesbian Equality v Minister of Justice* (1998) 6 BHRC 127 (re South African laws prohibiting sodomy).

are thrown onto mattresses or, swathed in Velcro, onto walls. The winner of the contest is the one who throws the dwarf furthest or highest.

The police in Morsang-sur-Orge and Aix-en-Provence took a dim view of this, and banned it. The issue went to the Conseil d'Etat, who decided that 'dwarf tossing was an attraction that affronted human dignity, respect for human dignity being part of public order and the authority vested in the municipal police being the means of ensuring it'.[33]

One of the dwarfs, Manuel Wackenheim, was not prepared to be deprived of his livelihood without a struggle. He contended before the International Committee convened under the International Covenant on Civil and Political Rights that:

> banning him from working has had an adverse effect on his life and represents an affront to his dignity. He claims to be the victim of a violation by France of his right to freedom, employment, respect for private life and an adequate standard of living, and of an act of discrimination. He further states that there is no work for dwarves in France and that his job does not constitute an affront to human dignity since dignity consists in having a job.[34]

The Committee found against him, saying that:

> the State party has demonstrated, in the present case, that the ban on dwarf tossing as practised by the author did not constitute an abusive measure but was necessary in order to protect public order, which brings into play considerations of human dignity that are compatible with the objectives of the Covenant. The Committee accordingly concludes that the differentiation between the author and the persons to whom the ban ordered by the State party does not apply was based on objective and reasonable grounds.[35]

If this decision is right, it is right because dignity is the right lens through which to look at the problem. If it is wrong, it is wrong either because dignity is the wrong lens, or because the right lens has been misapplied in some way. But this is a pure dignity decision: no other principle is in play.[36] The determinations of the Conseil d'Etat and the International Committee are painfully frustrating. Though they base their decision on dignity, they do not say what they mean by dignity. But in a sense it doesn't matter. Dignity in some sense it certainly was: it couldn't have been anything else.

Assume for the purposes of argument that this is the right decision (which I happen to think it was). How, other than via dignity, could one have arrived at it? Autonomy? No: just like the hypothetical mentally incapacitate girl on the hospital trolley, all of the obviously affected parties (the dwarfs, the dwarf-throwers and the spectators in one example; the girl and the lascivious youths in the other) were entirely happy with the throwing and the leching. One might argue that the autonomy interests of the outraged populations of Morsang-sur-Orge and

---

[33] Taken from the summary of the Conseild'Etat's position in the determination of the Human Rights Committee, established under Art 28 of the International Covenant on Civil and Political Rights para 2.5: see www.bayefsky.com/html/france_t5_iccpr_854_1999.php.

[34] Ibid para 3.

[35] Ibid, para 7.4.

[36] See the discussion by Stephen Wilkinson in his chapter 'Commodification' in R Ashcroft, A Dawson and H Draper (eds), *Principles of Healthcare Ethics* (London, Wiley, 2007) 287.

Aix-en-Provence, or France, or Europe, or those countries that have signed the International Covenant on Civil or Political Rights, were infringed by the throwing, but it would be tortuous. They didn't have to watch if they didn't want to. Was their ability happily to exercise their autonomy affected in any way by the knowledge that this was going on, on their moral or legal watch? In no real sense. And if it was, then at the bottom of their outrage must be something like dignity.

The autonomist's reasoning must be along the lines of: 'We wouldn't feel that we were living in the sort of place in which we had originally chosen to live, and in which we have a right to stay, if that sort of thing is happening in clubs regulated by laws to which we are a party and which in turn govern us. And that's because we think that dwarf-throwing is an affront to human dignity.'

There is no escape from that final line. And the same happens if one substitutes any other principle you choose in the place of autonomy.

Dignity as the Most Basic Legal Value

When, as a lawyer, you run out of other ideas, you pick up dignity. That may sound like a slight to dignity. In fact it is the opposite. It is an indication that when you are forced to basics (as in the PVS cases, to which we will shortly come), you are forced to dignity. We have met this idea already, in the course of a brief discussion about whether rights can do the job of dignity,[37] and we will meet it again in the course of our look at the way in which dignity has been used in specific bioethical contexts. A few short examples illustrate the point.

In the Constitutional Court of South Africa, Sachs J in *National Coalition for Gay and Lesbian Equality and Another v Minister of Justice and Others*, said: 'It will be noted that the *motif* which links and unites equality and privacy, and which, indeed, runs right through the protections offered by the Bill of Rights, is dignity.'[38]

In the same case, Ackermann J observed that: 'the right to dignity is a cornerstone of our Constitution'.[39]

In *Airedale NHS Trust v Bland*, Hoffmann LJ said that 'the dignity of an individual is an intrinsic value'.[40]

In *R (A, B, X and Y) v East Sussex County Council (No 2)*, Munby J said: 'The recognition and protection of human dignity is one of the core values—in truth the core value—of our society and, indeed, of all the societies which are part of the European family of nations and which have embraced the principles of the Convention'.[41]

As we have already seen, in *Pretty v UK*, the ECtHR said that: 'The very essence of the Convention is respect for human dignity and human freedom.'[42]

---

[37] See above, pp 66–67.
[38] *National Coalition for Gay and Lesbian Equality and Another v Minister of Justice and Others* [1998] 2 ZACC 15 para 120.
[39] At para 30.
[40] *Airedale NHS Trust v Bland* [1993] AC 789, 826.
[41] *R (A, B, X and Y) v East Sussex County Council (No 2)* (2003) 6 CCLR 194 para 86.
[42] (2002) 35 EHRR 1 para 65.

The West German Constitutional Court spoke of 'human dignity, the centre of the value system of the constitution'.[43]

The South African and German examples are comments on the constitutions of those countries, and it might be said that they are, for that reason, of little general interest. But that cannot be so. It would be strange if the United Kingdom, for instance, declared that dignity was less fundamental to it than to Germany. Indeed, in the light of the ECtHR's observations in *Pretty v UK*, such a declaration is not open to it.

I accept, though, that to say that dignity is important is not at all the same thing as to say that it is foundational, or more important than all other principles. Even in *Pretty*, dignity shares its throne with freedom. The nearest one gets to a judicial sound-bite establishing dignity's predominance is in *R (A, B, X and Y) v East Sussex County Council (No 2)*.[44] In medical ethics and bioethics, that predominance must be established by demonstration, not sound-bite. Outside the bioethical context, David Feldman probably represents the mainstream academic consensus in saying that dignity 'can never be more than one of a number of values, principles, and policies which pull decision-makers in different directions'.[45] There is probably no such consensus in bioethics. Bioethics forces lawyers to fundamentals in a way that other areas of ethics and law do not. Even outside bioethics, the prognosis 'can never be more than one of a number' is unduly pessimistic. It is not my brief, but I suspect that if one traces other principles of public and private law to their root, one might well arrive at dignity.

Dignity in the Bioethics Context: Have the Courts said Definitively what they mean by Dignity?

We have already noted:

(a) that although there are many international instruments that mention dignity in contexts relevant to bioethics and healthcare, they do not prescribe the meaning of dignity;

(b) that in areas other than bioethics and healthcare, the courts have not consistently adopted a particular interpretation of dignity.

---

[43] Decision of the Federal Constitutional Court, 35, 202, 225.

[44] And even that has to be read in the light of Munby J's further comments in *Burke* (see below).

[45] D Feldman, *Civil Liberties and Human Rights in England and Wales* (Oxford, OUP, 2002) 133. He illustrates this, at p 132, by quoting from Dawn Oliver's chapter, 'The Underlying Values of Public and Private Law', in M Taggart (ed), *The Province of Administrative Law* (Oxford, Hart, 1997), in which she suggests that dignity (along with autonomy, respect, status and security) is one of the values underlying both private and public United Kingdom law. Professor Feldman comments: 'Even among the values that Professor Oliver identifies, dignity would appear, from its concrete effects in law, to rank below autonomy and security, on which legal institutions such as property are founded.' This is fair, outside the bioethical context.

We will turn shortly to look at the way in which, in the major specific healthcare and bioethics contexts, the courts have wielded dignity (insofar as they have wielded it at all). The conclusion will be, as in (a) and (b) above, that there is no authority that forces us to read dignity in a way that precludes the version I am advancing. From a legal point of view, then, there is a point in going on with this argument. *Stare decisis* has not shut the door.

But before we get specific, it is worth pausing to look at some of the general judicial comments made in a healthcare/bioethics setting about dignity. They serve as an introduction to the specific areas, and citing them here will mean that we can move more swiftly through the specifics, referring back to the more general observations. Because of the industry of Munby J, this survey can be done by citing directly only two cases. Both are from the United Kingdom.[46]

Airedale NHS Trust v Bland

Bland[47] is the House of Lords' famous determination of the lawfulness of withdrawal of artificial nutrition and hydration from a patient in persistent vegetative state (PVS). PVS cases are the classic hard cases which may or may not make bad law. They force the judges to confront issues that can normally be sidestepped: the question of what is life and what is not; what is a human being and what is not; which rights prevail over which.

But before the case got to the House of Lords (which was apparently uninterested in the dignity arguments), of course it went to the Court of Appeal, and the judgment of Hoffmann LJ, as he then was, is an important and much-cited comment on dignity and its relationship to other principles.[48] He referred to 'a cluster of ethical principles which we apply to decisions about how we should live'.

---

[46] Of course this does not mean that other jurisdictions have not considered what dignity means. On the contrary (for instance), the Canadian case of *Rodriguez* was crucial in *Pretty v United Kingdom*, as we will see. One purported definition, promulgated in Canada, has received some attention from the commentators. This is *Law v Canada* [1999] 1 SCR 497. There, Iacabucci J said, at para 53: 'Human dignity means that an individual or group feels self-respect and self-worth. It is concerned with physical and psychological integrity and empowerment ... Human dignity ... does not relate to the status or position of an individual in society per se, but rather concerns the manner in which a person legitimately feels when confronted with a particular law.' For Bates, this definition is adequate to make dignity ubiquitously useful: see J Bates, 'Human Dignity—An Empty Phrase in Search of Meaning?' (2005) 10 *Judicial Review* 165. To rest dignity on a *feeling* that someone may or may not have makes it useless in many cases of incapacity, and to say that it is '*concerned* with physical and psychological integrity' is insufficiently specific to be helpful in most medical contexts. I agree with Bates's conclusion, at p 168: 'it is clear that by having a stable definition, the concept of "human dignity" is capable of being litigated and is capable of being put before the courts for adjudication ... Until a definition is available, human dignity will be just another empty phrase, of little use to either the courts or those who appear before them.'

[47] *Airedale NHS Trust v Bland* [1993] 1 All ER 821 HL.

[48] Cited in, for instance, *Portsmouth NHS Trust v Wyatt* [2004] EWHC 2247 (Fam), per Hedley J. This concerned the withdrawal of life-sustaining treatment from an infant. Hedley J, at para 21, said that the case 'evokes some of the fundamental principles that undergird our humanity. They are not to be found in Acts of Parliament or decisions of the courts but in the deep recesses of the common psyche of humanity whether they be attributed to humanity being created in the image of God or whether it be simply a self-defining ethic of a generally acknowledged humanism', and that these

I start with the concept of the sanctity of life ... we have a strong feeling that there is an intrinsic value in human life, irrespective of whether it is valuable to the person concerned or indeed to anyone else. Those who adhere to religious faiths which believe in the sanctity of all God's creation and in particular that human life was created in the image of God himself will have no difficulty with the concept of the intrinsic value of human life. But even those without any religious belief think in the same way. In a case like this we should not try to analyse the rationality of such feelings. What matters is that, in one form or another, they form part of almost everyone's intuitive values. No law which ignores them can possibly hope to be acceptable. Our belief in the sanctity of life explains why we think it is almost always wrong to cause the death of another human being, even one who is terminally ill or so disabled that we think that if we were in his position we would rather be dead. Still less do we tolerate laws such as existed in Nazi Germany, by which handicapped people or inferior races could be put to death because someone else thought that their lives were useless. But the sanctity of life is only one of a cluster of ethical principles which we apply to decisions about how we should live. Another is respect for the individual human being and in particular for his right to choose how he should live his own life. We call this individual autonomy or the right of self-determination. And another principle, closely connected, is respect for the dignity of the individual human being: our belief that quite irrespective of what the person concerned may think about it, it is wrong for someone to be humiliated or treated without respect for his value as a person. The fact that the dignity of an individual is an intrinsic value is shown by the fact that we feel embarrassed and think it wrong when someone behaves in a way which we think demeaning to himself, which does not show sufficient respect for himself as a person.[49]

This is tantalisingly incomplete. One would have liked to see a description of the relationship between the principle of the 'sanctity of life' and that of the 'intrinsic value' of the dignity of an individual. Two such intrinsic properties are surely intimately related. And indeed he did go on to say a little more about the relationship, in a passage cited by Munby J in *Burke*, reproduced at paragraph 79 in the judgment,[50] in which he said that the sanctity of life may have to give way to dignity. But such a bold assertion is no substitute for a detailed dissection of the concepts.

It may well be that Hoffmann LJ is pragmatically biting his tongue. He is one of the most philosophically literate of the judges, and surely knew well that, as we have seen, it is easy to devalue dignity's currency if one exposes too obviously the debates between the false dichotomisers—the proponents of 'dignity as status' and 'dignity as quality'.

Lord Hoffmann's overall track record shows that he cannot be accused of undervaluing dignity. He may well have thought that it was best defended by not over-defining it—by keeping its powder dry. I have two comments on that.

---

principles were 'powerfully captured' by the judgment of Hoffmann LJ in *Bland*; *An NHS Trust v D (By her Litigation Friend, the Official Solicitor), Mr and Mrs D* [2005] EWHC 2439 (Fam); cp *Re A (a minor)* [1992] 3 Med LR 303.

[49] At p 826.
[50] See below, pp 109–10.

First, the only point of keeping powder dry is so that it can ultimately be fired. And second, there are conflicts ahead, in the realm of enhancement technologies, in which dry powder will not be an option.

But something more mundane may well have been operating too. There is a prudent judicial tendency to do only what is necessary for the purposes of the case, and in the context of *Bland* it was arguably only necessary, for the purposes of getting the right result, to give readers of the judgment a quick flash of the dignity flag.

Munby J in R (Burke) v General Medical Council

In *Burke*, which concerned the question of whether the General Medical Council's guidelines on the withdrawal of life-sustaining treatment accurately summarised the law, Munby J, at first instance,[51] produced a masterly survey of the embryonic law relating to dignity, starting with Hoffmann LJ's observations in *Bland* and moving through several jurisdictions. It is far and away the most thorough expression of judicial thinking about dignity in a medico-legal context, and despite (or rather because of) its length, it is reproduced in full below. While the Court of Appeal concluded that Munby J had ranged more widely than was necessary for the determination of the narrow issue before the court (making much of the passage cited below technically obiter),[52] his comments on dignity were not disapproved.

The Court of Appeal was surely wrong in its criticism of the breadth and depth of the analysis. Munby J was right to deploy dignity as the lodestone. And if that was right, someone, sometime, had to grasp the nettle that successive courts had refused or failed to grasp—to say what dignity meant, and to indicate how, if at all, it could be described in the language of the ECHR.

A lot of water had passed under the bridge since *Bland*. In *Bland*, agnosticism about dignity's meaning, and a broad assertion that it was in some inchoate way important and fundamental, were just about enough. But by the time that *Burke* came before Munby J, dignity was being used as a buzzword in judicial and professional discourse; it was said to be the lifeblood of the ECHR. No competent judgment could fail to invoke dignity expressly. And no judge could properly invoke it without trying to tie it down.

Here is Munby J's attempt.[53] Under the heading 'Dignity', he said this:

57. I venture to repeat here what I said in *R (A, B, X and Y) v East Sussex County Council (No 2)* 6 CCLR 194, para 86:

The recognition and protection of human dignity is one of the core values—in truth the core value—of our society and, indeed, of all the societies which are part of the European family of nations and which have embraced the principles of the

---

[51] *R (Burke) v General Medical Council* [2004] EWHC 1879 (Admin).
[52] See [2006] QB 273.
[53] [2005] QB 424.

Convention. It is a core value of the common law, long pre-dating the Convention ... The invocation of the dignity of the patient in the form of declaration habitually used when the court is exercising its inherent declaratory jurisdiction in relation to the gravely ill or dying is not some meaningless incantation designed to comfort the living or to assuage the consciences of those involved in making life and death decisions: it is a solemn affirmation of the law's and of society's recognition of our humanity and of human dignity as something fundamental.

58. But it is not just the sentient or self-conscious who have dignity interests protected by the law. Referring to one of the arguments in *Bland* [1993] AC 789, 829 Hoffmann LJ made this important point:

> I think that the fallacy in this argument is that it assumes that we have no interests except in those things of which we have conscious experience. But this does not accord with most people's intuitive feelings about their lives and deaths. At least a part of the reason why we honour the wishes of the dead about the distribution of their property is that we think it would wrong them not to do so, despite the fact that we believe that they will never know that their will has been ignored. Most people would like an honourable and dignified death and we think it wrong to dishonour their deaths, even when they are unconscious that this is happening. We pay respect to their dead bodies and to their memory because we think it an offence against the dead themselves if we do not. Once again I am not concerned to analyse the rationality of these feelings. It is enough that they are deeply rooted in our ways of thinking and that the law cannot possibly ignore them. Thus I think that counsel for the Official Solicitor offers a seriously incomplete picture of Anthony Bland's interests when he confines them to animal feelings of pain or pleasure. It is demeaning to the human spirit to say that, being unconscious, he can have no interest in his personal privacy and dignity, in how he lives or dies. Anthony Bland therefore has a recognisable interest in the manner of his life and death which can help the court to apply the principles of self-determination and the value of the individual. We can say from what we have learned of Anthony Bland from those closest to him that, forced as we are to choose, we think it is more likely that in his present state he would choose to die than to live. There is no suggestion that he was, for example, motivated by any religious principles which would have made him want his life in its present state prolonged. We can also say that in allowing him to die, we would be showing more respect to him as an individual than by keeping him alive.

As he added, at p 833: 'The best interests of the patient in my judgment embrace not only recovery or the avoidance of pain ... but also a dignified death.' I respectfully agree.

Autonomy, dignity and the Convention

59. It is important to note that personal autonomy and dignity are both aspects of the 'private life' respect for which is guaranteed by article 8 of the Convention. As the Strasbourg court said in *Pretty v United Kingdom* (2002) 35 EHRR 1, para 61:

> the concept of 'private life' is a broad term not susceptible to exhaustive definition. It covers the physical and psychological integrity of a person. It can sometimes embrace aspects of an individual's physical and social identity ... Article 8 also protects a right to personal development, and the right to establish and develop relationships with other human beings and the outside world. Though no previous case has established as such any right to self-determination as being contained in article 8 of the Convention,

the court considers that the notion of personal autonomy is an important principle underlying the interpretation of its guarantees.

And it added, at para 65: 'The very essence of the Convention is respect for human dignity and human freedom.'

60. In *Bensaid v United Kingdom* (2001) 33 EHRR 205, para 47 the court had earlier identified another aspect of 'private life' which is also important in this context:

Mental health must also be regarded as a crucial part of private life associated with the aspect of moral integrity. Article 8 protects a right to identity and personal development, and the right to establish and develop relationships with other human beings and the outside world. The preservation of mental stability is in that context an indispensable precondition to effective enjoyment of the right to respect for private life.

61. I note that in *R (Razgar) v Secretary of State for the Home Department* [2004] 2 AC 368, para 9 Lord Bingham of Cornhill said: 'Elusive though the concept is, I think one must understand "private life" in article 8 as extending to those features which are integral to a person's identity or ability to function socially as a person', and quoted with approval Professor Feldman's observation, ('The Developing Scope of Article 8 of the European Convention on Human Rights' [1997] EHRLR 265, 270), that:

Moral integrity in this sense demands that we treat the person holistically as morally worthy of respect, organising the state and society in ways which respect people's moral worth by taking account of their need for security,

whilst Lord Carswell accepted, at para 74, that 'the preservation of mental stability can be regarded as a right protected by article 8'.

62. It is also important to note what the court said in *Pretty* 35 EHRR 1, paras 63–66:

63. While it might be pointed out that death was not the intended consequence of the applicants' conduct in the above situations, the court does not consider that this can be a decisive factor. In the sphere of medical treatment, the refusal to accept a particular treatment might, inevitably, lead to a fatal outcome, yet the imposition of medical treatment, without the consent of a mentally competent adult patient, would interfere with a person's physical integrity in a manner capable of engaging the rights protected under article 8(1) of the Convention. As recognised in domestic case law, a person may claim to exercise a choice to die by declining to consent to treatment which might have the effect of prolonging his life.

64. In the present case, though medical treatment is not an issue, the applicant is suffering from the devastating effects of a degenerative disease which will cause her condition to deteriorate further and increase her physical and mental suffering. She wishes to mitigate that suffering by exercising a choice to end her life with the assistance of her husband. As stated by Lord Hope, the way she chooses to pass the closing moments of her life is part of the act of living, and she has a right to ask that this too must be respected.

65. The very essence of the Convention is for human dignity and human freedom. Without in any way negating the principle of sanctity of life protected under the Convention, the court considers that it is under article 8 that notions of the quality of life take on significance. In an era of growing medical sophistication combined with longer life expectancies, many people are concerned that they should not be forced

to linger on in old age or in states of advanced physical or mental decrepitude which conflict with strongly held ideas of self and personal identity.

66. In *Rodriguez v Attorney General of Canada* [1994] 2 LRC 136, which concerned a not dissimilar situation to the present, the majority opinion of the Supreme Court considered that the prohibition on the appellant in that case from receiving assistance in suicide contributed to her distress and prevented her from managing her death. This deprived her of autonomy and required justification under principles of fundamental justice. Although the Canadian court was considering a provision of the Canadian Charter framed in different terms from those of article 8 of the Convention, comparable concerns arose regarding the principle of personal autonomy in the sense of the right to make choices about one's own body.

In other words, the personal autonomy which is protected by article 8 embraces such matters as how one chooses to pass the closing days and moments of one's life and how one manages one's death.

63. Dignity is, of course, also protected by article 3. In *D v United Kingdom* (1997) 24 EHRR 423, an AIDS sufferer was threatened with removal from the United Kingdom to the island of St Kitts where no effective medical or palliative treatment for his illness was available and where he would have been exposed to the risk of dying under most distressing circumstances. The court held that there would be a breach of article 3. Explaining why, it said:

51. The court notes that the applicant is in the advanced [stages] of a terminal and incurable illness. At the date of the hearing, it was observed that there had been a marked decline in his condition and he had to be transferred to a hospital. His condition was giving rise to concern. The limited quality of life he now enjoys results from the availability of sophisticated treatment and medication in the United Kingdom and the care and kindness administered by a charitable organisation. He has been counselled on how to approach death and has formed bonds with his carers.

52. The abrupt withdrawal of these facilities will entail the most dramatic consequences for him. It is not disputed that his removal will hasten his death. There is a serious danger that the conditions of adversity which await him in St Kitts will further reduce his already limited life expectancy and subject him to acute mental and physical suffering. Any medical treatment which he might hope to receive there could not contend with the infections which he may possibly contract on account of his lack of shelter and of a proper diet as well as exposure to the health and sanitation problems which beset the population of St Kitts. While he may have a cousin in St Kitts no evidence has been adduced to show whether this person would be willing to or capable of attending to the needs of a terminally ill man. There is no evidence of any other form of moral or social support. Nor has it been shown whether the applicant would be guaranteed a bed in either of the hospitals on the island which, according to the Government, care for AIDS patients.

53. In view of these exceptional circumstances and bearing in mind the critical stage now reached in the applicant's fatal illness, the implementation of the decision to remove him to St Kitts would amount to inhuman treatment by the respondent state in violation of article 3. The court also notes in this respect that the respondent state has assumed responsibility for treating the applicant's condition since August 1994. He has become reliant on the medical and palliative care which he is at present receiving and is no doubt psychologically prepared for death in an environment which is both

familiar and compassionate. Although it cannot be said that the conditions which would confront him in the receiving country are themselves a breach of the standards of article 3, his removal would expose him to a real risk of dying under most distressing circumstances and would thus amount to inhuman treatment.

64. As Cazalet J succinctly summarised it in *A National Health Service Trust v D* [2000] 2 FLR 677, 695: 'article 3 of the Convention, which requires that a person is not subjected to inhuman or degrading treatment includes the right to die with dignity.' I agree. I agree also with Mr Francis when he submits that article 3 encompasses a right to be protected from treatment—or, I would add, a lack of treatment—which will result in dying in avoidably distressing circumstances.

65. There are three points that I should add. The first is this. As we have already seen, 'private life' covers the 'physical and psychological integrity of a person'. Consistently with this, as the court recognised in *Raninen v Finland* (1997) 26 EHRR 563, para 63, there may be circumstances in which article 8 can be regarded as affording a protection in relation to conditions which do not attain the level of severity required by article 3. As the court said in *Bensaid v United Kingdom* 33 EHRR 205, para 46:

> Not every act or measure which adversely affects moral or physical integrity will interfere with the right to respect to private life guaranteed by article 8. However, the court's case law does not exclude that treatment which does not reach the severity of article 3 treatment may none the less breach article 8 in its private life aspect where there are sufficiently adverse effects on physical and moral integrity.

66. The second point is the one I made in *R (A, B, X and Y) v East Sussex County Council (No 2)* 6 CCLR 194, paras 121–122 about what is meant in this context by 'dignity'. We have to remember that:

> Dignified ends may sometimes demand the use of undignified means ... But this does not mean that means must be allowed to triumph over ends. There is a balance to be held—and it is often a very difficult balance to strike. It is difficult enough to balance the utility or possible futility of means against the utility or possible futility of ends: it is all the more difficult when one has to assess in addition the dignity or possible indignity of the means against the end in view. Modern medical law and ethics illustrate the excruciating difficulty we often have in achieving the right balance between using undignified means in striving to achieve dignified ends.

Moreover, we have to remember that views as to what is dignified or undignified are highly personal. What is dignified to one may be undignified to another. And vice versa. So, as Ms Rose correctly observes, we must guard against assuming that ANH is in all circumstances a good thing conducive to human dignity merely because that is, if indeed it is, the claimant's strongly held view.

67. The final point is very important and it relates to the enhanced degree of protection, and the increased vigilance in reviewing whether the Convention has been complied with, which is called for in the case of the vulnerable. I can start with what the Strasbourg court said in *Herczegfalvy v Austria* (1992) 15 EHRR 437, para 82:

> The court considers that the position of inferiority and powerlessness which is typical of patients confined in psychiatric hospitals calls for increased vigilance in reviewing whether the Convention has been complied with.

In *Keenan v United Kingdom* (2001) 33 EHRR 913 the court said, at paras 90, 110 and 112:

90. ... persons in custody are in a vulnerable position and ... the authorities are under a duty to protect them.

...

110. ... the authorities are under an obligation to protect the health of persons deprived of liberty. The lack of appropriate medical treatment may amount to treatment contrary to article 3. In particular, the assessment of whether the treatment or punishment concerned is incompatible with the standard of article 3 has, in the case of mentally ill persons, to take into consideration their vulnerability and their inability, in some cases, to complain coherently or at all about how they are being affected by any particular treatment.

...

112. ... While it is true that the severity of suffering, physical or mental, attributable to a particular measure has been a significant consideration in many of the cases decided by the court under article 3, there are circumstances where proof of the actual effect on the person may not be a major factor. For example ... treatment of a mentally ill person may be incompatible with the standards imposed by article 3 in the protection of fundamental human dignity, even though that person may not be capable of pointing to any specific ill-effects.

68. I need also to refer to the separate, concurring, opinion of Judge Greve in *Price v United Kingdom* (2002) 34 EHRR 1285, 1296–1297:

In this case there is a lack of immediate compatibility between the applicant's mere situation and detention in any ordinary prison facility. The applicant is confined to her wheelchair and has an extensive need for assistance, to the extent that at night she is unable to move enough to keep a normal human temperature if the room in which she stays is not specially heated or, as *in casu*, she is not wrapped, not just in blankets, but in a space blanket.

In this the applicant is different from other people to the extent that treating her like others is not only discrimination but brings about a violation of article 3 ...

It is obvious that restraining any non-disabled person to the applicant's level of ability to move and assist herself, for even a limited period of time, would amount to inhuman and degrading treatment—possibly torture. In a civilised country like the United Kingdom, society considers it not only appropriate but *a basic humane concern* to try to ameliorate and compensate for the disabilities faced by a person in the applicant's situation. In my opinion, these compensatory measures come to form part of the disabled person's bodily integrity. It follows that, for example, to prevent the applicant, who lacks both ordinary legs and arms, from bringing with her the battery charger to her wheelchair when she is sent to prison for one week, or to leave her in unsuitable sleeping conditions so that she has to endure pain and cold—the latter to the extent that eventually a doctor had to be called—is in my opinion a violation of the applicant's right to bodily integrity. Other episodes in the prison amount to the same.

The applicant's disabilities are not hidden or easily overlooked. It requires no special qualification, only a minimum of ordinary human empathy, to appreciate her situation and to understand that to avoid unnecessary hardship—that is, hardship not implicit in the imprisonment of an able-bodied person—she has to be treated differently from other people because her situation is significantly different.

69. Now the *Herczegfalvy, Keenan* and *Price* cases were all, of course, cases of persons who were vulnerable in part because they were detained by the state. But the principle is not confined to those who are vulnerable because they are confined, or whose vulnerability is increased because they are confined. It extends, for example, to the severely disabled living in their own homes: see *Botta v Italy* (1998) 26 EHRR 241 (in particular the concurring opinion, at pp 250–252, of Mr N Bratza, in the proceedings before the Commission) and *R (A, B, X and Y) v East Sussex County Council (No 2)* 6 CCLR 194. And *D v United Kingdom* 24 EHRR 423, as it seems to me, shows that exactly the same principle extends to a vulnerable patient in hospital: in that case, a terminally ill AIDS sufferer.

70. In *R (A, B, X and Y) v East Sussex County Council (No 2)* 6 CCLR 194, having set out the passage from Judge Greve's opinion which I have just quoted I continued, at para 93:

> This brings out the enhanced degree of protection which may be called for when the human dignity at stake is that of someone who is ... so disabled as to be critically dependent on the help of others for even the simplest and most basic tasks of day to day living. In order to avoid discriminating against the disabled ... one may, as Judge Greve recognised, need to treat the disabled differently precisely because their situation is significantly different from that of the able-bodied. Moreover, the positive obligation of the state to take reasonable and appropriate measures to secure the rights of the disabled under article 8 of the Convention ... and, in particular, the positive obligation of the state to secure their essential human dignity, calls for human empathy and humane concern as society, in Judge Greve's words, seeks to try to ameliorate and *compensate* for the disabilities faced by persons in A and B's situation.

71. I was pressed in that case by the Official Solicitor with the argument (see paras 138–139) that matters of dignity and respect weigh heavily with people who are already shut out from much of what is available to the vast majority. Agreeing, I said, at para 148:

> With [this argument]—the enhanced weight which is properly to be attached to the article 8 rights of those who through disability are already deprived of so much of what makes life enjoyable and enriching for the majority—I have no difficulty. It is, for the very reasons articulated by Judge Greve, a compelling argument. The claims of the disabled and the obligations of the state to give effect to their article 8 rights in the ways identified by Judge Greve in her separate opinion in Price and by Mr Bratza in his concurring opinion in *Botta*—analyses with each of which I entirely agree—are powerful indeed. I agree, therefore, that A and B's article 8 rights weigh heavily in the balance.

72. Very recently in her 2004 Paul Sieghart Memorial Lecture, 'What can the Human Rights Act do for my Mental Health?', Baroness Hale of Richmond made much the same point, at p 22:

> human dignity is all the more important for people whose freedom of action and choice is curtailed, whether by law or by circumstances such as disability. The Convention is a living instrument ... We need to be able to use it to promote respect

for the inherent dignity of all human beings but especially those who are most vulnerable to having that dignity ignored. In reality, the niceties and technicalities with which we have to be involved in the courts should be less important than the core values which underpin the whole Convention.

I respectfully agree.

The tension between these principles

73. Having identified these key ethical (and legal) principles—the sanctity of life, autonomy and dignity—Hoffmann LJ continued in *Bland* [1993] AC 789, 826–827 with this important observation:

> No one, I think, would quarrel with these deeply rooted ethical principles. But what is not always realised, and what is critical in this case, is that they are not always compatible with each other. Take, for example, the sanctity of life and the right of self-determination. We all believe in them and yet we cannot always have them both. The patient who refuses medical treatment which is necessary to save his life is exercising his right to self-determination. But allowing him, in effect, to choose to die, is something which many people will believe offends the principle of the sanctity of life. Suicide is no longer a crime, but its decriminalisation was a recognition that the principle of self-determination should in that case prevail over the sanctity of life ... A conflict between the principles of the sanctity of life and the individual's right of self-determination may therefore require a painful compromise to be made. In the case of the person who refuses an operation without which he will certainly die, one or other principle must be sacrificed. We may adopt a paternalist view, deny that his autonomy can be allowed to prevail in so extreme a case, and uphold the sanctity of life. Sometimes this looks an attractive solution, but it can have disturbing implications. Do we insist upon patients accepting life-saving treatment which is contrary to their strongly held religious beliefs? Should one force-feed prisoners on hunger strike? English law is, as one would expect, paternalist towards minors. But it upholds the autonomy of adults. A person of full age may refuse treatment for any reason or no reason at all, even if it appears certain that the result will be his death.

74. This crucially important point was adopted and elaborated by Lord Goff in the same case when he said in what, if I may say so, is an equally important passage, at p 864:

> it is established that the principle of self-determination requires that respect must be given to the wishes of the patient, so that if an adult patient of sound mind refuses, however unreasonably, to consent to treatment or care by which his life would or might be prolonged, the doctors responsible for his care must give effect to his wishes, even though they do not consider it to be in his best interests to do so ... To this extent, the principle of the sanctity of human life must yield to the principle of self-determination ... and, for present purposes perhaps more important, the doctor's duty to act in the best interests of his patient must likewise be qualified.

75. Striking examples of the respect the law shows for the principle of autonomy or self-determination, and examples, moreover, which emphasise its absolute nature, are to be found in such well-known cases as *In re C (Adult: Refusal of Treatment)* [1994] 1 WLR 290, *Secretary of State for the Home Department v Robb* [1995] Fam 127, *In re JT (Adult: Refusal of Medical Treatment)* [1998] 1 FLR 48, *St George's Healthcare NHS Trust v*

S [1999] Fam 26, *In re AK (Medical Treatment: Consent)* [2001] 1 FLR 129 and *In re B (Consent to Treatment: Capacity)* [2002] 1 FLR 1090.

76. Now all this, of course, presupposes that there is in fact a conflict, that we are in fact dealing with a competent patient or a patient who has competently expressed his wishes in a binding and effective advance directive. But this may not be at all clear as a matter of fact. What then? In *In re T (Adult: Refusal of Treatment)* [1993] Fam 95, 112, Lord Donaldson of Lymington MR referred to:

> a conflict between two interests, that of the patient and that of the society in which he lives. The patient's interest consists of his right to self-determination—his right to live his own life how he wishes, even if it will damage his health or lead to his premature death. Society's interest is in upholding the concept that all human life is sacred and that it should be preserved if at all possible. It is well established that in the ultimate the right of the individual is paramount.

He continued:

> But this merely shifts the problem where the conflict occurs and calls for a very careful examination of whether, and if so the way in which, the individual is exercising that right. In case of doubt, that doubt falls to be resolved in favour of the preservation of life for if the individual is to override the public interest, he must do so in clear terms.

77. In *In re T* the problem arose in the context of a dispute as to whether or not the patient had in fact made a valid advance directive at all. But the issue may be whether an advance directive is still effective. That is the problem which Lord Goff addressed in *Bland* [1993] AC 789, 864:

> the same principle applies where the patient's refusal to give his consent has been expressed at an earlier date, before he became unconscious or otherwise incapable of communicating it; though in such circumstances especial care may be necessary to ensure that the prior refusal of consent is still properly to be regarded as applicable in the circumstances which have subsequently occurred ...

It is the problem that I recently had to consider in *HE v A Hospital NHS Trust* [2003] 2 FLR 408. I summarised my conclusion, at para 46:

> Where life is at stake the evidence must be scrutinised with especial care. Clear and convincing proof is required. The continuing validity and applicability of the advance directive must be clearly established by convincing and inherently reliable evidence.

78. So much for autonomy.

79. However, as Hoffmann LJ went on to point out in *Bland* [1993] AC 789, 830 it is not only autonomy which may have to take priority over the sanctity of life. Human dignity may also on occasions properly take priority:

> There is no formula for reconciling this conflict of principles and no easy answer. It does no good to seize hold of one of them, such as the sanctity of life, and say that because it is valid and right, as it undoubtedly is, it must always prevail over other principles which are also valid and right. Nor do I think it helps to say that these principles are all really different ways of looking at the same thing. Counsel appearing as amicus said that there was 'no inherent conflict between having regard to the quality of life and respecting the sanctity of life; on the contrary they are complementary;

the principle of sanctity of life embraces the need for full respect to be accorded to the dignity and memory of the individual'. To my mind, this is rhetoric intended to dull the pain of having to choose. For many people, the sanctity of life is not at all the same thing as the dignity of the individual. We cannot smooth away the differences by interpretation ... In my view the choice which the law makes must reassure people that the courts do have full respect for life, but that they do not pursue the principle to the point at which it has become almost empty of any real content and when it involves the sacrifice of other important values such as human dignity and freedom of choice.

Conclusions

80. Pausing to take stock at this point I can summarise my conclusions as follows. (1) Personal autonomy—the right of self-determination—and dignity are fundamental rights, recognised by the common law and protected by articles 3 and 8 of the Convention. (2) The personal autonomy which is protected by article 8 embraces such matters as how one chooses to pass the closing days and moments of one's life and how one manages one's death. (3) The dignity interests protected by the Convention include, under article 8, the preservation of mental stability and, under article 3, the right to die with dignity and the right to be protected from treatment, or from a lack of treatment, which will result in one dying in avoidably distressing circumstances. (4) Important as the sanctity of life is, it has to take second place to personal autonomy; and it may have to take second place to human dignity. (5) An enhanced degree of protection is called for under articles 3 and 8 in the case of the vulnerable.

As an exegesis of the UK authorities concerned explicitly with medical decision-making, these conclusions seem to me, with respect, to be right. It is true to say that UK judges have often talked about autonomy in terms that suggest that it is a rival of dignity. *Re T* is the classic example. And they have often talked, too, about autonomy being the all-trumping principle. Again, *Re T* is a good illustration. But, as I have illustrated at length elsewhere, if one casts one's net wider, one sees that autonomy's inadequacy as the chair of all medico-legal discussions is well acknowledged by the judges.[54] That acknowledgment should have filtered into Lord Donaldson's determination in *Re T*, tempering his pro-autonomy dogmatism, and should accordingly have altered the conclusion of Munby J in *Burke*.

What should Munby J have concluded? That whatever dignity is, it is a deeper concept than autonomy, and so has a right to priority. That autonomy rights, crucially important though they are, are rights that are rooted in and find their only conceivable justification in dignity: autonomy is a *manifestation* of dignity. That autonomy, in medical ethics, is often in conflict with other second-order principles, such as justice, and that when one is trying to resolve such conflicts, one should always go back to the parent principle—dignity—which gave rise to the warring factions.

As to the meaning of dignity, it was not open to Munby J to concur with my formulation. That formulation is not implicit in the judicial authorities. But nor is it excluded by them.

We now turn to look at some of the specific areas of medicine and bioethics.

---

[54] C Foster, *Choosing Life, Choosing Death* (Oxford, Hart, 2009).

8

Consent, Confidentiality, Privacy, Medical Research and Resources

This chapter deals with the question of how dignity, as I have defined it, might work in the areas of consent to medical treatment, clinical confidentiality, medical research, and the allocation of resources.

Consent, confidentiality and research are close relatives. It is logical and not unconventional to deal with them together. Resource allocation, however, is not conventionally discussed alongside the other three. The reason that I deal with it here, in connection with the other three, is because rarely have the judges chosen explicitly to use the notion of dignity in relation to any of the four issues.[1] This is in contrast to other issues to which we will come (the status of the foetus, gene patenting, end-of-life decision-making and the use of body parts)— in relation to all of which there are some judicial comments at which we will need to look (albeit that the conclusion will be, in each case, that the comments are more or less window-dressing). While end-of-life decision-making falls squarely within the law of consent, the judges have sometimes used dignity-language to talk about it, and so I will consider it separately.

This chapter also serves as a general introduction to the issue, relevant to all subsequent chapters, of why, as a matter of basic principle rather than because of its demonstrated usefulness, dignity ought to be the foundational principle of bioethics. The usefulness in specific areas will still need to be demonstrated.

Using the colourful case of *R v Brown*,[2] I seek to show that analyses other than dignity do not work in many cases, and that dignity analyses work in all. I introduce Article 8 of the European Convention on Human Rights, suggest that in its approach to the problems of bioethics it adopts a dignity analysis and a substantive account of dignity that is identical to mine, and suggest that the

---

[1] Another way of justifying bracketing them together would be to adopt Freeman's line of thought. 'The current concepts of autonomy, surrogate autonomy and informed consent often lead to futile and expensive care at the ends of life. They may impinge on the dignity of the patient as well as subject society to unwarranted expense. In order to provide affordable healthcare for all, these concepts are in need of modification.' J Freeman, 'Rights, Respect for Dignity and End-of-life Care: Time for a Change in the Concept of Informed Consent' (2010) 36 *Journal of Medical Ethics (JME)* 61. I broadly agree with his comment, but would (of course) modify it to assert that autonomy and informed consent don't really need to be *modified*: they just need to acknowledge their origins and sometimes adjust their attitude accordingly. See too S Brooks 'Dignity and Cost-effectiveness: A Rejection of the Utilitarian Approach to Death' (1984) 10 *JME* 148.

[2] *R v Brown* [1994] 1 AC 212.

transactional approach to bioethics is what judges necessarily do when they make Article 8 determinations.

Having identified the dignity analysis implicit in *Brown*, and noted how that would translate into the language of Article 8, we will be able to move swiftly through confidentiality, research and resources. The points that can be made in those contexts are identical to those raised by the issue of consent.

Consent

Basics

In *Choosing Life, Choosing Death*, I surveyed the ethical principles deployed by the judges in struggling with the law of consent, noting that at first blush, autonomy seemed to dictate every passage of every judgment, but that if one looks a little deeper it is plain that other things are going on.[3] That is because other things *have* to go on: one cannot get the results that are obviously right using one simple rule.

How Judges Judge

Consent cases illustrate well the general strategy used by judges in dealing with cases of any type, and so I deal with that strategy here.

Very few judges are led entirely by reason. They are humans, and generally decent humans. Chronologically, all of them were human beings before they were judges, and philosophically most of them are human beings before they are judges. They strive to reach the answer that they, as humans, think is right, and then they justify it according to the law.

The legal process known as 'distinguishing' a troublesome authority into irrelevance is one of the fig-leaves used to cover up the embarrassment that some judges might otherwise have in reconciling this procedure with the judicial oath, by which they swear to uphold and apply the law without fear or favour. I'm not for a moment suggesting that judges are intellectually dishonest: I'm suggesting that they recognise that honesty involves fidelity to their instincts as humans as well as to the doctrine of *stare decisis*. They don't stop being mothers and children when they sit down on the bench, as can be poignantly seen in some of the expressions of judicial agonising, most visibly and audibly in the Family Division. I hope that we wouldn't want it any other way.

There are various tools they can use in helping them justify the decision that they have identified as the right one. In the realm of medical law those tools include a number of ethical principles.

---

[3] (Oxford, Hart, 2009) 83–125.

Medical law, interestingly, is one area where the judges can be less cautious than elsewhere about importing their own views. *Bolam*[4] has long been the touchstone of professional acceptability in the realm of clinical negligence, and has a place, too, in the determination of best interests and (via the *Source Informatics* reference to the conscience of the reasonable professional),[5] in the law of clinical confidentiality. Most conceivable judicial conclusions about the 'right answer' are likely to be accommodated within the penumbra of *Bolam* acceptability. The guidelines of the various professional bodies are wheeled into the substantive law on the back of *Bolam* (how can a doctor claim to be acting *Bolam*-responsibly if he ignores the dictates of the GMC, for instance?), but those guidelines are generally sufficiently wide to encompass, without much damage, most of the conclusions to which rational judges might come. In medical law, then, judges have a licence to *judge* overtly (with the caveat that their own judgment will have to be expressed as that of a responsible doctor), that is denied to judges in many other areas of law.

Since medical practitioners are presumed (and required by their professional organisations) to act in an ethically coherent way, judges too are allowed to be explicitly ethical. I have criticised the guidelines of (for instance) the GMC as being drafted by autonomy,[6] but the reality is that the imbalance in those guidelines is easy enough to correct when it comes to judicial decision-making. The judges listen to the experts, to their own experiences and consciences, nod to the GMC, and pick up whatever principles they need to reach the 'right' answer. So, when we read the judgments, we see judicial pluralism.

The Problems of Ethical and Legal Pluralism

If all one is interested in is the right answer, then pluralistic use of Beauchamp and Childress's Four Principles will, in many cases, allow one to reach it. But there are problems with that approach. We have touched on them already:

(a) Two of the principles necessarily appeal for substantive content to something outside itself. The injunction 'Do good' requires a definition of 'good'. The statement 'Do no harm', also implies an idea of the good of which 'harm' is presumably the converse, and the statement imposes no obligation on anybody actually to do anything at all. And all the principles beg the question: 'Why is this important?'—an answer not inherent in the principle itself.

Tracing the roots of principle X isn't just academically titillating. There is a practical point to it—a point that is particularly pertinent when X is being used in the law courts, and might affect not only people in the instant case, but others who come after. The point is that there are often unforeseen

---

[4] *Bolam v Friern Hospital Management Committee* [1957] 1 WLR 583; cp *Bolitho v City and Hackney Health Authority* [1998] AC 232; see ch 1 n 15 above.

[5] *R v Department of Health ex p Source Informatics Ltd* [2000] Lloyd's Rep Med 76. For detailed discussion of this decision, see Foster, *Choosing Life, Choosing Death* 72.

[6] Foster, *Choosing Life, Choosing Death*, esp 5–6.

consequences of deploying X. Principles that seem safe and appropriate in a particular forensic arena can do monstrous things when they metastasise out of that arena (borne in the brains of creative lawyers). So before invoking X, one needs to look not only at the wider corollaries of X, but also, and very critically, at its origins. If X is endorsed, and it turns out that it can be demonstrated that it is the offspring of Y, it may prove hard to resist a later argument that Y should be the ruling principle.

Pluralism is generally a good thing, because it implies humility and lack of dogmatism on the part of the pluralist. But where the pluralism is actually a failure to recognise relationships, it shouldn't be applauded.

(b) If one adopts the 'make-do' pluralistic approach, one runs into real practical and philosophical trouble when that approach manifestly fails—as it does with (for instance) transhumanism. What does one do then? Create a separate discipline of ethics and law to deal with transhumanist problems? A discipline which one acknowledges has no intellectual continuity with the principles used to solve easier problems? If one is going to crack bioethical nuts, one should use the same type and size of hammer to crack them all, ignoring the jibe that dignity is an inappropriately big tool to use on, for instance, the day-to-day problems of confidentiality. It may be (in fact it certainly is) the case that most problems facing most clinicians on most wards most days can be solved by an appropriate interplay of Beauchamp and Childress's four principles. But why adopt an approximation when, with no greater practical difficulty, you can use a formula that gets it right?

(c) One problem with pluralism is that, if it is to work properly, each of the voices in the debate needs to be listened to with respect. But that hasn't happened in bioethics. One—autonomy—has been strident and intolerant, drowning out the voices of the others.

(d) Another problem with the 'Four Principles' type of pluralism is that it doesn't obviously take into account all the relevant material. Notably absent from the four principles is something that the intuitions of clinicians, patients and carers, as well as many of the relevant guidelines, think is central: dignity. This might, of course, be another way of saying that the 'good' in beneficence must include or be dignity, or that the 'harm' in non-maleficence is or includes the absence of dignity. If this is conceded, this quibble adds nothing to that in (a) above.

Does Dignity add Anything to the Conventional Ways of Looking at Consent?

The inadequacy of autonomy alone is easy enough to demonstrate. One need not go to the small print of any decision. The very existence of law—at least most of which is about the regulation of autonomy—will do. But if one needs supporting footnotes, they can be found, for instance, in *Reeves v Commissioner of Police for the Metropolis,*[7] (in which the police were found liable for negligently failing to prevent the entirely autonomous suicide of a wholly capacitate prisoner), in the many cases where pregnant women have been ordered, against their will, to have Caesarean sections saving their own lives and those of their foetuses,[8] in the criminalisation of sadomasochistic practice,[9] and in the whole notion of the best interests test used in determining what treatment should and should not be given to people labouring under a chronological or other incapacity.

In commenting on the law of consent in relation to children, I said that notwithstanding that some of the decisions made by children and subsequently overridden by the courts were, strictly speaking autonomous, it was still right that they were overruled. Why? Because:

> autonomy's perspective is too narrow. Autonomy makes a judgment at time X based on the information then available. The law sees the broader picture: it bases its judgment on what it knows about how human beings change over time and what the general criteria for human happiness are, as well as on its knowledge of and respect for the individual preferences and situation of the patient. When the law trumps a child's decision, it is wisdom trumping impulse. Wisdom ... is catholic in her choice of counsellors.[10]

The adjudication of wisdom—the adjudication of something that has taken into account everything possible, and particularly the accumulated knowledge of the species about what is best for members of the species—is an adjudication by dignity in the sense that I have defined it.

Surely this is recognised widely, although sometimes without using the word dignity. It is sometimes so obvious that it is easily missed. Why do patients put themselves into the hands of doctors in the first place? Because physical compromise is generally thought of as a bad thing. Bodily integrity matters because we are embodied animals—an observation that, as we have seen, has some momentous consequences. No doctor says: 'I could mend your fractured tibia, but I'm not going to. It's more important to get your soul in good shape.' The doctor knows, if she is any good, that there is a tight, if complex, relationship between the patient's overall well-being and the state of his tibia. Equally, a doctor who sees her treatment as merely an accurate placement of a plate is guilty of shameful dereliction of duty—neglecting two thirds of her patient, who is a mind-body-spirit unity.[11]

What happens in the process of consenting a capacitate patient for medical treatment? The clinician gives the patient the benefit of information accumulated in the course of the treatment of other members of the species facing similar situ-

---

[7] *Reeves v Commissioner of Police for the Metropolis* [2000] AC 360.

[8] See, eg, *Re MB (An Adult: Medical Treatment)* [1997] 2 FLR 426; *Re L (Patient: Non-Consensual Treatment)* [1997] 2 FLR 837.

[9] See *R v Brown* [1994] 1 AC 212; *Laskey, Jaggard and Brown v United Kingdom* (1997) 24 EHRR 39.

[10] Foster, *Choosing Life, Choosing Death* 125.

[11] C Foster, 'Why Doctors Should get a Life' (2010) 102 *Journal of the Royal Society of Medicine* 519–20.

ations. The factual information about outcomes that is found in the professional literature and in the doctor's own experience is filtered through the doctor's own intellect, intuition and personality until it becomes an opinion tailored to the patient's own circumstances. It emerges as an expression of what, for the patient, is the route most likely to make the patient thrive as a human being.

This is an unusual way to put the conclusion. It is only unusual because it is assumed to be so blindingly obvious that humans thrive better with intact tibias than with fractured ones that there is no point in spelling it out. But the advice, which will include an implicit statement to the effect 'Your leg is better off fixed than unfixed', will in fact be a statement of what the doctor knows—from studying the wider experience of the species—of how to solve the tibia problem in the way most likely to ensure thriving.

As a matter of fact, the patient is likely autonomously to agree with the suggestion that his tibial fracture is better off mended. Indeed autonomous choices are likely in most cases to overlap with what objectively will engender thriving. That is no surprise, but the overlap often obscures the contribution made by dignity to the process of deciding what is best. We will look in a moment at some cases where a patient's autonomous wishes depart from the dictates of dignity.

When we come to incapacitate patients, the focus on 'thriving' is all the more obvious. United Kingdom law says that it eschews the substituted judgment test, and focuses instead on a determination of the patient's best interests. This is no less the case in the compulsory treatment of children. Talk about parental consent to the treatment of their children can be misleading: a parent can only validly consent to something that is in the child's best interests. The starting point (but often not the ending point), is that the parent's view about what should be done is indeed an expression of the child's best interests.

The courts have repeatedly emphasised, in medical treatment decision cases, that the 'best interests' to which the decision-maker must have regard are all the relevant interests—not just the 'medical best interests'. The assessment required (often unrealistically, given the exigencies of medical practice) is a holistic one. The Mental Capacity Act 2005 similarly provides that the assessor of 'best interests' 'must consider *all* the relevant circumstances'[12] (added emphasis). The courts have observed that 'best interests are not limited to best medical interests',[13] that 'best interests encompasses medical, emotional and all other welfare issues'[14] and that '[i]t would be undesirable and probably impossible to set bounds to what is relevant to a welfare determination.'[15]

---

[12] S 4(2).

[13] *Re MB (Medical Treatment)* [1991] 2 FLR 426, 439 (Butler-Sloss LJ).

[14] *Re A (Male Sterilisation)* [2000] 1 FLR 549, 555 (Butler-Sloss P).

[15] *Re S (Adult Patient: Sterilisation)* [2001] Fam 15, 30 (Thorpe LJ). The importance of a wide-ranging determination of best interests was emphasised in *A v A Health Authority, Re J (A child), R (on the application of S) v Secretary of State for the Home Department* [2002] Fam 213; cp *Re B (A Minor) (Wardship: Sterilisation)* [1988] AC 199; *Re K (Minors) (Children: Care and Control)* [1977] Fam 179; *Re T (A minor) (Wardship: Medical Treatment)* [1997] 1 WLR 242.

Implicit in any purported holistic determination of 'best interests' is a notion of the Good Life; or of human thriving. The assessor looks at the situation that will pertain if the proposed intervention occurs, compares it with that that will pertain if the intervention does not occur, and decides, using a metaphysical measure derived from his understanding of what makes life worth living, whether the balance lies in favour of intervention or non-intervention. The best interests determination is supposed to be an *objective* determination. In *Re S (Sterilisation: Patient's Best Interests)*, Butler-Sloss P said:

> When the doctor moves on to consider the best interests of the patient he/she has to choose the best option, often from a range of options. As Mr. Munby has pointed out, the best interests test ought, logically, to give only one answer.
>
> In these difficult cases where the medical profession seeks a declaration as to lawfulness of the proposed treatment, the judge, not the doctor, has the duty to decide whether such treatment is in the best interests of the patient. The judicial decision ought to provide the best answer, not a range of alternative answers. There may, of course, be situations where the best answer may not be obvious and alternatives may have to be tried. It is still at any point the best option of that moment which should be chosen.[16]

An objective determination of best interests means that there is an objective account of how humans can best thrive being applied. At least in the case of very young infants, the infants can have provided no indication of how they would like to be treated: there is no element of substituted judgment. Autonomy doesn't come into it.

The law sometimes explicitly recognises that it may be in the best interests of X to undergo something whose primary purpose is to help Y. Thus, for instance, donation of bone marrow to a sibling may be justified, because of the likely beneficial effect on the emotional and psychological state of the donor.[17] A blood test to determine a child's paternity may be justified, even if its primary purpose is to resolve an issue of adultery in divorce proceedings,[18] as may ritual circumcision.[19] Here, the court is saying that to determine the best interests of the child or patient, one has to look at the nexus of relationships in which it exists. The child/patient will thrive best if that nexus is happy and healthy (bone marrow), if the basic facts on which self-understanding and consequent relationships rest are known (blood tests), and if the child/patient is able to slot into the religious community in which he/she naturally belongs. There is no room here for atomism.[20]

---

[16] *Re S (Sterilisation: Patient's Best Interests)* [2000] 2 FLR 389, 400.

[17] *Re Y (Mental Patient: Bone Marrow Donation)* [1997] Fam 110.

[18] *S v McC, W v W* [1972] AC 24; *B(BR) v B(J)* [1968] P 466.

[19] *Re J (Specific Issue Orders: Muslim Upbringing and Circumcision)* [1999] 2 FLR 678; *Re S (Specific Issue Order: Religion: Circumcision)* [2005] 1 FLR 236; *Secretary, Department of Health and Community Services v JWB and SMB* (1992) 175 CLR 218.

[20] For further examples of the courts using the idea of dignity to enshrine the importance of identity, see the German Constitutional Court case *BVerfGE 79*, 256 (268) (31 January 1989), and two ECJ

While autonomy comes into many other consent cases, it often doesn't win. One of the most dramatic examples is *R v Brown*.[21]

The defendants were homosexual sadomasochists. This account of their activities is taken from the speech of Lord Templeman:

> The victim was usually manacled so that the sadist could enjoy the thrill of power and the victim could enjoy the thrill of helplessness. The victim had no control over the harm which the sadist ... might inflict. In one case a victim was branded twice on the thigh ... The charges against the appellants were based on genital torture and violence to the buttocks, anus, penis, testicles and nipples. The victims were degraded and humiliated, sometimes beaten, sometimes wounded with instruments and sometimes branded. Bloodletting and the smearing of human blood produced excitement. There were obvious dangers of serious personal injury and blood infection ... Some activities involved excrement ... Cruelty to human beings was on occasions supplemented by cruelty to animals in the form of bestiality.[22]

All the defendants were convicted of offences under s 47 of the Offences Against the Person Act 1861 (assault occasioning actual bodily harm), and some to offences under s 20 (assault occasioning grievous bodily harm). Their defence was that no offences had been committed because the 'victims' had all consented. This was rejected by a majority of the House of Lords.

Lord Templeman said:

> My Lords, the authorities dealing with the intentional infliction of bodily harm do not establish that consent is a defence to a charge under the 1861 Act. They establish that the courts have accepted that consent is a defence to the infliction of bodily harm in the course of some lawful activities. The question is whether the defence should be extended to the infliction of bodily harm in the course of sadomasochistic encounters ... The question whether the defence of consent should be extended to the consequences of sado-masochistic encounters can only be decided by consideration of policy and public interest ... Counsel for the appellants argued that consent should provide a defence to charges under both ss 20 and 47 because, it was said, every person has a right to deal with his body as he pleases. I do not consider that this slogan provides a sufficient guide to the policy decision which must now be made. It is an offence for a person to abuse his own body and mind by taking drugs. Although the law is often broken, the criminal law restrains a practice which is regarded as dangerous and injurious to individuals and which if allowed and extended is harmful to society generally. In any event the appellants in this case did not mutilate their own bodies. They inflicted bodily harm on willing victims. Suicide is no longer an offence but a person who assists another to commit suicide is guilty of murder or manslaughter.

The assertion was made on behalf of the appellants that the sexual appetites of sadists and masochists can only be satisfied by the infliction of bodily harm and that the law

---

cases concerned with discrimination on the grounds of perceived sexual identity: *P v S and Cornwall County Council* [1996] ECR I-2143 and *KB v NHS Pensions Agency* [2004] ECR I-541.

[21] *Brown* (n 9).
[22] Ibid 236.

should not punish the consensual achievement of sexual satisfaction. There was no evidence to support the assertion that sado-masochist activities are essential to the happiness of the appellants or any other participants but the argument would be acceptable if sado-masochism were only concerned with sex as the appellants contend. In my opinion sado-masochism is not only concerned with sex. Sado-masochism is also concerned with violence. The evidence discloses that the practices of the appellants were unpredictably dangerous and degrading to body and mind ... Society is entitled and bound to protect itself against a cult of violence. Pleasure derived from the infliction of pain is an evil thing. Cruelty is uncivilised.[23] (emphasis added).

Lord Lowry thought that the question of consent was immaterial to the question of whether s 47 and/or s 20 offences had been committed, and accordingly the remaining question was whether there were good policy reasons for excluding sado-masochistic acts from the definition of those offences. He said:

In my opinion, the answer to that question is No.

In adopting this conclusion I follow closely my noble and learned friends Lord Templeman and Lord Jauncey. What the appellants are obliged to propose is that the deliberate and painful infliction of physical injury should be exempted from the operation of statutory provisions the object of which is to prevent or punish that very thing, the reason for the proposed exemption being that both those who will inflict and those who will suffer the injury wish to satisfy a perverted and depraved sexual desire. Sado-masochistic homosexual activity cannot be regarded as conducive to the enhancement or enjoyment of family life or conducive to the welfare of society. A relaxation of the prohibitions in ss 20 and 47 can only encourage the practice of homosexual sado-masochism, with the physical cruelty that it must involve, (which can scarcely be regarded as a 'manly diversion') by withdrawing the legal penalty and giving the activity a judicial imprimatur. As well as all this, one cannot overlook the physical danger to those who may indulge in sado-masochism ... So far as I can see, the only counter-argument is that to place a restriction on sado-masochism is an unwarranted interference with the private life and activities of persons who are indulging in a lawful pursuit and are doing no harm to anyone except, possibly, themselves. This approach, which has characterised every submission put forward on behalf of the appellants, is derived from the fallacy that what is involved here is the restraint of a lawful activity as opposed to the refusal to relax existing prohibitions in the 1861 Act ... The position is as simple as that, and there is no legal right to cause actual bodily harm in the course of sado-masochistic activity.[24]

There were blistering dissents from Lord Mustill and Lord Slynn of Hadley. That from Lord Mustill is particularly enlightening in our context. He wanted, he said:

---

[23] Ibid 234–37.

[24] Ibid 255–56. Lord Jauncey of Tullichettle decided the appeals on the basis that the infliction of actual or more serious bodily harm is an unlawful activity to which consent is no answer (ibid 245), but nonetheless went on to comment on, and dismiss, the defendants' submissions that consent to their activities would not be injurious to the public interest. His reasons for dismissing this submission are not completely clear, but the physical dangerousness of the activities seems to have weighed heavily with him: ibid 246.

to stress two considerations of cardinal importance. Lawyers will need no reminding of the first, but since this prosecution has been widely noticed it must be emphasised that the issue before the House is not whether the appellants' conduct is morally right, but whether it is properly charged under the 1861 Act. When proposing that the conduct is not rightly so charged I do not invite your Lordships' House to indorse it as morally acceptable. Nor do I pronounce in favour of a libertarian doctrine specifically related to sexual matters. Nor in the least do I suggest that ethical pronouncements are meaningless, that there is no difference between right and wrong, that sadism is praiseworthy, or that new opinions on sexual morality are necessarily superior to the old, or anything else of the same kind. What I do say is that these are questions of private morality; that the standards by which they fall to be judged are not those of the criminal law; and that if these standards are to be upheld the individual must enforce them upon himself according to his own moral standards, or have them enforced against him by moral pressures exerted by whatever religious or other community to whose ethical ideals he responds. The point from which I invite your Lordships to depart is simply this, that the state should interfere with the rights of an individual to live his or her life as he or she may choose no more than is necessary to ensure a proper balance between the special interests of the individual and the general interests of the individuals who together comprise the populace at large. Thus, whilst acknowledging that very many people, if asked whether the appellants' conduct was wrong, would reply 'Yes, repulsively wrong', I would at the same time assert that this does not in itself mean that the prosecution of the appellants under ss 20 and 47 of the Offences against the Person Act 1861 is well founded.[25]

What is to be made of this? The views both of the majority and the majority were concerned in part with the reach of the law. Should the law reach into such private territory? The majority concluded that it should; the minority that it should not. That matter, although of course crucial when formulating and applying the law, is of relatively minor interest to us. What is of much more interest is what was said about the reasons for approving or disapproving of the defendants' conduct.

All agreed that those reasons could be categorised as 'public policy'. Where the majority and the minority differed was what public policy should say. But even there their *criteria* for deciding what public policy should say were very similar: they differed primarily about what the criteria meant for the crystallisation of ethical conclusions into law. They broadly agreed that public policy should condemn those things that, taken as a whole, did not tend to humanise.

So we have Lord Templeman frowning on violent behaviour that was 'degrading to body and mind', and on cruelty because it was 'uncivilised'. And we have Lord Lowry denouncing 'perverted and depraved sexual desire' (a denunciation that implies a normal, humanising type of sexual expression), and commenting that 'Sado-masochistic homosexual activity cannot be regarded as conducive to the enhancement or enjoyment of family life or conducive to the welfare of society'. This observation fits squarely within the notion that when law is in the

---

[25] Ibid 273.

business of encouraging a particular ethical purpose, that purpose is based on the encouragement of human flourishing, and contains an assertion that human flourishing (at least insofar as the law is concerned with it), is quintessentially a relational idea (note the mention of 'family life' and 'society').

Lord Mustill expressed his disapproval of the defendants' conduct in a very similar way as did the judges in the majority. Ethically there is little to distinguish him from them. He observed:

> It is sufficient to say that whatever the outside might feel about the subject matter of the prosecutions—perhaps horror, amazement or incomprehension, perhaps sadness—very few could read even a summary of the other activities without disgust. The House has been spared the video tapes, which must have been horrible.[26]

He certainly would not have agreed that public policy should encourage the defendants' behaviour, and the reason that it should not was that the activities were not the sort that facilitate human thriving. His reasons for not wanting to criminalise their behaviour were more political than anything else. They were to do with the legitimate reach of the state. So for him, as for the others, the starting point in deciding what public policy should say—the principle that grounds all later reasoning—is to do with the dignity both of the participants and of the society through which any public policy declaration would reverberate.

Lord Mustill's reasoning in deciding that public policy should not criminalise this behaviour (the reasoning that I have described as political), can coherently be described as dignity reasoning too. On the basis of the same conclusion as the majority in relation to the engaged dignity interests of the defendants, he nonetheless concluded that, taken in the round, and considering the dignity that haemorrhages away in any truncation by the state of individual liberty, a public policy prohibition would be more dignity-diminishing than dignity-enhancing.

It is not my purpose to suggest either that *Brown* was rightly decided or that it was wrongly decided. My only points are:

(a) that it was a case solved by, and only soluble by, the application of the notion of dignity; and

(b) the notion of dignity deployed is the one that I have articulated.

Support for this view comes from *National Coalition for Gay and Lesbian Equality v Minister of Justice*,[27] where the Constitutional Court of South Africa considered whether a law criminalising sodomy was unconstitutional. Ackermann J, with whom the majority concurred, found that it was. Such a law was contrary to the dignity of gay men, as well as contrary to their right to equality with heterosexuals (a right, the Court found, intimately related to dignity, and, I contend, dependent on it and ultimately derived from it). Ackermann J said that:

---

[26] Ibid 256–57.
[27] *National Coalition for Gay and Lesbian Equality v Minister of Justice* (1998) 6 BHRC 127; cp *Vriend v Alberta* [1998] 1 SCR 493 (Supreme Court of Canada).

the common-law crime of sodomy also constitutes an infringement of the right to dignity which is enshrined in section 10 of our Constitution. As we have emphasised on
several occasions, the right to dignity is a cornerstone of our Constitution. Its importance is further emphasised by the role accorded to it in section 36 of the Constitution
which provides that:

> The rights in the Bill of Rights may be limited only in terms of law of general appli-
> cation to the extent that the limitation is reasonable and justifiable in an open and
> democratic society based on human dignity, equality and freedom....

Dignity is a difficult concept to capture in precise terms. At its least, it is clear that the
constitutional protection of dignity requires us to acknowledge the value and worth of
all individuals as members of our society. The common-law prohibition on sodomy
criminalises all sexual intercourse per annum between men: regardless of the relationship of the couple who engage therein, of the age of such couple, of the place where
it occurs, or indeed of any other circumstances whatsoever. In so doing, it punishes a
form of sexual conduct which is identified by our broader society with homosexuals. Its
symbolic effect is to state that in the eyes of our legal system all gay men are criminals.
The stigma thus attached to a significant proportion of our population is manifest.
But the harm imposed by the criminal law is far more than symbolic. As a result of the
criminal offence, gay men are at risk of arrest, prosecution and conviction of the offence
of sodomy simply because they seek to engage in sexual conduct which is part of their
experience of being human. Just as apartheid legislation rendered the lives of couples
of different racial groups perpetually at risk, the sodomy offence builds insecurity and
vulnerability into the daily lives of gay men. There can be no doubt that the existence of
a law which punishes a form of sexual expression for gay men degrades and devalues gay
men in our broader society. As such it is a palpable invasion of their dignity and a breach
of section 10 of the Constitution, the rights of equality and dignity are closely related, as
are the rights of dignity and privacy.[28]

Sachs J added:

> One of the great gains achieved by following a situation-sensitive human rights approach
> is that analysis focuses not on abstract categories, but on the lives as lived and the injuries
> as experienced by different groups in our society. The manner in which discrimination is
> experienced on grounds of race or sex or religion or disability varies considerably–there
> is difference in difference. The commonality that unites them all is the injury to dignity
> imposed upon people as a consequence of their belonging to certain groups. Dignity in the
> context of equality has to be understood in this light. The focus on dignity results in empha-
> sis being placed simultaneously on context, impact and the point of view of the affected
> persons. Such focus is in fact the guarantor of substantive as opposed to formal equality.[29]

It couldn't have been done any other way. Whether you want to criminalise or
decriminalise sadomasochism, sodomy or, ultimately, any behaviour that involves
anything other than a trivial expression of one's humanity, you have to rely on
dignity or one of the lesser principles, such as autonomy, which dignity has

---

[28] *National Coalition for Gay and Lesbian Equality v Minister of Justice* (n 27) para 30.
[29] Ibid para 126.

spawned and in which dignity remains crucially rooted. And you might as well go each time for the root. It will ultimately save a lot of trouble.

In Chapter 1 I noted that I was happy to accept Duff's idea of humanisation as (for most bioethical purposes at least), identical to my idea of dignity. Duff has applied his idea specifically to the context of *R v Brown*. He begins by asking why we think (as right-thinking people do), that gladiatorial contests are wrong:

> If we tried to explain what is so disturbing about the gladiatorial example (apart from the likely further effect of such activities), we might talk not just of the 'objective regret-tability of millions deriving pleasure from brutal bloodshed', but of the dehumanization or degradation perpetrated by the gladiators on each other, and by the spectators on the gladiators and on themselves. We might talk in similar terms, though with less emphatic insistence, about the sadomasochism of *R v Brown*. Whilst there were no spectators to degrade or be degraded, we might still say that the participants were degrading or dehumanizing themselves and each other. This would involve an appeal, in both cases, to a normative conception of 'humanity'—of what it is to be human and to recognise the humanity of others, and of what it is to deny or fail to respect that humanity in others or in oneself.[30]

Here, Duff hints at the marriage of the empirical and the normative. Even if one can definitively exclude the possibility that physical or emotional harm results from a particular activity, one might properly object to that activity on the ground that it is not an activity within the normative rules of the human game, and that it is actively good for oneself and others (in a way described by the notion of flourishing or thriving) to play that game.

Brown was of course decided before the enactment of the Human Rights Act 1998, but European Convention of Human Rights points were argued, and were the facts to occur again, Article 8 of the Convention would undoubtedly be very prominent. Indeed it would be the main battlefield of the debate.

The Article provides:

(1) Everyone has the right to respect for his private and family life, his home and his correspondence.

(2) There shall be no interference by a public authority with the exercise of this right, except such as is in accordance with the law and is necessary in a democratic society in the interests of national security, public safety or the economic well-being of the country, for the prevention of disorder or crime, for the protection of health or morals, or for the protection of the rights and freedoms of others.

This is the most elastic of the Convention articles, stretching to places that the original draftsman could never have imagined would even exist.[31] In *R (Countryside Alliance) v Attorney-General*, Baroness Hale said that 'Article 8 is the right most capable of being expanded to cover everything that anyone might

---

[30] R Duff, 'Harms and wrongs' (2002) 5 *Buffalo Criminal Law Review* 13, 39.

[31] See D Feldman, 'The developing scope of Article 8 ECHR' (1997) 3 *European Human Rights Law Review* 270.

want to do.'[32] Or *be*, one might add.[33] She did not in fact expand it there as far as the claimants hoped, but although it may not be infinitely elastic, it certainly covers most situations pertinent to the establishment of the basic conditions for flourishing. Article 2 of course is relevant too, and Article 3 refers specifically to inhuman and degrading treatment, and may therefore seem a more natural home for dignity, but except in the extreme situations to which Article 3 is directed, Article 8 is the place in which the jurisprudence of dignity is being worked out. In a medical context it has been used to prohibit compulsory medical examinations,[34] compulsory psychiatric treatment[35] and other medical treatment.[36]

In *Pretty v United Kingdom* the Strasbourg Court said:

> the concept of 'private life' is a broad term not susceptible to exhaustive definition. It covers the physical and psychological integrity of a person ... It can sometimes embrace aspects of an individual's physical and social identity ... Elements such as, for example, gender identification, name and sexual orientation and sexual life fall within the personal sphere protected by Article 8 ... Article 8 also protects a right to personal development, and the right to establish and develop relationships with other human beings and the outside world ... Though no previous case has established as such any right to self-determination as being contained in Article 8 of the Convention, the court considers that the notion of personal autonomy is an important principle underlying the interpretation of its guarantees.[37]

In this passage the Court started holistically and well. Article 8, it was saying, was about protecting what one needs to be quintessentially human and to thrive while doing it. Thriving involves relationship—hence the need to protect the relationships. There is no point in passing a law giving special status to flowers if there is no legal obstacle to contaminating all flower beds.

The extension of the notion of 'private life' to 'the right to establish and develop relationships with other human beings', including in a work context, was expressly recognised by the Court in *Niemietz v Germany*.[38] It is clear, too, that the Article protects other preconditions of flourishing, including mental health. In asserting that this is the case the ECtHR uses the word 'integrity'—an interesting, resonant word, which implies that there is a model of wholeness to which we can more or less approximate. It said, in *Bensaid v United Kingdom*:

---

[32] *R (Countryside Alliance) v Attorney-General* [2008] 1 AC 719 para 115.

[33] 'Article 8 encompasses ... the right to *be* oneself, to *live* as oneself, and to *keep* to oneself ...': A Lester and D Pannick, *Human Rights Law and Practice* (London, LexisNexis, 2009) 367.

[34] *Matter v Slovakia* (2001) 31 EHRR 783.

[35] *Storck v Germany* (2006) 43 EHRR 96.

[36] *Glass v United Kingdom* (2004) 39 EHRR 341; cp *R (Wilkinson) v Broadmoor Special Hospital Authority* [2002] 1 WLR 419; *R (Wooder) v Feggetter* [2003] QB 219; *R (B) v S* [2006] 1 WLR 810.

[37] *Pretty v United Kingdom* (2002) 35 EHRR 1 para 61; cp *Van Kuck v Germany* (2003) 37 EHRR 973; *Bensaid v United Kingdom* (2001) 33 EHRR 205 para 47.

[38] *Niemietz v Germany* (1993) 16 EHRR 97 paras 29–30.

Mental health must ... be regarded as a crucial part of private life associated with the aspect of moral integrity. Article 8 protects a right to identity and personal development, and the right to establish and develop relationships with other human beings and the outside world ... The preservation of mental stability is in that context an indispensable precondition to effective enjoyment of the right to respect for private life.[39]

The last quoted sentence in *Pretty* ('the notion of personal autonomy is an important principle underlying the interpretation of its guarantees') has been seized upon by some who see it as the whole ratio of the case.[40] Of course, the exercise of autonomy is of central importance. But there is more to life and law than autonomy. And indeed the application of Article 8 to situations akin to *Brown*, and to cases involving children and incompetent adults, is an express recognition of this.

The structure of Article 8 indicates how it is used in practice. First the would-be relier on the Article establishes that Article 8(1) is engaged. But if it is, there will be no breach of the Article unless it is shown that the offence against Article 8(1) that is made out cannot be justified on a ground falling within Article 8(2).

Article 8(2) is concerned, too, with human thriving, but its focus is more obviously social than that of 8(1).

Article 8(2) says two things. First, and most obviously, society's interests, represented by Article 8(2), may be in competition with an individual's interests. Article 8(2), then, is the voice of the many. But Article 8(2) may also speak for the individual, saying things that are in his interests, but which he does not have the perspective to recognise, or the means to utter. It recognises that the Article 8(1) interests have no meaning, or only truncated meaning, in a social vacuum. They need relational context to be fully meaningful, to flourish.

Article 8(2) takes its flavour from 8(1). If 8(1) is, at least in a bio-medical context, about flourishing, then so is 8(2). 8(2) is a protector of the dignity rights of the many, and a facilitator of the dignity rights of the individual who is asserting his 8(1) rights.

My contention simply is, then, that the thesis I advanced in Chapter 1 (namely that dignity is the most fundamental bioethical principle from which all right principles derive, and that in analysing bioethical problems one should look at the dignity of everyone affected by an action or inaction, and decide on the right course by seeing whether the net amount of dignity is increased or decreased by the action or inaction) is legally old hat. It is what judges do anyway (and clinicians should do anyway) when they look at bioethical problems (as they should) through the prism of Article 8. Article 8 is all about dignity; Article 8(2) demands that the dignity interests of all conceivable stakeholders be assessed and a decision made in the light of that assessment.

---

[39] *Bensaid* (n 37) para 47. See too *Peck v United Kingdom* (2003) 36 EHRR 719.

[40] Eg, by campaigning organisations such as 'Dignity in Dying', and by the House of Lords in *R (Purdy) v DPP* [2009] UKHL 45.

In *Brown* itself there was rather cursory consideration of Article 8. Lord Templeman said that, on the assumption that Article 8(1) was engaged, 'I do not consider that Article 8 invalidates a law which forbids violence which is intentionally harmful to body and mind'.[41] Lord Mustill said that he believed that:

> the general tenor of the decisions of the European court does furnish valuable guidance on the approach which the English court should adopt, if free to do so, and I take heart from the fact that the European authorities, balancing the personal considerations invoked by Article 8(1) against the public interest considerations called up by Article 8(2), clearly favour the right of the appellants to conduct their private lives undisturbed by the criminal law.[42]

Lords Templeman and Mustill came to different conclusions about where the right balance between 8(1) and 8(2) lay, but both sets of observations are, as I see it, about Article 8(2)'s protection of the defendants against their own anti-flourishing behaviour, and of society against that same behaviour (both by declaring in what flourishing consists, and by the direct prohibition of that behaviour).[43] Both support my basic contention.

Brown went to Strasbourg, sub nom *Laskey, Jaggard and Brown v United Kingdom*.[44] In a rather bland judgment the Court unanimously concluded that there had been no breach of Article 8, observing that:

> 43. The Court considers that one of the roles which the State is unquestionably entitled to undertake is to seek to regulate, through the operation of the criminal law, activities which involve the infliction of physical harm. This is so whether the activities in question occur in the course of sexual conduct or otherwise.

> 44. The determination of the level of harm that should be tolerated by the law in situations where the victim consents is in the first instance a matter for the State concerned since what is at stake is related, on the one hand, to public health considerations and to the general deterrent effect of the criminal law, and, on the other, to the personal autonomy of the individual.

A more interesting comment came from Judge Pettiti, who agreed with the conclusion, but who added this, inter alia:

> It seemed to me necessary to expand para. 43 by noting:

> > to regulate and punish practices of sexual abuse that are demeaning even if they do not involve the infliction of physical harm.

> The dangers of unrestrained permissiveness, which can lead to debauchery, paedophilia (see para. 11 of the judgment) or the torture of others, were highlighted at the Stockholm World Conference. The protection of private life means the protection of a

---

[41] *Brown* (n 9) 237.

[42] Ibid 272.

[43] Lord Lowry commented on Art 8 at ibid 256. Much of what he said is now of only historical interest.

[44] *Laskey, Jaggard and Brown v United Kingdom* (1997) 24 EHRR 39.

person's intimacy and dignity, not the protection of his baseness or the promotion of criminal immoralism.

This final prescient sentence is in the modern tones of Article 8. Article 8 is about being, as well as doing. It recognises that good doing presupposes good being, that bad being breeds bad doing, and that bad doing is actually bad being.

It may be thought wrong to take *Brown* (on any view, an extreme and remarkable case), comment that it cannot be solved without a notion at least akin to dignity, and to suggest that this means that dignity is needed throughout the law of consent in bioethics. But that is not what I am doing.

Brown, like the PVS cases, is useful because it forces us back to fundamentals. That the fundamental we find beneath *Brown* just happens to be dignity does not necessarily imply that dignity is necessarily what we find if we dig deep enough into all consent cases, although it might tend in that direction.[45] But, once *Brown* has alerted us to the nature of a fundamental, that fundamental is easier to spot elsewhere. And in fact it is there. I have indicated that, if we look properly, we see it even in the most basic medical fact—that patients go to doctors at all. The fact that the unquestionably dignity-infused Article 8 has been used to unlock consent problems far removed from *Brown*-type situations indicates that the judges have identified a continuous sub-stratum of dignity that extends all the way from a patient who validly consents to a doctor examining a wart, to the withdrawal of life-sustaining treatment.

Confidentiality and Privacy

The issues raised by confidentiality and privacy are very similar to those raised by consent. The analysis of those questions within the ambit of Article 8 is methodologically identical.

In *Z v Finland* the ECtHR said:

> The protection of personal data, not least medical data, is of fundamental importance to a person's enjoyment of her right to respect for private and family life as guaranteed by Article 8 of the Convention.[46]

If I am right to argue that Article 8 is about dignity, then the ECtHR agrees that the Convention protects confidentiality for dignity reasons.

---

[45] *Brown*, of course, is not a case about medical ethics, but it is not so far removed from situations that often occur in medical ethics. Take, for instance, the case of a request for gender reassignment surgery (see *R v North West Lancashire Health Authority ex p A* [2000] 1WLR 977; cp *Goodwin v United Kingdom* (2002) 35 EHRR 447 and *Van Kuck v Germany* (2003) 37 EHRR 973), or mutilating surgery to treat body-image dysphoria.

[46] *Z v Finland* (1998) 25 EHRR 371 para 95.Cp *MS v Sweden* (1997) 28 EHRR 313; *Ashworth Hospital Authority v MGN Ltd* [2002] 1 WLR 2003; *Ackroyd v Mersey Care NHS Trust (No 1)* 73 BMLR 88; *Mersey Care NHS Trust v Ackroyd (No 2)* [2008] EMLR 1; *Archer v Williams* [2003] EMLR 869.

It has long been recognised in UK law that to encourage the flow of medical information (which of course is in the interests both of the doctor and the patient), but also because it is a basic right, medical confidences should be kept unless the public interest in keeping them is outweighed by the public interest in disclosing them.

In *Attorney-General v Guardian Newspapers Ltd (No 2)*, Lord Goff of Chieveley put it like this:

> although the basis of the law's protection of confidence is that there is a public interest that confidences should be preserved and protected by the law, nevertheless that public interest may be outweighed by some other countervailing public interest which favours disclosure. This limitation may apply ... to all types of confidential information. It is this limiting principle which may require a court to carry out a balancing operation, weighing the public interest in maintaining confidence against a countervailing public interest favouring disclosure.[47]

In *W v Egdell*, a case about keeping medical confidences, it was made crystal-clear that no private rights were in play:

> In so far as the judge referred to the 'private interest' of W, I do not consider that the passage in his judgment ... accurately stated the position. There are two competing public interests ... Of course W has a private interest, but the duty of confidence owed to him is based on the broader ground of public interest.[48]

In an Article 8 analysis, of course, the language would be slightly different. The Article 8(1) right to have a confidence kept would normally be thought of as a private right in competition with public interests under Article 8(2). But it is inconceivable that a traditional common law analysis (based on competing public interests), would reach a different conclusion from the Article 8 analysis. Indeed in *W v Egdell*, where the common law was applied, Article 8 was also considered by Bingham LJ, who expressly said that the common law and the Convention gave the same result.[49]

How can this be? It is a matter of basic algebra. The public right in nondisclosure which is an element of the common law formulation is identical with the private right under 8(1). And why? For the reason at which I have already hinted: the law sees individual rights as being able to flower fully only in societal, relational soil. It is another way of saying that the dignity rights in play both in the common law and under the Article need to be approached transactionally.

For confidentiality, so, with no caveats in the present context, for privacy.[50]

---

[47] *Attorney-General v Guardian Newspapers Ltd (No 2)*[1990] 1 AC 109, 282. Followed in the context of clinical confidentiality by, eg, *X v Y* [1988] 2 All ER 648; *H (A Healthcare Worker) v Associated Newspapers Ltd and N (A Health Authority)* [2002] Lloyd's Rep Med 210.

[48] *W v Egdell* [1990] 1 Ch 359, 416 (Sir Stephen Brown P). Bingham LJ agreed: ibid 420.

[49] Ibid 424–25.

[50] See, eg, *Peck v United Kingdom* (2003) 36 EHRR 719; *Campbell v Mirror Group Newspapers Ltd* [2004] 2 AC 457; *Von Hannover v Germany* (2005) 40 EHRR 1; *Murray v Express Group Newspapers plc* [2008] 3 WLR 1360. Graham Laurie discusses (in the context of genetic privacy) the relationship

We can now return to one of the problems posed in Chapter 1—that of the mentally incapacitate girl lying undraped but happy on a hospital trolley, enjoying the lascivious attentions of the youths in the neighbouring Accident and Emergency Department.

If this reached a court, the court would undoubtedly find that the girl's Article 8 right was engaged, and also that there was nothing in 8(2) that prevented a finding of an overall breach of Article 8. They could not do so if autonomy were the only actuating principle.

The court would in effect be saying:

Notwithstanding the fact that the girl likes being admired, there is something about that admiration that offends against her right to be treated as humans have a right to be treated. It is objectively wrong for her to be exposed because, objectively speaking, humans thrive best when respected. We do not fall into Ruth Macklin's trap of thinking that 'respect for persons' is a sufficient guide for our decision, because it begs the question 'Why should a person be respected?'

It is not only the girl's dignity interests that we need to consider. It is also the interests of the boys. They are doing nothing criminal in looking lustfully at her, and nor can we say seriously that they are being depraved or corrupted. But we can say that by looking at the girl they fail to honour her dignity, and, because dignity is by its very nature reciprocal and relational, they fail to honour their own. Call that paternalism if you like. But sometimes fathers know a bit more about life than their children, and their wisdom and perspective can help children to thrive. We do not forget, either, the importance of expressing in our judgment the values of a healthy society, which is the only context in which healthy humans can grow.

This case, like *Brown*, is a hard case. As in *Brown*, it does not necessarily follow that dignity is really the actuating principle behind all bioethical confidentiality and privacy cases. But in defence of the contention that as a matter of fact it is, I repeat what I said about *Brown* in this context.

Medical Research

Again, there is little more to say than has already been said in the context of consent and confidentiality. We have already noted that there are several international instruments dealing with medical research, and that they expressly invoke dignity, but without saying expressly what they mean by it.[51] These express mentions will at some stage have to be handled by the judges.

---

between dignity, privacy, autonomy and liberty, seeing the latter three as adjuncts to dignity: see G Laurie, *Genetic Privacy: A Challenge to Medico-Legal Norms* (Cambridge, CUP, 2002) 84. The book is also noteworthy for its criticism of the ability of autonomy alone to deliver the right answers to problems of genetic privacy.

[51] In ch 7.

For all the reasons already discussed, judges in countries that are signatories to the ECHR will undoubtedly find that those mentions have the substantive content given to them by the jurisprudence of Article 8 (and, in more extreme cases, Article 3).

Resources

There is an infinite amount of suffering in the world, and a distinctly limited amount of money to spend alleviating it. To treat one patient is to withhold treatment from another. Various devices have been devised, all of them more or less unsatisfactory, to help clinicians, fundholders and courts make agonising and unavoidable decisions about who should get what.

Why do we agonise? Why do people write papers about resource allocation? Why are we not content with caprice? Surely it is perhaps an indication of some instinctive belief in the equal status of human beings—a belief that is best described as rooted in some sort of status-dignity concept. If you say it is rooted in rights, I will simply (the procedure is becoming familiar now) rejoin: 'And why should X have the same rights as Y? From where do those rights spring?'

By and large, the courts have been rather timid, preferring to shift the burden of decision to fundholders, and being prepared to intervene only if a resource-allocation decision is manifestly unreasonable in a public law sense.[52] The House of Lords expressly said in *Airedale NHS Trust v Bland* that the question of how the funds that kept Tony Bland alive might be reallocated was an irrelevant consideration in deciding whether or not his treatment should be withdrawn.[53]

This judicial reluctance to be involved indicates something significant that is pertinent to our discussion. We have noted already that academics worry about resource allocation for reasons that must be located in dignity. The judicial distaste for weighing one life against another is a similar indication of an often

---

[52] For an overview of the position, see C Foster, 'Simple Rationality? The Law of Healthcare Resource Allocation in England' (2007) 33 *JME* 404.

[53] *Airedale NHS Trust v Bland* [1993] AC 789. Lord Browne-Wilkinson, for instance, said (ibid 879): 'it is not legitimate for a judge in reaching a view as to what is for the benefit of the one individual whose life is in issue to take into account the wider practical issues as to allocation of limited financial resources or the impact on third parties of altering the time at which death occurs.' Lord Mustill said (ibid 896): 'The large resources of skill, labour and money now being devoted to Anthony Bland might in the opinion of many be more fruitfully employed in improving the condition of other patients, who if treated may have useful, healthy and enjoyable lives for years to come. This argument was never squarely put, although hinted at from time to time. In social terms it has great force, and it will have to be faced in the end. But this is not a task which the courts can possibly undertake. A social cost-benefit analysis of this kind, which would have to embrace "mercy killing" to which exactly the same considerations apply, must be for Parliament alone, and the outcome of it is at present quite impossible to foresee. Until the nettle is grasped, we must struggle on with the existing law, imperfect as it is.'

undiagnosed belief in dignity—a belief echoed in judicial comments about the sanctity of life and the strong presumption in favour of the maintenance of life.[54,55]

Sometimes dignity is prominent in the distributivist writing. McDougall, talking about human reproductive cloning, and having rejected other dignity-based arguments against cloning, contends nonetheless that dignity does have a role to play in the cloning debate. The argument, in outline, goes like this:

1. A person's dignity is violated when he or she is prevented from exercising his or her basic rights or liberties.
2. A certain level of health (the liberties-level) is a necessary condition for the exercise of basic rights and liberties.
3. There are people whose level of health falls below the liberties-level.
4. Lack of resources prevents improvements to these people's health.
5. Allocating resources to cloning precludes the resources being used to improve the health of those below the liberties-level.
6. Allocating resources to cloning is an affront to human dignity.'[56]

---

[54] See, for instance, Lord Goff of Chieveley in *Bland* (ibid 863–64): 'The fundamental principle is the principle of the sanctity of human life—a principle long recognised not only in our own society but also in most, if not all, civilized societies throughout the modern world'; also see Taylor LJ's formulation of the 'intolerability test' in *Re J (A Minor) (Wardship: Medical Treatment)* [1991] Fam 33, 35; cp *W Healthcare NHS Trust v KH* [2004] EWCA Civ 1324 para 26, and *Re B (A Minor) (Wardship: Medical Treatment)* [1981] 1 WLR 1421, 1424.

[55] That distaste is illustrated very well in *Re A (Children) (Conjoined Twins: Surgical Separation)* [2001] Fam 147. For instance, Ward LJ said: 'I repeat that the balancing exercise I have just conducted is *not* a balancing of the quality of life in the sense that I value the potential of one human life above another. I have already indicated that the value of each life in the eyes of God and in the eyes of law is equal. Remember Lord Mustill's observation in *Bland's* case ... In this unique case it is, in my judgment, impossible not to put in the scales of each child the manner in which they are individually able to exercise their right to life. Mary may have a right to life, but she has little right to be alive. She is alive because and only because, to put it bluntly, but none the less accurately, she sucks the lifeblood of Jodie and she sucks the lifeblood out of Jodie. She will survive only so long as Jodie survives. Jodie will not survive long because constitutionally she will not be able to cope. Mary's parasitic living will be the cause of Jodie's ceasing to live. If Jodie could speak, she would surely protest, "Stop it, Mary, you're killing me." Mary would have no answer to that. Into my scales of fairness and justice between the children goes the fact that nobody but the doctors can help Jodie. Mary is beyond help. Hence I am in no doubt at all that the scales come down heavily in Jodie's favour. The best interests of the twins is to give the chance of life to the child whose actual bodily condition is capable of accepting the chance to her advantage even if that has to be at the cost of the sacrifice of the life which is so unnaturally supported. I am wholly satisfied that the least detrimental choice, balancing the interests of Mary against Jodie and Jodie against Mary, is to permit the operation to be performed' (ibid 197). Earlier he had referred to the notion of dignity, commenting that 'Mary's life, desperate as it is, still has its own ineliminable value and dignity' (ibid 188). Robert Walker LJ suggested that allowing separation from her sister gave Mary, (although it would kill her), the benefit, denied to her by nature, of being separated from her sister. 'The operation would give her, even in death, bodily integrity as a human being' (ibid 259). Ward LJ's comment on this was: 'The only gain I can see is that the operation would, if successful, give Mary the bodily integrity and dignity which is the natural order for all of us. But this is a wholly illusory goal because she will be dead before she can enjoy her independence and she will die because, when she is independent, she has no capacity for life' (ibid 184).

[56] R McDougall, 'A Resource-based Version of the Argument that Cloning is an Affront to Human Dignity' (2008) 34 *JME* 259, 260. Cp M Williams, 'Resource *Expenditure* not Resource Allocation: Response to McDougall on Cloning and Dignity' (2009) 35 *JME* 330.

Of course this argument is not unique to cloning. It is an objection to any sophisticated healthcare at the expense of those who do not have the basic pre-requisites of a decent life. The argument fits squarely into the notion of dignity as thriving.

There are various tools used by health economists to help to make resource-allocation decisions. One of the best known is the QALY—the Quality Adjusted Life Year. The user works out how many patient life-years will be gained by a particular mooted intervention, and then adjusts the figure to take account of the quality of those years. In a young patient in PVS, many decades might be bought by artificial nutrition and hydration, together with treatment of infection, but from the patient's own perspective, assuming the diagnosis is right, those years will mean little. In a young patient with a family, Avastin treatment of a colon cancer might buy only a few months, but they may be extraordinarily precious. Avastin might thus have a higher overall QALY score than the PVS maintenance treatment.

Of course the QALY is crude, and imports many rankly subjective judgments. It notoriously does not work well with palliative care (an area which most people, however strenuously utilitarian their instincts, consider worthwhile) where, usu-ally and almost by definition, the patient will not be alive for very long at all. I mention it only because it has fairly widespread acceptance, and because, at its best, it is an indication of the dignity-principle in action.[57] What is the QALY? Beneath the veneer of objectivity that all acronyms magically apply, it is one of the few ways of trying to structure the application of our intuitions.

Those intuitions are entirely in tune with the substantive idea of dignity as thriving, assessed transactionally. Take the PVS and Avastin examples. If there were an absolute choice between funding Avastin and funding the PVS patient, all rational decision-makers would tend to lean towards Avastin. Why? Because in the few Avastin-delivered months there would be a good deal of thriving on the part both of the patient and the people with whom he was in relationship. That is not to say that the continued biological existence of the PVS patient is irrelevant, or that there is no thriving to take account of. To the contrary, that patient is likely to be the focus of intense and agonised relationship, just as was Tony Bland. And it would be rightly regarded as just as deplorable to refuse to fund the PVS patient's maintenance for the period necessary for his family and carers to say goodbye as it would be to say no to Avastin—and for many of the same reasons. In each of the cases, whatever the outcome, the approach would be essentially a dignity-transaction approach, weighing the interests not only of the patient but of his family, his carers and the wider community (or, rather, acknowledging that it was impossible neatly to disentangle the patient's interests from those others, so gloriously entangled are they as a result of their joint participation in the human journey).

---

[57] Jonathan Herring disagrees, contending that the QALY places no weight on concepts such as dignity: J Herring, *Medical Law and Ethics* (Oxford, OUP, 2010) 78.

The holistic nature of the assessment that is routinely made in resource-allocation cases would be more accurately expressed by a change of name to the TADALY—the Transactionally Assessed Dignity Adjusted Life Year.

There is no reason in legal theory why this way of looking at resource allocation could not be accommodated within existing jurisprudential frameworks—for instance within Article 8 of the ECHR. It has to be acknowledged, though, that Article 8 has some work to do to establish its resource allocation credentials.[58]

---

[58] In, eg, *Sentges v Netherlands* (2004) 7 CCL Rep 400, *Pentiacova v Moldova* (2005) 40 EHRR SE 23 and *R (Condliff) v North Staffordshire Primary Care Trust* [2011] EWHC 872 (Admin), it was held that Article 8 was not *generally* engaged in medical resource allocation cases. It would require no great mutation of the law (or national budgets), to hold that it was generally engaged.

9

Human Enhancement and Cloning Technologies

Here already, or waiting in the wings, are some techniques which will allow normal human capacities to be enhanced. There is every reason to suspect that very soon we will be able to create humans who can leap 20 feet in the air, upload into their brain huge quantities of facts, go without sleep for long periods, be free of depression or cancer, and be incapable of unkindness.

Should we embrace these technologies? If not, why not?

Last night, hoping to be able to write this demanding chapter coherently, I went to bed early. Just now, hoping that I would be able to work on it faster, I had a two-shot espresso.

This morning I took my son to school. There he will go through a series of academic exercises which will create neuronal connections in his brain. Those changes are physical. You could see them with an electron microscope. If I produced physical changes on his buttocks by beating him, I would rightly be denounced as a child abuser. But those bruises would go away in a few days. The changes in his neurones will never go away, and are likely to have a much more profound effect on his life than any bruise. Are his teachers guilty of child abuse? If not, why not?

It may not show, but I have spent years of my life trying to enhance my own brain by education, and every night I read my children bedtime stories in an attempt to enhance theirs. If I send them to private schools I will be paying to mould their brains in an attempt to give them a competitive advantage over their peers.

I married someone whose brain as well as whose body I find attractive. In choosing her, there was no doubt operating, at some level, the Darwinian imperative that goes: 'If you mate with someone beautiful and clever, you stand a much higher chance of having beautiful, clever children than if you pick randomly.'

I want my children to be disease-free. They have had their standard childhood vaccinations.

I wear shoes on my feet. I use a notebook to help me remember things, and a computer to help me write.[1]

---

[1] Bostrom and Savulescu observe that 'In one sense *all* technology can be viewed as an enhancement of our native human capacities, enabling us to achieve certain effects that would otherwise require more effort or be altogether beyond our power.' 'Human Enhancement Ethics: The State of the Debate', in J Savulescu and N Bostrom (eds), *Human Enhancement* (Oxford, OUP, 2009) 2.

So: I'm an enhancer. We all are. Is there anything wrong with it?

This chapter looks broadly at some of the arguments about enhancement technologies. It has two main purposes. First, to show that none of the existing ways of looking at bioethical problems help very much in this area. And second, to suggest that dignity, in the way that I have defined it and used it, can enlighten.

I deal in this chapter too with the question of cloning. This is not because it is an enhancement technology—it is not—but because it raises similar questions of how ethics and law should react on the frontiers of technology, where questions of identity might come into play. It also introduces some ideas that we meet later when we deal with enhancement.

Erik Parens, in a recent essay, recalls how 'Jonathan Glover observed that enhancement technologies force us to think anew about the oldest, most pressing, and most infuriatingly difficult questions: What does human flourishing consist in?'[2] Quite right.

Cloning

Cloning is the creation of genetically identical individuals.[3] Identical twins are clones of each other.

For the purpose of this argument we will ignore the fact that currently available technologies do not produce true clones, since they involve the insertion of the nucleus (which contains most but not all of the genetic material), leaving in the host cell its original cytoplasm with a complement of cytoplasmic DNA which will be different from that of the cell from which the nucleus was taken.

Therapeutic and reproductive cloning must be distinguished. Therapeutic cloning is the creation of embryos from which cells can be harvested for therapeutic purposes. The embryos themselves may be used for research. I deal with the ethical benefits and detriments of this in Chapter 10, where I discuss the status of the early embryo. Reproductive cloning involves placing the embryo inside a uterus, with the intention that it develops to term.

Reproductive cloning might be used to help otherwise intractably childless couples to have children, or, where the woman is capable of child-bearing but

---

[2] E Parens, 'Toward a More Fruitful Debate about Enhancement' in Savulescu and Bostrom (eds) *Human Enhancement* 196.

[3] The definition adopted by the US President's Council on Bioethics is: 'The asexual production of a new human organism that is, at all stages of development, genetically virtually identical to a currently existing or previously existing human being. It would be accomplished by introducing the nuclear material of a human somatic cell (donor) into an oocyte (egg) whose own nucleus has been removed or inactivated, yielding a product that has a human genetic constitutions virtually identical to the donor of the somatic cell.' *Human Cloning and Human Dignity: The Report of the President's Council on Bioethics* (New York, Public Affairs, 2002) xliii. Of course, when a cloning technique of nuclear replacement is used, the individuals produced will be identical so far as their nuclear genetic material is concerned. Their cytoplasmic DNA will differ. The contribution to phenotype of that cytoplasmic DNA is unclear.

her partner has no or no functional sperm (eg lesbian couples) to have a child intimately connected to both of them without the use of donor sperm. It might also be used by a woman without a partner to create a child without any third party being involved—by inserting one of her own nuclei into one of her own eggs. It could be used to recreate a beloved child who had died.

It might be used to allow couples at risk of producing a child with a genetic disease to have unaffected children, to obtain ideal transplant donors from whom cells or organs could be harvested with no risk of immunological rejection, or to replicate individuals of prodigious talent.[4]

What are the objections? They are summarised well in a thoroughly referenced text by Jonathan Herring,[5] and I adopt some of his structure.

(a) Given the present state of technology, cloning is too risky, in the sense that it would produce an unacceptable rate of miscarriage, or disease/disability in the offspring.[6]

     This is an uninteresting and unimpressive objection. Even if it is true now, these practical problems are likely to be solved soon.

(b) Cloning would reduce the diversity of the human gene pool, with potentially deleterious effects, such as vulnerability to particular diseases.

     Again, this is hardly a potent objection. For this to be a serious worry, cloning would have to be a much more common means of reproduction than it is ever likely to be.

(c) Cloning denies the clone its right to be genetically unique.[7]

     Sexual reproduction, goes the argument, is a device that ensures that no two individuals are genetically alike. That individuality is one of the most fundamental bequests that nature can give, and to deprive someone of it is to deprive them of a unique status. It may inhibit their ability to plough their own furrow. I enlarge on this objection in (h) below, with the help of Sandel and Habermas.

     The obvious response is that the contribution of environment is massive. Identical twins—even those brought up together—are far from identical. Surely a clone, if asked, would be unlikely to say either: 'I'm not properly human because I'm not genetically unique', or 'I'd prefer not to exist at all.' Cloning isn't denying the clone any right at all. If you don't exist, it is meaningless to talk about your rights.[8]

(d) Cloning would distort the generational structure of the family.

     Thus if a clone were created by using a nucleus from her father, she would genetically be the daughter of her paternal grandparents, the sister of her

---

[4] These possibilities are listed in *Report of the President's Council on Bioethics* 86–88.
[5] J Herring, *Medical Law and Ethics* (Oxford, OUP, 2010) 387–90.
[6] See *Report of the President's Council on Bioethics* 99–105.
[7] Ibid 114–16.
[8] See C Foster, T Hope and J McMillan, 'Submissions from Non-existent Claimants: The Non-identity Problem and the Law' (2006) 25 *Medicine and Law* 1.

uncles and aunts, and the aunt of her cousins. The US President's Council on Bioethics noted:

> we freely admit that, like any child, [cloned children] might be welcomed into the cloning family. Nevertheless, the cloned child's place in the scheme of family relations might well be uncertain and confused. The usually clear designations of father and brother, mother and sister would be confounded ... What the exact effects of cloning-to-produce-children might be for families is highly speculative ... but it is still worth flagging certain troubling possibilities and risks. The fact that the cloned child bears a special tie to only one parent may complicate family dynamics ... the sins or failings of the father (or mother), if reappearing in the cloned child, might be blamed on the progenitor ... The problems of being and rearing an adolescent could become complicated should the teenage clone of the mother 'reappear' as the double of the woman the father once fell in love with.[9]

And so on.

(e)   The burden of cloning is likely to fall disproportionately on women.

Women, not men, will be the ones who go through the trauma of ovarian stimulation, egg harvesting, embryo transfer and pregnancy. And, as with other reproductive technologies, there may be, as many feminists have observed, a tendency for women's bodies to become commodified. Braidotti rather excitedly declared that 'the test tube babies of today mark the long-term triumph of the alchemists' dream of dominating nature through their self-inseminating, masturbatory practices'.[10] Corea, more realistically, contended that 'Reproductive technology is a product of the male reality. The values expressed in the technology—objectification, domination—are typical of male culture. The technology is male-generated and buttresses male power over women.'[11]

(f)   The 'yuck factor'.

This is a widespread intuition, and is relied upon by, inter alia, Leon Kass, who talks resonantly about the 'wisdom of repugnance'.[12] I have already noted John Harris's suspicion of 'olfactory philosophy'.[13]

While it is certainly unwise to ignore one's instincts (which are far older than at least many of the cognitive tools used in modern philosophy, and no doubt tell us deep and crucial things about ourselves), this should be an argument of last resort, on the grounds that it is hardly an argument at all. As I have already observed, it is reassuring, at the end of an argument that has proceeded on other grounds, to find that one's instincts are happy

---

[9] *Report of the President's Council on Bioethics* 123–25.

[10] R Braidotti *Nomadic Subjects* (New York, Columbia University Press, 1994) 88, cited in Herring, *Medical Law and Ethics* 351.

[11] G Corea, *The Mother Machine* (London, The Women's Press, 1985) 4: cited in Herring, *Medical Law and Ethics* 352.

[12] L Kass, 'The Wisdom of Repugnance: Why we should Ban the Cloning of Humans' in G McGee, (ed), *The Human Cloning Debate* (Berkeley, CA, Berkeley Hills Books, 2002).

[13] See ch 1.

with the conclusion. So it is a confirmatory check, like the final 'stand back and survey' check of a workman who, in putting up a shelf, has repeatedly ensured with the spirit level that it is straight. If the final eye-balling doesn't confirm what the spirit-level has said, then one is unwise not to go back and check with another spirit level, but if the two levels agree, then it would be even more unwise to go by the eye.

It is interesting to note, though, that the 'yuck factor' has some most unlikely but most welcome supporters. A good example is the arch reductionist, Daniel Dennett, who thinks that it would be harmful to ignore all traditional taboos because they have deep and real utility: they fulfil some deep longing in us, and to abide by them will make our lives better. He doesn't seem to be talking here about making our lives better as a chalk placebo helps our headache. He seems to believe in real effects. He's a mystic at heart. He peremptorily dismissed the soul as the seat of the fulfilled longings, of course, but one might be forgiven for thinking that he smuggles it back in under another name.

He uses a golfing analogy. Apparently if you keep your head down throughout a swing, even when the ball has left the tee, you hit the ball better. This seems irrational: how can keeping your head down affect the ball after it has gone? But, he says, biomechanics is a mysterious business. Who can plumb its wonders? It's similar, he says, to respect for corpses, patients in PVS, and so on. There's no very rational ground for treating them differently from a pound of sausages, and yet our instincts insist otherwise. We should abide by our instincts, he insists. Failure to do so might mess with something deep down.[14]

(g) 'Playing God'.

God, some say, created humans to reproduce sexually, with the corollary that each person is produced in accordance with a divine plan, and accordingly that to reproduce in any other way is to set oneself up in competition with him and frustrate the plan.

There are many responses. No heterosexual couple would ever choose cloning, with all its attendant physical and psychological traumas, if natural conception were possible. Cloning will only ever be a treatment for infertility or a way of mitigating catastrophe (for instance by seeking to replace a dead child).

Why is it different from any other therapy? One might argue that it was 'playing God' to give antibiotics for infections, or anaesthetics. Indeed precisely that argument was deployed against obstetric anaesthesia. God, in Genesis, had decreed that, because of the sin of Eve, she would have pain in

---

[14] D Dennett, 'How to Protect Human Dignity from Science', in E Pellegrino, A Schulman and T Merrill (eds), *Human Dignity and Bioethics* (Notre Dame, IN, University of Notre Dame Press, 2009) 39.

childbirth. To use chloroform to dull that pain was to frustrate his purposes. One rarely hears that view from modern pulpits.

Jewish scholars have traditionally been much more tolerant of reproductive technology in general, retorting to objections like those above that any new human life is good, and technology that helps to produce it is technology wielded in obedience to the Biblical injunction to 'go forth and multiply'.[15]

(h) Cloning is manufacture, to manufacture is to instrumentalise, to instrumentalise is to become Promethean, and to be Promethean is to be non-human.

The US President's Council on Bioethics was concerned that cloning raised important questions about the whole nature of human procreation. It began by observing that:

a child is not made, but begotten.[16] Procreation is not making but the outgrowth of doing. A man and a woman give themselves in love to each other, setting their projects aside in order to do just that. Yet a child results, arriving on its own, mysterious, independent, yet the fruit of the embrace. Even were the child wished for, and consciously so, he or she is the issue of their love, not the product of their wills; the man and the woman in no way produce or choose a particular child, as they might buy a particular car. Procreation can, of course, be assisted by human ingenuity (as with IVF). In such cases, it may become harder to see the child solely as a gift bestowed upon the parents' mutual self-giving and not to some degree as a product of their parental wills. Nonetheless, because it is still sexual reproduction, the children born with the help of IVF begin, as do all other children—with a certain genetic independence of their parents ... Gifts and blessings we learn to accept as gratefully as we can. Products of our wills we try to shape in accord with our desires. Procreation as traditionally understood invites acceptance, rather than reshaping, engineering, or designing the next generation. It invites us to accept limits to our control over the next generation. It invites us even—to put the point most strongly—to think of the child as one who is not simply our own, our possession. Certainly, it invites us to remember that the child does not exist simply for the happiness or fulfilment of the parents.[17]

In manufacturing rather than begetting, something crucial to our whole identity as humans is lost. The loss can be characterised in many ways, but one of the ways in which it can be noted most clearly is in the loss of continuity with the rest of humanity.

The Council felt compelled to use the language of dignity to describe the damage. It raised no objection in principle to the use of reproductive technologies per se, to the use of genetic technologies to treat individuals with

---

[15] Another reason is that (perhaps because being human involves being in a relationship with another human), Jewish thought does not credit pre-implantation embryos with any legal status. They are akin to gametes: see M Gross and V Ravitksy, 'Israel: Bioethics in a Jewish-Democratic State' (2003) 12 *Cambridge Quarterly of Healthcare Ethics* 247, 250.

[16] This distinction is enlarged upon by O O'Donovan, *Begotten or Made?* (Oxford, OUP, 1984).

[17] *Report of the President's Council on Bioethics* 111–12.

genetic diseases (even *in utero*).[18] The problem is to do with 'the control of the entire genotype, and the production of children to selected specifications'.[19]

Why does this matter? It matters because human dignity is at stake. In natural procreation, two individuals give life to a new human being whose endowments are not shaped deliberately by human will, whose being remains mysterious, and the open-endedness of whose future is ratified and embraced. Parents beget a child who enters the world exactly as they did—as an unmade gift, not a product. Children born of this process stand equally beside their progenitors as fellow human beings, not beneath them as made objects. In this way, the uncontrolled beginnings of human procreation endow each new generation and each new individual with the dignity and freedom enjoyed by all who came before.[20]

In similar vein, Michael Sandel (writing about enhancement, but his observations apply equally here), comments that the greatest danger of such technologies is:

that they represent a kind of hyperagency—a Promethean aspiration to remake nature, including human nature, to serve our purposes and satisfy our desires. The problem is not the drift to mechanism but the drive to mastery. And what the drive to mastery misses and may even destroy is an appreciation of the gifted character of human powers and achievements.

To acknowledge the giftedness of life is to recognise that our talents and powers [and in the context of cloning, our children] are not wholly our own doing ... It is also to recognise that not everything in the world is open to whatever use we may desire or devise. Appreciating the gifted quality of life constrains the Promethean project and conduces to a certain humility. It is in part a religious sensibility. But its resonance reaches beyond religion.[21]

Habermas, too, notes that reproduction is essentially uncontrollable and unforeseeable, and contends that we must have gone through the normal process of reproduction (must each be the randomly occurring result of a shake of millions of genetic dice) in order for us to be properly ourselves (to avoid co-authorship of our lives) and to ensure egalitarian human relationships.[22] Like Sandel and the President's Council, he fears obliteration of the 'boundary between persons and things',[23] and loss of an 'appropriate ethical self-understanding of the species' which sustains 'an autonomous morality'.[24] If we were made, rather than begotten, our self-perception would be

---

[18] Ibid 118.

[19] Ibid 118.

[20] Ibid 118.

[21] M Sandel, 'The Case Against Perfection' (2004) 293 *Atlantic Monthly* 51. See too M Hauskeller, 'Human Enhancement and the Giftedness of Life' (2011) 40 *Philosophical Papers* 1 for an articulation of a similar thesis without the invocation of any religious ideas.

[22] J Habermas, tr H Beister and W Rehg, *The Future of Human Nature* (London, Polity Press, 2003) 13.

[23] Ibid 13.

[24] Ibid 40.

catastrophically devalued.[25] The clone herself (or the enhanced human) could not be sure that she, herself lay behind her, intentions, initiatives and aspirations.[26] 'For the person to feel one with her body, it seems that this body has to be experienced as something natural.'[27]

These are powerful and subtle arguments that go at least close to the root of what we are.[28] They are true dignity arguments. They can be, and not surprisingly have been, criticised.[29] It might be said, for instance, that Sandel, despite disavowing 'mastery', is actually advocating mastery by the status quo, and that he doesn't really want the unbidden—he wants the predictable certainties of the known, rather than the uncertainties associated with developing technologies.[30] Certainly it needs to be accepted that not everything that is given is good. Any philosophy that dubs the unlooked for gift of multiple sclerosis 'good' is diabolically perverted.

But the arguments of Sandel et al are true arguments—by which I mean that they are not mere intuitions of the sort that I considered briefly above under the heading 'The "yuck factor"'. They are in principle testable. To test them one would simply allow reproductive cloning and see if it diminished an appreciation of the giftedness of human nature. Put like that, the idea sounds slightly ridiculous. Indeed it has been mischievously ridiculed by Julian Savulescu and Nick Bostrom, in their comments on Sandel's essay on enhancement:

> One could imagine an enhancement user who is under no illusion that her talents and powers are wholly her own doing, understanding clearly that without the contributions from Nature, God, or Fortune, she would be literally nothing.

> Perhaps one solution would be for the FDA to require appropriate labelling of enhancement products. A bottle of memory-boosting pills could come with the inscription: 'May cause constipation, dry mouth, skin rashes, and loss of openness to the unbidden. If symptoms persist after 48 hours, consult your physician and/or your spiritual adviser.'[31]

---

[25] Ibid 81.

[26] Ibid 57.

[27] Ibid 58.

[28] See S Wheatley, 'Human Rights and Human Dignity in the Resolution of Certain Ethical Questions in Biomedicine'(2001) 3 *European Human Rights Law Review*, 312, 318–19, for an examination of the way in which dignity arguments might affect identity-changing manipulations.

[29] See, eg M Tooley, 'The Moral Status of the Cloning of Humans' in J Humber and R Almeder (eds), *Human Cloning* (Totowa, Humana Press, 1998); J Harris, *On Cloning* (London, Routledge, 2004); F Kamm, 'What is and is Not Wrong with Enhancement' in Savulescu and Bostrom (eds) *Human Enhancement* 91–130; J Harris, 'Is Cloning an Attack on Human Dignity?' (1997) 387 *Nature* 754; J Harris, *Clones, Genes and Immortality* (Oxford, OUP, 1998); P Singer and D Wells, *The Reproduction Revolution: New Ways to Making Babies* (Oxford, OUP, 1984).

[30] G Kahane, presentation at the MacDonald Centre Conference on Human Enhancement, Christ Church, Oxford, October 2010.

[31] Bostrom and Savulescu, 'Human Enhancement Ethics: The State of the Debate' 6.

This is (genuinely) very amusing, but should not be allowed to obscure the fact that the sort of self-truncation of which Sandel and Habermas warn will have genuine psychological sequelae. An existential crisis might not be quite as demonstrable as a skin rash, but it is likely to cause sufficiently tangible unhappiness for one to be able to conclude that cloning is a bad thing for the reasons so solemnly feared.

But should one allow the experiment? Should one allow reproductive cloning in order to gather the data that might show conclusively that it should not continue? The answer must be no. While it is true that we do not know whether Sandel's spectre is real, it does not seem wholly ridiculous. Add it to the other factors, weigh them cumulatively against the potential goods, remind yourself that these are humans you're dealing with, not equations, and the experiment becomes unacceptable. The President's Council referred rightly to the 'precautionary principle'.[32] The evolutionary perspective might give our precautions some more biological literacy. We have been evolving for a very long time. It may be, as we shall observe again when we come to look at enhancement technologies, that there are very good reasons, accredited by that very diligent Darwinian laboratory, why natural selection has frowned on asexual reproduction in humans.[33]

Most of these reasons for and against cloning will be very familiar to anyone who knows anything about bioethics. They are listed here for one reason: so that I can make the observation that they are all based on claims about human thriving. They are all, at root, dignity claims. At stake is not only the dignity of the cloned person, but also that of the person who has been cloned (whose identity has been diluted), everyone else involved in the cloning procedure,[34] and (by genetic fallout, expressivist damage, and the diversion of resources away from more pressing health concerns), the entire human species. It is a classic case for a transactional audit of any proposed action. Beauchamp and Childress can't help (except to the limited extent that one might point to some of the more organic sequelae of botched cloning technology and say: 'There's harm: it should have been avoided'). People disagree about the way of maximising human thriving, but not that that is the ultimate objective.

This might seem to be fatal to my contention that a 'thriving' formulation of dignity is actually useful. Am I not just articulating a banal truism—that the point of ethics and of good laws is to help us to live our lives well?

---

[32] 'This principle would suggest that scientists, technologists, and, indeed, all of us should be modest in claiming to understand the many possible consequences of any profound alteration of human procreation, especially where there are not compelling reasons to proceed. Lacking such understanding, no one should take action so drastic as the cloning of a human child. In the absence of the necessary human wisdom, prudence calls upon us to set limits on efforts to control and remake the character of human procreation and human life.' *Report of the President's Council on Bioethics* 128.

[33] See N Bostrom and A Sandberg, 'The Wisdom of Nature: An evolutionary heuristic for human enhancement' in Savulescu and Bostrom (eds) *Human Enhancement* 375–416.

[34] Kass, 'The Wisdom of Repugnance' 94.

I have several observations:

(1) If the formulation is a truism, it is so because it is generally held to be true. Which means that I start with most people agreeing with me about the objective. That's not a bad start.

(2) If I am right about dignity being essentially about human thriving (a claim I have sought to make by looking at the literature), then it follows from (1) that most people would agree that dignity is the way to look at hard bioethical problems. I would regard that as a major triumph.

(3) The fact that both the friends and enemies of cloning are talking, when we listen to them carefully, in the same language, means that there is hope for dialogue. It does not always seem that way in the bioethical arena.

(4) If I am right that the question of what constitutes human thriving is empirically ascertainable, then the dialogue has some prospect of a peaceful resolution. Failing that, the courts have a prospect of reaching an evidence-based determination.

(5) There is one important caveat to (4). That relates to those who, through religious conviction or instinctual distaste, take a particular view. It may be too much to expect them to come round and fall in line with the evidence. Cognitive dissonance is terrifyingly powerful. The greater the evidence for a massively old Universe, the greater the strength with which a young Universe will be proclaimed in Kentucky. But in the context of bioethical problems in general, and cloning in particular, I think that there are grounds for tentative confidence. They stem from the example of anaesthesia in childbirth, and of religious objections to medical intervention in general. No one now maintains any theological objection to obstetric anaesthesia, or to the use of antibiotics to stem plagues of Biblical proportions. Why? Because religious people have been the beneficiary of these blessings, and they have seen that the moon didn't turn to blood when they were blessed. Granted, some Jehovah's Witnesses still let their children die for want of an easily available blood transfusion, but they are unusual. Self-interest (or, in our terms, demonstrated human thriving with its communitarian ramifications) usually gets the better of mumbo-jumbo. If their children died for asserting that the world was only 3,000 years old, Southern US fundamentalists would soon find a way to reinterpret the early chapters of Genesis, just as they did when faced with the challenge from chloroform.

What about the Law?

We have seen already that the Additional Protocol to the Convention on Human Rights and Biomedicine on the Prohibition of Cloning Human Beings and the

UNESCO Declaration on the Human Genome and Human Rights prohibit human cloning, both specifically, but shortly, invoking dignity as they do so. Article 6 of the Directive on the Legal Protection of Biotechnological Inventions[35] forbids the grant of a patent for human cloning processes, and the United Nations has produced a Declaration calling on member states to prohibit 'all forms of human cloning inasmuch as they are incompatible with human dignity and the protection of human life.'[36] The United Kingdom, concerned about stifling therapeutic cloning and research with cloned embryos, voted against this Declaration. There is, however, no reason to doubt the UK's commitment to banning reproductive cloning.[37]

The legislative control of cloning, then, is in the hands of instruments that either use the word 'dignity' or are inspired by it. The instruments themselves do not specify any particular definition of dignity, but the lawmakers have heard the arguments for and against reproductive cloning that are outlined above. If I am right to contend that those arguments are arguments that fall within my definition of dignity, it follows that the lawyers' version of dignity is either guided by a similar notion, or could be so guided without any damage to the existing legal understanding of the control of reproductive cloning.

Any legal attempt in Europe to justify human reproductive cloning would undoubtedly be framed in terms of Article 8 of the ECHR, and possibly also in terms of Article 12—the right to found a family.

Article 12 provides: 'Men and women of marriageable age have the right to marry and found a family according to the national laws governing the exercise of this right.' Only those who have first married have an Article 12 protected right to found a family.[38] Non-natural methods of founding a family may well fall within Article 12.[39] In theory, this might include cloning. But contracting states have a very wide margin of appreciation in relation to the regulation of reproduction, and in practice it is inconceivable that a state would be held in breach of Article 12 for failing to allow cloning, even where that gave a couple their only chance of reproducing. It seems, too, that in cases concerning reproductive technology, Article 12 will have little or nothing to add to Article 8.[40] In any event the considerations under Article 12 would be more or less identical, both substantively and procedurally, to those under Article 8.

The Article 8 exercise of balancing the individual interests against the societal interests that would be carried out would be the one with which we are now

---

[35] Council Directive 98/44/EC of 30 July 1998 on the Legal Protection of Biotechnological Inventions [1998] OJ L 213.

[36] The Declaration and the surrounding documentation are at www.un.org/law/cod/sixth/57/docs. htm#162.

[37] See the Human Reproductive Cloning Act 2001.

[38] Application 39051/03, *Emonet v Switzerland*; judgment of the ECtHR, 13 December 2007, para 92.

[39] Cp *X, Y and Z v United Kingdom* (1997) 24 EHRR 143 and *Dickson v United Kingdom* (2007) 46 EHRR 927—both in the context of Art 8 claims.

[40] *Dickson v United Kingdom* (n 39) para 86.

familiar—the one whose substantive considerations are essentially those of thriving-dignity, and whose procedural considerations are those of the transactional analysis.

Enhancement

As we have noted, we're all enhancers. There is no difference in principle between a good night's sleep, a cup of coffee, or a medically prescribed attention-enhancing drug. There may be a difference in principle between those things and a tweak to my genome that makes me a better concentrator. And even if there isn't, it might be different if that tweak was heritable.

Is it that personality-changing transformations are illegitimate, and everything else is permissible? But what's a personality? And how do I change it? If I change the shape of my nose, I will feel different about myself, and (literally) project a different face to the world and to myself. If I drink a bottle of claret my temperament changes radically. I'm sunny, garrulous, and Falstaffian. Does it make any difference to the ethics of my claret-induced personality change that in the morning I'll have reverted to my grey, introspective 'real' self? If I have been subjected to an arduous university course for years, I may well have acquired an ability to concentrate, and an attitude to life, that I might not have acquired if I'd worked in the corner shop.

Should deaf parents be allowed to deafen their foetuses *in utero* so that the resultant child can have the benefit (as the parents see it) of the peculiarly intimate communion with the parents, the rest of the deaf community, and the wider world, that comes from being deaf? If not, is that because deafening is not 'enhancement' but detriment? Who's to say which is which, and applying what criteria?

We can multiply troubling examples ad nauseam, but the point is clear enough. How are we to think about these things? It is not my intention here to summarise the huge literature on enhancement. The necessary points can be made very shortly.

First: in all genuinely difficult enhancement problems, everyone recognises that something other than the traditional four principles of bioethics needs to be used.

The simple, uninteresting, untroubling cases can be analysed traditionally. If someone wants to take anabolic steroids so that he can run, alone and non-competitively, rather faster around a track, then, subject to properly informed consent, and the usual societal concerns (which will include all sorts of slippery slope arguments), he should be allowed to do so.

If he wants to take the same drugs for the purpose of competition then, provided everyone knows about it, and the level pharmacological playing field upon which justice would insist is provided, there is no great problem.

Although our holistic 'thriving' analysis may give a more nuanced and satisfactory answer (and would be the approach taken by an Article 8-wielding judge), Beauchamp and Childress would ensure that most of the relevant issues were brought to the table.

It is different, though, if we get even slightly more controversial. Take the (at the moment theoretical) example of an injection that permanently increases IQ by 50 points. Is there anything further to say than: 'As long as one knows what one is doing, it is not only fine to exercise one's autonomy so to choose to have the injection, but wrong to stop it'? Everyone agrees that there is more to say. The analysis isn't made satisfactory simply by bolting on a contribution from justice, to the effect that it might be wrong if rich people could pay for the enhancement, but poor people couldn't, and that the enhancement might cause unacceptable inequalities, or dangerously exacerbate existing ones.

Autonomy won't work, or won't work satisfactorily, because, at least arguably (depending on your view of the effect of such a gargantuan jump in processing power), at the moment the syringe plunger is pressed, the person who requested the injection ceases to exist. Further: at the time that the intervention is requested, there is no one to whom the benefit of the intervention accrues.

It is worth reflecting more widely on Kant's impotence in the enhancement arena. For Kass, Kant is hopeless because he 'dualistically sets up the concept of "personhood" in opposition to nature and the body', and so 'fails to do justice to the concrete reality of our embodied lives ... Precisely because it is universalistically rational, it denies the importance of life's concrete particularity, lived always locally, corporeally, and in a unique trajectory from zygote in the womb to body in the coffin ... Not all of dignity consists in reason or freedom.'[41] Accordingly, while Kant will have plenty to say about informed consent and excessive medical paternalism, he would be 'perfectly comfortable with embryo farming, surrogate motherhood, cloning, the sale of organs, performance-enhancing drugs, doctoring of memory, chemical happiness, man-machine hybrids, and even extra-corporeal gestation.'[42] Why?

> [B]ecause these peculiar treatments of the body or uses of our embodiments are no harm to that homunculus of personhood that resides somewhere happily in a morally disembodied place. *Pace* Kant, the answer for the threat to human dignity arising from sacrificing the humanly high to the humanly urgent, the soul to the body, is not a teaching of human dignity that severs mind from body, that ignores the urgent, or that denies dignity to human bodily life as lived. The defense of what is humanly high requires an equal defense of what is seemingly 'low'.[43]

Kass has many critics, but even those who see him as incurably (if covertly) religious, and over-zealous in his suspicion of autonomy, follow him to the extent of acknowledging that Kant is not the Virgil we need when we get to the lower circles of bioethical hell—those circles closest to the core of whatever a human being is.

---

[41] L Kass, 'Defending human dignity' in Pellegrino et al (eds), *Human Dignity and Bioethics* 313.
[42] Ibid 313.
[43] Ibid 313.

Second: having acknowledged the inadequacy of other analytic tools, most commentators turn expressly to dignity, and the others to something that looks very like dignity dressed up in other clothes.[44] A good example of the former is Nick Bostrom, one of the high priests of human enhancement. He doesn't pretend that the ethical language in which the enhancement debate has to rage is anything other than that of dignity.[45]

Third: Some of the debates about dignity and enhancement are carried out at cross-purposes, with combatants disagreeing hotly about what 'dignity' decrees, when in fact they are each assuming a wholly different definition of dignity. But, that said, there is quite enough agreement about the definition to make the better debates very meaningful. That between Bostrom and Rubin is a good example.[46]

Fourth: Having agreed that horns must lock over the question of what dignity must dictate, the disagreements begin.

Many anti-enhancers begin, and all end, with apocalyptic fears. Enhancement makes philosophers grimly eloquent. Here is Leon Kass:

> the final technical conquest of his own nature would almost certainly leave mankind utterly enfeebled. This form of mastery would be identical with utter dehumanization. Read Huxley's *Brave New World*, read C. S. Lewis's *Abolition of Man*, read Nietzsche's account of the last man, and then read the newspapers. Homogenization, mediocrity, pacification, drug-induced contentment, debasement of taste, souls without loves or longings—these are the inevitable results of making human nature the last project of technical mastery. In his moment of triumph, Promethean man will also become a contented cow.[47]

The road to this conclusion differs depending on the version of dignity used. I have outlined those versions already. I have also expressed already most of the main reasons for thinking that Kass's apocalyptic vision is a real possibility.

In relation to significant enhancement (ie that where ordinary autonomy-type arguments falter), the pro-enhancers have three complementary strategies. They say:

(a)   We're all enhancers anyway.

(b)   Some enhancements are dignity-enhancing.

(c)   One can put into place workable legislative safeguards against abuse.

---

[44] In this second class I would put Ruth Macklin, who would have to accept that autonomy didn't work for difficult enhancement problems, and would thus presumably fall back on 'respect for persons', which in the enhancement context would have to mean something like respect both for Bostrom's 'dignity as a quality' and 'Menschenwurde', the ground on which, according to some, rests the moral status of humans.

[45] N Bostrom, 'Dignity and enhancement' in Pellegrino et al (eds), *Human Dignity and Bioethics* 173–206.

[46] Bostrom, 'Dignity and enhancement'; C Rubin, 'Human Dignity and the Future of Man' in Pellegrino et al (eds), *Human Dignity and Bioethics* 155–72; and 'Commentary on Bostrom' in Pellegrino et al (eds), *Human Dignity and Bioethics* 207–11. I have already surveyed the various meanings given to dignity by representatives of the main factions: see chs 3, 4 and 5. It will be apparent from that survey that there is enough common ground for the conversation to continue.

[47] L Kass, *Life, Liberty and the Defense of Dignity: The Challenge for Bioethics* (San Francisco, CA, Encounter Books, 2002) 48.

I propose to deal only with the first two of these. The arguments about (c) are important, but would take us far from the focus of our inquiry.

So:

(a) We're all enhancers anyway

I have acknowledged this. But it is no argument at all for unrestricted enhancement. Such an argument would be not a *reductio ad absurdum,* but an *inflatio ad absurdum.*[48] Yes, coffee-drinking is only different in degree from genetic enhancement of my ability to concentrate. Likewise, stealing a lollipop from a shop is only different in degree from a multi-million pound jewel theft. Both are thefts. Yet no one would seriously argue that they should be treated the same way. Clear demarcations between categories are unusual, both in ethics and in law. Ethicists are used to dealing with fuzzy concepts that connect with others. The fact of a continuum doesn't begin to imply that there is no real moral difference between the two ends.

Autonomy is perhaps to blame for the fact that the *inflatio ad absurdum* is appealing. Lawyers especially are fond of autonomy because it does seem more hard-edged and definite than other principles. Ms B can insist on the withdrawal of her own life-sustaining treatment[49] for precisely the same reason as I can insist on my right to pick my own nose. Yet they are very different situations. I am not criticising the identical operation of autonomy in those two situations; I am simply pointing out (a) that this is an unusual example of a principle working identically at two ends of an ethical spectrum, and should not be taken to indicate a general rule; and (b) that this false analogy with enhancement technology has given the 'you're all enhancers anyway' argument an intellectual authority that it does not deserve.

All that said, there is enough in the argument to cause us to think more critically than we normally do, using the notion of dignity to do so, about many of the things that we take for granted.

Two examples:

(1) Is educating my son abusive, on the grounds that I'm allowing his teachers to mould his brain in a way incompatible with his dignity? Well, his brain will be moulded whether he is at school or not. But it is strongly arguable (and I would in fact argue) that the moulding is illegitimate on dignity grounds except insofar as it gives him the set of neuronal connections that he will need for self-realisation—to be more fully himself.

It will be noted that I am importing a notion of my son being one person as opposed to another, and of it being possible for him to be more or less what he 'really' is. I am unembarrassed by this observation. It is central to my notion of human dignity as thriving: (a) that there is an identifiable person about whom we can meaningfully talk, whose thriving is in issue in

---

[48] Thanks to Louise Bralsford for this expression.
[49] *B v An NHS Trust* [2002] 2 All ER 449.

the conversation; and (b) that the thriving in issue, so far as it relates to that individual, consists at least in part in that person being themselves. Whether there is more to individual thriving than that is something about which I'm agnostic. I would also counter-note that objections to this kind of talk (objections that often take the form: 'You're being teleological') are generally levelled by thoroughgoing autonomists who are not similarly critical of the ontological basis for asserting, as they do, that an individual's autonomy should be sovereign.

(2)   The distinction between enhancement and therapy is easy enough to criticise. If I have a stainless steel hip inserted as a consequence of osteoarthritis, I am enhancing the body I have. I am enhancing it to improve my performance. Is there really a difference of any moral weight between this and a non-competitive athlete who has his own perfectly serviceable gastrocnemius tendon replaced by a carbon-fibre tendon whose biomechanical properties will allow him to run faster and more joyfully? If there is, I can't see it.

We tend to assume that because there is no difference between these two scenarios, it follows, on dignity grounds, that because (obviously) one should allow the hip replacement, one should also allow the athlete to have his new tendons. But what if the opposite is true? What if the similarity points up to us something that, in our assumption that healthcare is a good thing, we often miss—namely that the hip replacement might itself be an affront to dignity?

Ryuichi Ida points out that in Japan and some other Asian countries, human beings are understood as a part of nature, and, since it is hard to think that humans could (or should) change or improve nature, there is a resistance to technologies that purport to change or improve humans. She continues:

> There is an objection. If we cannot change nature, what about the role of the medicine, which, in fact, changes the state of health of a diseased person? It should be remembered that oriental medicine does not stand on the same footing as Western medicine. Oriental medicine has as its basic principle the re-establishment of the balance of body and soul. All the diseases come from the imbalance of the patient. It is true that this type of medicine does not practice big operations, like organ transplants, or brain operations. Oriental medicine sees the conditions that might call for such interventions as natural, simply a consequence of human mortality, and it accordingly sees such a patient as entering a stage of returning to nature, ie dying.[50]

---

[50] R Ida, 'Should we Improve Human Nature? An Interrogation from an Asian Perspective' in Savulescu and Bostrom (eds), *Human Enhancement* 65. The theologian Edward Schillebeeckx noted that 'The basic mistake of many conceptions about creation lies in the fact that finitude is felt to be a flaw, a hurt which as such should not really have been one of the features of the world ... there is the feeling that ... mortality, failure, mistakes and ignorance should not be a part of the normal condition of our humanity'; cited and discussed in W Wing Han Lamb and H Thomson, 'Wholeness, Dignity and the Aging Self: A Conversation between Philosophy and Theology' (2002)12 *Journal of Religious Gerontology* 58–59.

Whatever one thinks of this, embodied in the thinking is a clear and high view of human dignity—a view that is intensely relational (humans are defined in terms, inter alia, of their relationship to the rest of the natural order) and would strike a chord with all those who describe as dignified those who go bravely and acceptingly to their deaths. It is, certainly, a view of dignity that is concerned with how best to thrive on this curious, complex ball of rock. And yet it is a view of dignity that would make illegitimate most significant medical intervention.

Were this view of dignity to be adopted, medical ethics would be a great deal simpler, simply because there would be little legitimate medicine, or little that was ethically difficult. It would put a blue pencil through much of bioethical discourse (which in itself would be a dignity-enhancing mercy), and render our lives simpler. It is not just our philosophical agonies that are caused by medical cleverness and ambition. It is many actual agonies: the *timor mortis*; the existential dread; the tremulous look into the doctor's face for his verdict; the long, sophisticated prolongation of the inevitable; the medicalisation of life and death; the violating insertion of a needle where there should be a caress; the bleep of the monitor that drowns out the baby's first and the grandmother's last breath. It is not just the romantic Luddite in me that tends towards this iconoclastic conclusion. Wouldn't we *thrive* more if dehumanising technology didn't take our eyes off the ontological ball?

There is nothing necessarily Eastern about this conclusion. I expect that Amish medical ethicists think in a similar way.

(b) Some enhancements are dignity-enhancing

Bostrom can stand well for the mainstream enhancers. He contends that some enhancements would plainly increase dignity as a quality; for instance composure, distinctiveness, inaccessibility to destructive or subversive influences, and so on. Perhaps, also, the ability to withstand mild pains and discomforts and to self-regulate the consumption of food, exercise and sleep.[51]

Other 'enhancements', he accepts, while apparently being good in themselves, might reduce dignity as a quality. For instance a greatly enhanced capacity for empathy and compassion might (since the world is such a turbulent place), diminish composure and serenity; boosting personal motivation might destabilise our equilibrium; an increased ability to adapt to changing circumstances might make us more susceptible to corrosive influences and 'undermine our ability to stand firm and quietly defy the world.'[52]

In response to the suggestion that the act of 'enhancement' might in itself lower our dignity as a quality, or that capacities generated artificially might contribute less to our dignity than naturally occurring 'authentic' characteristics, he powerfully counters that self-shaping might enhance our dignity if we deliberately

[51] Bostrom, 'Dignity and Enhancement' 180.
[52] Ibid 180–81.

choose good characteristics for ourselves.[53] His argument is strengthened by his moderation, and in particular his important concession that, other things being equal, defiance in the face of the natural vicissitudes of life seems more dignified than compliance and adaptation, and accordingly that one might gain in un-dignity by picking up a bottle of self-enhancer in order to cope.[54]

Less nuanced thinkers than Bostrom might contend simply that the transhumanist project is suffused with the sort of defiance in the face of the universe that most would associate with the highest expressions of human dignity: that it is essentially a refusal to accept the design flaws in humanity (in which they include all limitations imposed by biology). For such transhumanists, it's undignified to accept what nature bestows.

Charles Rubin deals robustly with these extreme expressions of transhumanist optimism:

> by defining dignity in terms of ceaseless self-overcoming, the transhumanists open the door to an incomprehensible human future. In so doing, they deprive the term 'dignity' of any determinate moral meaning.[55]

There are many other strands to the discussion. I cannot and need not do justice to them all. The only comment necessary for present purposes can be made by reference to a trite example.

Suppose a man wants to be enhanced (say by the alteration of his vision and his associated neurological ability to compute angles), so that he unerringly pots snooker balls every time. Surely he should be permitted to do so, so long as he does not take part in snooker tournaments with unenhanced individuals without notifying them of his advantage. There are two reasons why he should not take part in such competitions.

The first is fairness. This, on the facts of the scenario, is the least important. It doesn't matter much in the great scheme of things who wins a snooker match. But on other sets of facts it might matter very much indeed. Enhancement might create an underclass.

The second, and more fundamental reason, is that the game that the enhanced player would be playing is not snooker at all. Snooker is by definition a game played by people with unenhanced functions who do their best to overcome nerves, colds, sleepless nights, the naturally bestowed curvatures of their corneas, and so on. Snooker is not just about putting balls into pockets. There are far easier ways of doing that than prodding them with thin sticks.[56]

The same two points can be made about any enhancement. I suggest that they are really the only two points to be made about any enhancement. There will

---

[53] Ibid 181–84.

[54] Ibid 184–85.

[55] C Rubin, 'Human Dignity and the Future of Man' in Pellegrino et al (eds), *Human Dignity and Bioethics* 160.

[56] See J Savulescu and N Bostrom, 'Human Enhancement Ethics: The State of the Debate', in Savulescu and Bostrom (eds) *Human Enhancement* 13.

always be concerns about equality. And there may be concerns about whether the enhancement means that the enhanced person is not playing the human game at all. 'Not playing the human game' is entirely synonymous with 'being undignified', 'failing to thrive as a human', 'being dehumanised', or any of the other ways in which I have suggested that dignity and un-dignity can be framed.

Of course it will often be nightmarishly difficult to decide whether a particular enhancement means that one isn't playing the game. Few cases, in practice, will be of obvious transhumans. A person with an IQ boosted by, say, 50 points, will still be plainly human. But will they be 'them'? The game isn't just being a member of the human species; it's about being oneself. There may be enhancements which allow one to be more fully oneself. As I've suggested already, the only justifiable education is education that allows that. Alleged enhancements that diminish one's ability to be oneself are not enhancements at all: they are truncations. They are wrong in the same way and for the same reasons as it is wrong for someone to be manipulated by advertising or peer pressure into wearing clothes that they do not themselves like.

The enhancement/therapy distinction cannot be ducked. What if 'oneself' is generally perceived to be less favourably placed in the human scheme than are others?

Suppose a 10-year-old achondroplastic child could be treated so as to be of 'normal' height and appearance. Should it be done? Few will agree with me, but no, it should not. The only justification for any intervention is the maintenance or boosting of human dignity. Human dignity is simply not in play in the achondroplastic example. Yes, we are embodied animals, and our dignity has to be read in a fleshly context. Of course 'thriving' not only has physical corollaries, but presupposes physicality. My conclusion about the treatment is a consequence of my insistence on the importance of embodiment, not a contradiction of it.

The first question to ask when one is thinking about thriving is: '*Whose* thriving are we talking about?' An achondroplastic child's thriving is a thriving in its body. If you gave it another body—a taller body, say—that child would stop thriving. It wouldn't have *its* body in which to thrive. It wouldn't be itself. The child is inextricable from its body. To say otherwise is to lapse into the sort of dualism that has long emasculated religious contributions to bioethics, but with which secular commentators are so often nastily infected.

This is not a politically correct point, made out of slavish deference to the disability rights lobby. I can see that it might be different if the child were, say, six months old. I entirely accept that there is a neurodevelopmental component to 'being oneself'. Which brings me back to my original insistence that dignity questions have to be empirically grounded. 'Being oneself', for the purposes of deciding whether it is legitimate to alter oneself, may turn on one's capacity for Theory of Mind. Of course one must be careful about generalising that observation. It does not begin to follow, for instance, that an entity without Theory of Mind (say an early embryo, or a patient in PVS) has no dignity. We come to those cases shortly.

In the end I am not far from Sandel, but I have reached his position by a round-about journey through Asia.

It only remains to say, as one would now expect, that if these matters were to hit a European courtroom they would be under the umbrella of Article 8. 8(1) would look after the 'being oneself'/dehumanisation parts. 8(2) would be interested in the wider societal fallout of those elements, and would scrutinise the equality issues particularly closely.

10

Reproductive Choice and the Unborn

Many of the arguments behind many of the issues of reproductive choice, the use of technology to facilitate reproduction, the status of the embryo, and abortion, have already been aired in Chapter 9. Usually it is obvious how they apply to this chapter's issues. Where that is so, I do not spell out the arguments.

Reproductive Choice Generally

Nobody suggests that humans should be required to reproduce against their will.[1] But sometimes claimants have suggested that their desire to have a child should trump their partner's refusal. Those claims, framed in terms of Articles 8 and 12 of the ECHR, have failed.[2] They were viewed (or would now be viewed) as a straight-forward cases of competition between opposing Article 8 claims.[3]

Dignity could argue these cases both ways. Is having a child connected with human thriving? Yes: it goes close to the root of one's self-identity and sense of purpose. In *Evans v Amicus Healthcare* Arden LJ commented:

> Infertility can cause the woman or man affected great personal distress. In the case of a woman, the ability to give birth to a child gives many women a supreme sense of fulfilment and purpose in life. It goes to their sense of identity and to their dignity.[4]

But by precisely the same reasoning, not having a child is similarly connected. One's sense of identity, integrity and purpose may be diluted by the emergence into the world of a child to whose existence one was not a consenting party. It is arguably rather different if one has consented to the possibility of pregnancy by having sexual intercourse: we come to that consideration in a moment. But in

---

[1] See C Foster, *Choosing Life, Choosing Death* (Oxford, Hart, 2009) 33–34.

[2] See *Evans v United Kingdom* (2008) 46 EHRR 34; *R v Human Fertilisation and Embryology Authority ex p Blood* [1997] 2 WLR 806.

[3] For judicial guidance as to how to adjudicate this sort of competition, see *Campbell v Mirror Group Newspapers Ltd* [2004] 2 AC 457. See too S Choudry and H Fenwick, 'Taking the Rights of Parents and Children Seriously: Confronting the Welfare Principle Under the Human Rights Act' (2005) 25 *Oxford Journal of Legal Studies* 453.

[4] *Evans v Amicus Healthcare* [1994] Fam 94 para 81.

cases involving the impregnation of a willing woman with the stored semen of a no longer willing man, or the implantation into her of an embryo fathered by a man who no longer wishes to be a father, the civil war of the Article 8(1) claims is resolved by the adjudication of Article 8(2). It is possible to see this as a simple battle of autonomy claims, sub nom Article 8.[5] (Of course when the matter in issue is the implantation of an embryo, the embryo's own rights, if any, fall to be considered too: of that, more below.) But surely it is better to give Article 8 credit for rather more nuance than that, and to accept that the judges who spoke about dignity when addressing the issue were being sincere and legally accurate?

No one suggests that the balance is an easy one to strike. When *Evans* got to Strasbourg the majority concluded that:

> Respect for human dignity and free will, as well as a desire to ensure a fair balance between the parties to IVF treatment, underlay the legislature's decision to enact provisions permitting of no exception to ensure that every person donating gametes for the purpose of IVF treatment would know in advance that no use could be made of his or her genetic material without his or her continuing consent.[6]

But there was a powerful dissent.

> [U]nlike the majority we consider that the legislation has not struck a fair balance in the special circumstances of the case. Where the effect of the legislation is such that, on the one hand, it provides a woman with the right to take a decision to have a genetically related child but, on the other hand, effectively deprives a woman from ever again being in this position, it inflicts in our view such a disproportionate moral and physical burden on a woman that it can hardly be compatible with Art.8 and the very purposes of the Convention protecting human dignity and autonomy.[7]

The fact that dignity does not provide a definitive answer does not begin to suggest that it is not useful. *Evans* is an example of dignity-as-thriving in play.[8]

It is different, of course, when both partners want a child. Then, autonomy has little to say, and it is plain that Articles 8 and 12 are primarily the mouthpieces of dignity. I have outlined elsewhere the outcome and the reasons for it.[9] It is straightforward 8(1) v 8(2) territory, with the dignity considerations inherent in Article 8 outweighing the more absolute, couple-friendly language of Article 12.

---

[5] Indeed I have represented it this way myself: see *Choosing Life, Choosing Death* 31–34.

[6] *Evans v United Kingdom* (n 2) para 89.

[7] Ibid O–I14.

[8] See generally S Chan and M Quigley, 'Frozen Embryos, Genetic Information and Reproductive Rights' (2007) 21 *Bioethics* 439; C McLeod, *Self-Trust and Reproductive Autonomy (Basic Bioethics)* (Cambridge, MA, MIT Press, 2002); R Bennett and J Harris 'Are There Lives Not Worth Living? When is it Morally Wrong to Reproduce?' in D Dickenson (ed), *Ethical Issues in Maternal-Fetal Medicine* (Cambridge, CUP, 2002) 321; J McHale, 'Is there a Duty not to Reproduce?' in Dickenson, *Ethical Issues in Maternal-Fetal Medicine* 101.

[9] I consider this situation in detail in *Choosing Life, Choosing Death* 34–39; see too E Jackson, *Regulating Reproduction: Law, Technology and Autonomy* (Oxford, Hart, 2001).

General Dignity Observations on the Use of Therapeutic Cloning and other Reproductive Technology

We have covered much of this already when we looked at the notions of unnaturalness, of 'playing God', of 'giftedness', and so on.

What we have not yet examined is the status of the embryo and foetus. My comments here are deliberately limited, partly because the account in *Choosing Life, Choosing Death* gives me a complete defence to the charge of equivocation,[10] but mainly because I have a very limited purpose. I seek only to show that dignity is the right lens through which to examine these questions.

The metaphysical status of the embryo is deeply mysterious.[11] I do not presume to penetrate the mystery. But few would disagree with John Pilkinghorne:

> The very early embryo is entitled to a deep moral respect because of its potential humanity, so that it is not just a speck of protoplasm that you can do what you like with and then flush it down the sink; but it is not yet fully a human being.[12]

So: we respect early embryos because they are in a crucial continuity, or at least potential continuity, with beings (born humans) to whom we accord without caveat the sort of respect which, in previous chapters, we have seen is best, if ambiguously, regarded as dignity.[13] Another way of putting this is to say that our belief in human dignity is so instinctively strong that we accord some of its benefits (notably the protection against blithe destruction) to something that might ultimately and unequivocally have this full quality.

But is this the full story? Are we really refusing to treat embryos blithely *because* of their potentiality? Surely if we have concluded confidently that the embryo is only a potential human, we would be impressed into callousness by John Harris's sermons about natural embryo wastage[14] in a way that we are not. Or is the ground of our respect actually a queasy uncertainty about whether the embryo *as it is* should be treated as having dignity? I suspect the latter. This is the one place in this book where I depart from my original principle of not using instinct

---

[10] Foster, *Choosing Life, Choosing Death* 41–62.

[11] See the UK Parliament Science and Technology Committee 5th Report (2004), which deals with the status of the embryo, at: www.publications.parliament.uk/pa/cm200405/cmselect/cmsctech/7/705.htm.

[12] J Polkinghorne, 'The Person, the Soul, and Genetic Engineering'(2004) 30 *Journal of Medical Ethics (JME)*593. A similar view was held by the Warnock Committee, whose report led to the Human Fertilization and Embryology Act 1990. See also B Steinbock, 'A Philosopher Looks at Assisted Reproduction' (1995) 12 *Journal of Assisted Reproduction and Genetics* 543.

[13] Cp the decision of the French Conseil Constitutionnel, which saw dignity as the key guiding principle when considering the constitutionality of laws relating to medically assisted reproduction and prenatal diagnosis: Decision de 27 juillet 1994, nos 94-343-344, DC: relative au respect du corps humain et a l'utilisation des elements et produits du corps human, a l'assistance medicale a la procreation et au diagnostique prenatal (lois no 94-653 et no 94-654 du 29 juillet 1994).

[14] J Harris, '"ARTBs": Assisted Reproductive Technological Blunders' (2003) 29 *JME* 205.

as a guide. I do so reluctantly, and because there is no alternative. Uncertainty, anyway, is often the basis for rather good law-making.[15] We're going to have to become increasingly used to legislating about matters of existential mystery.

But let's not despair of argument quite yet. Are there any grounds for thinking that the embryo does have dignity? The UK judges don't help. It is perhaps unsurprising, and it is certainly depressing, that the House of Lords[16] and the Administrative Court[17] managed to negotiate three fairly recent cases concerning the status of the embryo without once invoking the idea of dignity.

Is the embryo human? This is a big and rather unhelpful question. Pamphlets often point out that the early embryo has all the genetic information necessary to generate the whole organism. That is true. But where does it take us? A flake of dandruff similarly has all the information necessary to clone the person from whom it came, but no one suggests that it should be treated with the respect due to a child. The difference between the flake and the embryo is that the embryo needs no more done to it in order for it to become a human, other than (and this is an important consideration when we come to consider abortion) continued accommodation within, and draining biological support from, the mother.

The real question is whether there are grounds for distinguishing between the embryo's potential and the born human's actuality. Of course there are dangers associated with gestation and birth. Embryonic and foetal loss are real issues. But assume for the purposes of argument that, if left alone, the embryo will grow and be delivered. It is likely to have a longer likely life span than the average born human. In that sense its capacity for human thriving might be said to be greater than that of the born human. Certainly, even if one factors in the possibility of intra-uterine death, one would put one's QALY-audited money on the embryo rather than on an elderly patient with angina. So can it coherently be said that the elderly patient has something material, describable as dignity, that the embryo does not?

The elderly patient has cognition (which might, of course be compromised by dementia), preferences, relationships and a past. All of these might be said to be relevant to dignity-thriving.

The embryo, on the other hand, has no cognition (but it is likely to develop in a few weeks or months, and, when it does, is unlikely to be compromised for

---

[15] I am thinking particularly of the utility of the intolerability principle, deployed where one is considering the withdrawal of life-sustaining treatment, but there is uncertainty about the quality of life. See the discussion at Foster, *Choosing Life, Choosing Death* 145 et seq.

[16] *R (Quintavalle) v Secretary of State for Health* [2003] 2 AC 687, which concerned the definition of an embryo in the 1990 Act; *R (Quintavalle) v Human Fertilisation and Embryology Authority* [2005] 2 AC 561, which concerned the lawfulness of pre-implantation genetic diagnosis for the production of a 'saviour sibling'.

[17] *R (Quintavalle) v Human Fertilisation and Embryology Authority* [2008] EWHC 3395 (Admin), which concerned the creation of animal/human hybrid embryos. There is no substantive mention of dignity, although the judge commented that: '[t]he second claimant (CLC) is a public interest group, concerned to uphold the sanctity and dignity of human life in the fields of law, ethics and public policy'. (para 5)

_s), has no preferences (but in weeks will acquire at least a preference not to cut or poisoned, if not a preference for Bach over Pink Floyd), has relationships (albeit the enjoyment of those relationships is likely, again for a short time, to be rather unilateral), and a future as long as the past of the elderly patient.

If one objects that the embryo is still to be made, it might be countered that, as a matter of gruesome fact, the elderly patient will soon be biologically un-made. He will not long have the body which is the medium for his enjoyment of himself. In terms of made-ness, the embryo arguably has the upper hand. One could put the same point in terms of humanisation. In a little while the elderly patient will be, in some senses, dehumanised: he will be food for worms. (In other senses, as we see in Chapters 11 and 12, he remains humanised). In a little while, the embryo will certainly be fully humanised. Or one might talk about being oneself: the embryo is completely itself, and will remain so until it becomes a teenage fashion-victim.

None of these arguments is conclusive. But, together, they do provide a way of saying that the early embryo has dignity in the same sense, and for the same reasons (if not better) than we say that born humans have dignity.

Embryos aren't created in a vacuum, of course. They're not created for fun. They are created with a view either to implantation into a woman, or for research, or for the production of stem cells for therapeutic purposes (whether harvested directly from the embryo, or from the child at term, as in a 'saviour sibling' case). And as soon as we start looking at all the other dignity interests that are immediately relevant when we identify the context of the embryo's creation and fate, our considerations become messy in the way with which we are now very familiar. Assuming that the embryo has dignity interests, they have to be balanced against all the other interests. And it's not just dignity interests that are in play. If the embryo is to be regarded as human to the extent of attracting the protection (for instance) of Article 2 of the ECHR,[18] it is hard to see how any opposing Article 8 interests could outweigh that Article 2 interest. There is a plain hierarchy in the Convention,[19] which accords neatly and necessarily with all coherent ethical thinking.[20] A live body is a necessary prerequisite of the enjoyment of any rights that fall due under Article 8. So if the embryo or foetus has a crystallised right

---

[18] Article 2 provides: '1. Everyone's right to life shall be protected by law. No one shall be deprived of his life intentionally save in the execution of a sentence of a court following his conviction of a crime for which this penalty is provided by law. 2. Deprivation of life shall not be regarded as inflicted in contravention of this article when it results from the use of force which is no more than absolutely necessary: a. in defence of any person from unlawful violence; b. in order to effect a lawful arrest or to prevent the escape of a person lawfully detained; c. in action lawfully taken for the purpose of quelling a riot or insurrection.'

[19] R v Secretary of State for the Home Department, ex p Bugdaycay [1987] AC 514, 531; R v Lord Saville of Newdigate, ex p A [2000] 1 WLR 1855 paras 34–37; Venables v News Group Newspapers Ltd [2001] Fam 430.

[20] For instance in *State of Israel v Rahamin Gibli* (1996): Originating Motion 829/26A, which concerned force-feeding of a hunger-striker, an Israeli district judge observed that 'when there is direct conflict between human life and human dignity, human life must be given priority.' Cited by S Glick, 'Who Decides? The Patient, the Physician, or the Rabbi?' in *Jewish Medical Ethics 1989-2004* (Jerusalem, Falk Institute for Medical-Halakhic Research, 2004) 156.

to life (an issue on which the Strasbourg Court has been understandably but culpably equivocal),[21] all other competing Article 8 rights become irrelevant.

I observe that the arguments outlined above, to the effect that the embryo might have dignity interests, should work just as well as arguments for the application of Article 2 (and indeed work rather more urgently), as they do as arguments for the entitlement to some Article 8 rights. It need not follow, though, that the non-possession of an Article 2 right means automatic disentitlement to Article 8 rights. If the embryo is, for whatever reason, not entitled to the protection of Article 2, there is nothing in principle to stop it being protected by Article 8.

If the embryo possesses any of the potential dignity-characteristics that might engage Article 8, the propriety of any technology such as human-animal hybrid formation (a very obvious example of something that offends against dignity, because it stops something being itself),or PGD for saviour sibling creation, would be left for determination by 8(2) and (in the case of another engaged 8(1) interest—such as in the saviour sibling example), by comparing the weight of the competing 8(1) interest.

All this presupposes, of course, rejection of Sandel, and rejection of the Asian approach to 'big' interventions (which, on any view, include reproductive techno-logical manipulations that call into question the status of the embryo).

General Dignity Observations on Abortion

If dignity argues for the early embryo, invoking Articles 2, 3, 8 or 14, or any combination of them—if dignity has *locus standi* to represent them—a fortiori, dignity will argue against abortion. That is not to say that it will do so without professional embarrassment: it will, of course, argue also in favour of the woman's claim to be spared the burden of tyrannous, emetic inhabitation, followed by a lifetime of obligation.

I have sought previously to adjudicate this dispute, and nothing would be gained by reiteration.[22]

It is perhaps worth noting, though, the other briefs that dignity will hold. There are several other stakeholders, although in UK law at least they have rarely been allowed a voice. Fathers, notably, have not been allowed to say that the parts of their identity and aspiration that are bound up in the body of a foetus should be

---

[21] See *Vo v France* (2005) 40 EHRR 259; *H v Norway* (1992) 73 DR 155; *Paton v United Kingdom* (1980) 3 EHRR 408; *Boso v Italy* (Application 50490/99) 5 September 2002; *Poku v United Kingdom* (1996) 22 EHRR CD 94. Art 4 of the American Convention on Human Rights 1969, conversely, protects the right 'in general, from the moment of conception'. Of course this is subject to a number of caveats, upon which we will touch in looking at the law of abortion.

[22] See Foster, *Choosing Life, Choosing Death* 41–54.

weighed in the balance.[23] And expressivism is perhaps peculiarly important in the abortion debate.

Judgments of the UK courts in abortion cases have, by and large, been dry exercises in statutory construction.[24] One can well see why the judges would want to approach them that way. Dignity has not been expressly mentioned. Nor was it in the early US cases, where one might have thought that the religious/political climate might have compelled its use. It is not mentioned in *Roe v Wade*.[25] In the 1986 (unsuccessful) root and branch challenge to *Roe v Wade*, *Thornburgh v American College of Obstetricians and Gynecologists*,[26] Justice Blackmun, for the court, observed that:

> Few decisions are more personal and intimate, more properly private, or more basic to individual dignity and autonomy, than a woman's decision—with the guidance of her physician and within the limits specified in Roe—whether to end her pregnancy. A woman's right to make that choice freely is fundamental. Any other result, in our view, would protect inadequately a central part of the sphere of liberty that our law guarantees equally to all.[27]

There was no mention at all in *Webster v Reproductive Health Services*.[28]

It was not until 1992 that the Supreme Court said anything about dignity in the abortion context that even purported to be substantive. In *Planned Parenthood of Southeastern Pennsylvania v Casey*[29] the Court said:

> Our law affords constitutional protection to personal decisions relating to marriage, procreation, contraception, family relationships, child rearing, and education. *Carey v. Population Services International*, 431 U.S., at 685. Our cases recognize 'the right of the individual, married or single, to be free from unwarranted governmental intrusion into matters so fundamentally affecting a person as the decision whether to bear or beget a child.' *Eisenstadt v. Baird*, supra, at 453 [.....]. Our precedents 'have respected the private realm of family life which the state cannot enter.' *Prince v. Massachusetts*, 321 U.S. 158, 166 (1944). These matters, involving the most intimate and personal choices a person may make in a lifetime, choices central to personal dignity and autonomy, are central to the liberty protected by the Fourteenth Amendment. At the heart of liberty is the right to define one's own concept of existence, of meaning, of the universe, and of the mystery of human life. Beliefs about these matters could not define the attributes of personhood were they formed under compulsion of the State.

---

[23] See *Paton v Trustees of the British Pregnancy Advisory Service* [1979] QB 276; *C v S* [1988] QB 135.

[24] *Paton* and *C v S*, n 23 above, are good examples.

[25] *Roe v Wade* 410 US 113 (1973).

[26] *Thornburgh v American College of Obstetricians and Gynecologists* 476 US 747 (1986).

[27] *Thornburgh* (n 26) 476.

[28] *Webster v Reproductive Health Services* 492 US 490 (1989), a decision of the US Supreme Court, upholding a law of the State of Missouri imposing restrictions on how state funds and facilities could be used in performing, helping with, or counselling about abortion.

[29] *Planned Parenthood of Southeastern Pennsylvania v Casey* 505 US 833 (1992). This concerned the legality of several Pennsylvania state regulations concerning abortion. The details do not matter for our purposes. The Court upheld the constitutional right to abortion established in *Roe v Wade*.

These considerations begin our analysis of the woman's interest in terminating her pregnancy but cannot end it, for this reason: though the abortion decision may originate within the zone of conscience and belief, it is more than a philosophic exercise. Abortion is a unique act. It is an act fraught with consequences for others: for the woman who must live with the implications of her decision; for the persons who perform and assist in the procedure; for the spouse, family, and society which must confront the knowledge that these procedures exist, procedures some deem nothing short of an act of violence against innocent human life; and, depending on one's beliefs, for the life or potential life that is aborted.[30]

Dissenting, Stevens J observed that:

A woman considering abortion faces 'a difficult choice having serious and personal consequences of major importance to her own future-perhaps to the salvation of her own immortal soul.' *Thornburgh*, 476 U.S., at 781. The authority to make such traumatic and yet empowering decisions is an element of basic human dignity. As the joint opinion so eloquently demonstrates, a woman's decision to terminate her pregnancy is nothing less than a matter of conscience.[31]

In *Mazurek v Armstrong*,[32] a 1997 challenge to a state law restricting the performance of abortions to licensed physicians, the Supreme Court did not mention the word 'dignity' once.

In the 2000 case of *Stenberg, Attorney General of Nebraska v Carhart*, which concerned the constitutionality of partial birth abortion[33], Breyer J, giving the opinion of the court, noted that:

A State may take measures to ensure the medical profession and its members are viewed as healers, sustained by a compassionate and rigorous ethic and cognizant of the dignity and value of human life, even life which cannot survive without the assistance of others.[34]

And:

Nebraska could conclude the procedure presents a greater risk of disrespect and a consequent greater risk to the profession and society, which depend for their sustenance upon reciprocal recognition of dignity and respect.[35]

It also noted that the dignity interests of women were crucially relevant:

millions fear that a law that forbids abortion would condemn many American women to lives that lack dignity.[36]

---

[30] Ibid 851–52.
[31] Ibid 916.
[32] *Mazurek, Attorney General of Montana v Armstrong* 520 US 968 (1997).
[33] Surgical abortion, in which the intact foetus is removed from the uterus via the cervix and vagina.
[34] *Stenberg, Attorney General of Nebraska v Carhart* 530 US 914 (2000) para 962.
[35] Ibid para 963.
[36] Ibid para 920.

is on such observations that those who contend that dignity is mere window-dressing build their case.

We have already noted that Germany, for understandable historical reasons, has, along with Israel,[37] led the jurisprudential world in its explicit deployment of dignity. Its approach to abortion is a good example.

In 1975, two years after *Roe v Wade*, the German Federal Constitutional Court held that respect for human dignity meant that abortion should be criminalised.[38] It said that Article 1 of West Germany's Basic Law of 1949 (which protects dignity),[39] when read together with Article 2's assertion that 'Everyone has the right to life', meant that Article 2's protection extended into the womb:

> Where human life exists, human dignity is present to it; it is not decisive that the bearer of this dignity himself be conscious of it and know personally how to preserve it. The potential faculties present in the human being from the beginning suffice to establish human dignity.[40]
>
> ...
>
> Human life represents, within the order of the Basic Law, an ultimate value, the particulars of which need not be established ... it is the living foundation of human dignity and the prerequisite for all other fundamental rights.[41]
>
> ...
>
> A compromise which guarantees the protection of the life of the one about to be born and permits the pregnant woman the freedom of abortion is not possible since the interruption of pregnancy always means the destruction of the unborn life. In the required balancing, 'both constitutional values are to be viewed in their relationship to human dignity, the center of the value system of the constitution' (Decisions of the Federal Constitutional Court, 35, 202 225) ... The opinion expressed in the Federal Parliament during the third deliberation on the Statute to Reform the Penal Law, the effect of which is to propose the precedence for a particular time 'of the right to self-determination of the woman which flows from human dignity vis-a-vis all others, including the child's right to life' (German Federal Parliament, Seventh Election Period, 96th Session, Stenographic Reports, p. 6492), is not reconcilable with the value-ordering of the Basic Law.[42]

---

[37] See Israel's Basic Law: Human Dignity and Liberty 1992, amended in 1994, which reads, inter alia: '1. The purpose of this Basic Law is to protect human dignity and liberty, in order to establish in a Basic Law the values of the State of Israel as a Jewish and democratic state. 2. There shall be no violation of the life, body or dignity of any person as such. 3. There shall be no violation of the property of a person. 4. All persons are entitled to protection of their life, body and dignity.'

[38] *First Abortion Decision* 1975 BVerfGE 39, 1.

[39] It provides: 'The dignity of man shall be inviolable. To respect and protect it shall be the duty of all state authority.'

[40] *First Abortion Decision* (n 37) Pt1 (trs RE Jonas and JDGorby, 9 *The John Marshall Journal of Practice and Procedure* 605).

[41] Ibid Pt 2:1.

[42] Ibid Pt 2:2. For a detailed comparative legal perspective, see A Eser and H-G Koch, *Abortion and the Law: From International Comparison to Legal Policy* (The Hague, TMC Asser, 2005).

The European Court of Human Rights has tended to bolt to the margin of appreciation whenever the word 'abortion' is mentioned. That is an emotionally comfortable but intellectually uncomfortable place to be. But the Court will not give up that refuge easily. That, no doubt, is one of the reasons for its reluctance to accord the embryo or the foetus an Article 2 right. The absolute language of Article 2 must surely mean that there can be no margin of appreciation when it is engaged.[43]

What about dignity in relation to abortion? *Vo v France*, of course, did not concern abortion, but it did raise the question of Article 2's application to the foetus, and the Court did mention dignity.[44] As we have already observed, the Court equivocated on the question of whether or not the foetus was a 'person', for the purposes of Article 2, but the majority did note that:

> At best, it may be regarded as common ground between States that the embryo/foetus belongs to the human race. The potentiality of that being and its capacity to become a person—enjoying protection under the civil law, moreover, in many States, such as France, in the context of inheritance and gifts, and also in the United Kingdom—require protection in the name of human dignity, without making it a 'person' with the 'right to life for the purposes of Article 2.[45]

Dissenting, Judge Mularoni, joined by Judge Straznicka, considered that:

> as with other Convention provisions, Article 2 must be interpreted in an evolutive manner so that the great dangers currently facing human life can be confronted. This is made necessary by the potential that exists for genetic manipulation and the risk that scientific results will be used for a purpose that undermines the dignity and identity of the human being.[46]

In its most recent foray into abortion, (*A, B and C v Ireland*[47]), the ECtHR established (without mentioning dignity once, except when summarising the applicant's submissions under Article 3) that there was no Convention right to abortion per se, but that contracting states had an obligation, where there was a competition between the mother's life and that of the foetus, to ensure that the mother could win. And if that required abortion, so be it. The dignity analysis that I have been urging has no difficulty at all with that conclusion, and the Catholic

---

[43] See, on this point, the dissenting opinion of Judge Ress in *Vo v France* (n 21) para 8.

[44] See too *Tysiąc v Poland* (2007) (Application no 5410/03), in which a pregnant woman sought an abortion to prevent the deterioration of her eye disease. Several doctors refused. The baby was born, and her condition deteriorated. Claims against the doctors failed in Poland. The case found its way to the ECtHR, which found that the doctors were liable. Judge Barrago dissented, pointing out powerfully one of the corollaries of the majority's finding, and couching his distaste in the language of dignity. He said (para 15) 'All human beings are born free and equal in dignity and rights. Today the Court has decided that a human being was born as a result of a violation of the European Convention on Human Rights. According to this reasoning, there is a Polish child, currently six years old, whose right to be born contradicts the Convention. I would never have thought that the Convention would go so far, and I find it frightening.'

[45] *Tysiąc v Poland* (n 43) para 84.

[46] Ibid.

[47] *A, B and C v Ireland* [2010] ECHR 2032.

pro-life lobby's disquiet with the decision is (in the light of the Catholic Church's ancient reliance on the principle of double effect to justify abortion when the mother's life is threatened), incomprehensible.[48]

The point of these examples is to illustrate that (while noting the outlier of *A, B and C v Ireland*), there is an increasing tendency to use dignity language in the abortion debate. The references to dignity that there are in the judgments are few and philosophically sparse. One cannot spell out of them any particular account of dignity, but one can note, once again, that it is the lowest philosophical and forensic denominator to which the judges are sometimes forced to appeal. And one can say that whatever these various judges do understand by dignity, it is not inconsistent with the version articulated in Chapter 1.

---

[48] See C Foster, J Herring, T Hope and K Melham, 'The Double Effect Effect' (2011) 20 *Cambridge Quarterly of Healthcare Ethics* 56.

11

The End of Life

D ying is a part of living. So our instincts tell us, and so eventually, after a stutter, does UK law. The stutter was in *R (Pretty) v DPP*,[1] which held that Article 8 did not extend to end-of-life decision-making, essentially on the grounds that the Article was about how to live, not how to die. The Strasbourg Court, in *Pretty v United Kingdom*,[2] was 'not prepared to exclude' that Article 8 might go that far. The House of Lords, in *R (Purdy) v DPP*,[3] concluded that Article 8 stretched (at least) from the delivery suite to the death bed.

That means that everything we have said in the previous chapters about dignity during life applies equally here. Which means that we can be brief. That might seem strange. After all, much of the dignity rhetoric in popular use relates to the end of life. The Voluntary Euthanasia Society in the UK changed its name to Dignity in Dying, shrewdly realising that no one could coherently object to anyone having a dignified death.[4]

Part of the business of human thriving is connected with, if not actually identical with, being a unique *story*.[5] We thrive particularly when our story is a good one. One of the things about good stories is that they have a beginning, a middle and an end. The ending is important. The ending reaches back and colours the whole story. A good ending can rescue a whole book from banality; a bad ending can mar the whole.

---

[1] *R (Pretty) v DPP* [2002] 1 AC 800.

[2] *Pretty v United Kingdom*(2002) 35 EHRR 1.

[3] *R (Purdy) v DPP* [2010] 1 AC 345.

[4] For an overview of the subject, using some of the Aristotelian ideas referred to in ch 1, see J Gentzler, 'What is a Death with Dignity?' (2003) 28 *Journal of Medicine and Philosophy* 461. For a sophisticated dignity-based argument for euthanasia, see H Biggs, *Euthanasia: Death with Dignity and the Law* (Oxford, Hart, 2001), and the criticisms in M Otlowski, Review of *Euthanasia: Death with Dignity and the Law* (2002) 10 *Medical Law Review* (MLR) 238. See too K Amarasekara and M Bagaric, *Euthanasia, Morality and the Law* (New York, P Lang, 2002); P Miller, 'Death with Dignity and the Right to Die: Sometimes Doctors have a Duty to Hasten Death'(1987) 13 *Journal of Medical Ethics (JME)* 81; and P Allmark, 'Death with Dignity'(2002) 28 *JME* 255; cp L Gormally, 'Against Voluntary Euthanasia' in R Gillon (ed), *Principles of Health Care Ethics* (Chichester, Wiley, 1994) 763; and, generally, J Keown (ed), *Euthanasia Examined: Ethical, Clinical and Legal Perspectives* (Cambridge, CUP, 1995). Christopher Coope suggests that the phrase 'death with dignity' should simply be abandoned, on the grounds that its meaning is too unclear. C Coope, 'Death with Dignity' (1997) 27 *Hastings Center Report* 37.

[5] Cp W Wing Han Lamb and H Thomson, 'Wholeness, Dignity and the Aging Self: A Conversation between Philosophy and Theology' (2002) 12 *Journal of Religious Gerontology* 57, 63.

This sort of talk is common amongst the pro-euthanasia lobby. Their ethical lodestone is Kantian autonomy, as read by John Stuart Mill. Some of their representations are made on behalf of a person who almost certainly doesn't exist, and if he does (it would almost certainly be a 'he'), certainly isn't representative of general opinion, even in the autonomistic West. You wouldn't want him round for dinner. He's a frigid, entirely self-made man, who owes nothing to anybody, and wrote in stone, in the early years of his burgeoning self-possession, a life-plan. For him, the only sin is to divert from that plan. But it is a most terrible sin. He has no friends, no family, and no obligations to anybody but himself. His life-plan, since he's read the judgment of the House of Lords in *Purdy*, includes a detailed account of his death. This is very important to him. He hasn't planned anything very spectacular: he's not like that. There will be no dramatic twist at the end of this story. The crucial thing for him is consistency. He wants to die as he has lived, in perfect control.

I will be rightly accused here of making a straw man. But quite a lot of the work has been done for me by the pro-euthanasia theorists.

Beneath it all, I have a lot of sympathy for my straw man's position. I have agreed that endings are crucial. One very good type of end will be one in perfect artistic harmony with the story that has gone before. Consistency can be a real virtue—but only if one is consistent with something good. If one is consistent with a bad life, that's bad. But in the case of my straw man, my sympathy tends towards pity. He's sad. If he exists, he's never really smiled with anything other than self-satisfaction—and that gives the thinnest smiles of all. His perfectly controlled descent into the darkness will be unlamented. He didn't thrive in life, and he's not thriving in death. His story is terribly, inhumanly dull. He hasn't lived with dignity, and his only hope of dying with dignity—of having a good end to the story—is to be radically inconsistent with his values.

Real people, as we saw when we looked into the nursing homes in Chapter 5, don't look at all like him. They want to die as they have lived—in the nexus of relationships that gave their life its shape. Yes, they are concerned about their relatives seeing or smelling them 'in this state', but what are the relatives' real concerns? The relatives won't be disgusted. They won't think any the less of their father for soiling the bed. They'll remember how they wet their own bed for years, and that the father dutifully and joyfully changed the sheets in the early hours, and will be glad to get a chance to do the same for him. Their only concern about their father's state (apart, of course, from the queasiness that comes from knowing that they are about to lose him), probably comes from knowing that he'll be embarrassed about the damp bed. And he'll only be embarrassed because he thinks the children care. There's a nasty, vicious circle here that can only be broken if we recognise that the father has a dignity that has nothing to do with bladders or bowels.[6]

---

[6] Cp the view taken by the court in *Compassion in Dying v State of Washington* (1996) Ninth Circuit 79 F3d 790: 'A competent, terminally ill adult, having lived nearly the full measure of his life, has a strong liberty interest in choosing a dignified and humane death rather than being reduced at the end

If dying is part of living, then, is one thriving when one is dying? Yes indeed. As we've noted, the end of the story is often the best bit. It might be painful or frightening, but the whole story would be different—wouldn't be a story at all—without it. If my children misbehave during their bedtime story, and I refuse to finish it, they're distraught. To inject a fatal bolus of potassium chloride is slamming the book shut.

If you require someone (a doctor or nurse) to stop the story, their normal function as a friendly, if poignant character in the story is disastrously changed. That's not good for the specific story, for stories in general, for the specific doctor-character in question, for doctor-characters in general, or for people in general who might meet doctor-characters.[7] That will weigh heavily in our transactional audit of the flow of dignity in and out of the ward.

There are many other stories going on, too: wives, children, friends, carers. Our interconnectedness means that when someone in our nexus dies, something of us dies too. The stories of our friends are part of us. If their story loses its proper ending, we are diminished. Our story-likeness, which is part of our own dignity—our own ability to thrive as multi-dimensional relational beings processing from a beginning, via a middle, to an end—is pruned.

The potassium chloride stops endings. It's anti-story: it's dehumanising: it's undignified.

This is an argument against euthanasia. It might be said that it is an argument against palliative care, or indeed against medicine in general. It might be said that terminal pain and respiratory distress are part of the story, and that to cut out that part of the plot with a merciful prescription of analgesics is to spoil it.[8]

I accept the force of the argument. It may be that our dignity would be enhanced, were we willing to dive boldly into the great waves of terminal pain that can be held off with morphine. Some great saints have said so. But in the light of my own cowardice, I cannot insist on it.

The point about medicine, if it is different, is similarly well taken. I have accepted already (Chapter 9) that we over-treat, and that many of our medico-legal difficulties are an artefact of that over-treatment. The logic of the story metaphor similarly compels me to agree that to extend a story artificially is to distort it in a way that is inconsistent with human dignity. But, and this is important, the

---

of his existence to a childlike state of helplessness, diapered, sedated, incontinent.' (Cited by Gentzler, 'What is a Death with Dignity?' 481.)

[7] The mutation in the doctor–patient relationship was one of the principal concerns that pushed the British Medical Association to reject assisted dying. Its current policy is that it '(i) believes that ongoing improvement in palliative care allows patients to die with dignity; (ii) insists that physician-assisted suicide should not be made legal in the United Kingdom; (iii) insists that voluntary euthanasia should not be made legal in the United Kingdom; (iv) insists that non-voluntary euthanasia should not be made legal in the United Kingdom; and insists that if euthanasia were legalised, there should be a clear demarcation between those doctors who would be involved in it and those who would not.' See British Medical Association, *End of Life Decisions: Views of the BMA* (London, BMA, 2009).

[8] See, eg, S Nuland, *How We Die: Reflections on Life's Final Chapter* (New York, Knopf Doubleday, 1995).

extension is not undignified because during the extension the patient's bowels might be incompetent. It is undignified because that's not the story. Behind all this hovers the spectre of Sandel, insisting that we need to accept our gifts—which include the time necessary for the right telling of the story. Or, if you prefer a biblical spectre, we might substitute the shadowy, cynical, wining but never whining figure of the philosopher in Ecclesiastes, reminding us that there is a time for everything, including a time for dying.[9]

The argument is an ethical argument against some suicides: against Dianne Pretty's, for instance, or Debbie Purdy's. But not, of course, against the withdrawal of treatment from Miss B, or, in principle, from Tony Bland.

When translating ethics into law we should always be careful, and nowhere more so than here. There cannot and should not be an exact correspondence between the two. Such correspondence only happens in theocracies and the dictatorships of idealogues, all of which are abominable.

Forthright statutory expressivism, combined with a compassionate exercise of prosecutorial discretion, is the way forward. It is what we have in the UK after the House of Lords' decision in *R (Purdy) v DPP*.[10] It is right from both a practical and an expressivist point of view to have assisted suicide legislation on the statute book. Endings need to be declared to be important, and some who help to bring stories to a premature close need to be prosecuted. But some do not. Dignity does not insist on it. Indeed, dignity would often be outraged if the legal process were to mar further a premature ending by demanding that lawyers pore over it and cameras flash over it.

PVS cases are the classic creatures of technology. If I were to be consistently Japanese,[11] I would simply regret that PVS patients were alive at all, declare that their ends had come at the time that their cerebral cortices were ablated (while being careful not to equate lack of cerebral function in itself with dehumanisation), and endorse immediate withdrawal of life-sustaining treatment. But it is not that simple. We have to do medical ethics (and hence apply our notion of dignity), in the wards that actually exist, rather than those which would conform best to our idea of how things should be done.

Does a patient in PVS have dignity in my sense? Yes: I dealt specifically and explicitly with this case in Chapter 1. But not only does the patient have dignity;, there is lots of dignity in the transaction that falls to be considered. That of relatives, carers, and doctors, for instance. It was dignity-relevant in the *Ms B* case that her doctors and nurses thought that her treatment should be continued, and wanted nothing to do with its withdrawal.[12] Similarly in a PVS case. Might it be dignity-justifiable

---

[9] Ecclesiastes 3:1–2.
[10] *R (Purdy) v DPP* [2010] 1 AC 345. The *Purdy* litigation gave rise to the DPP's 'Policy for Prosecutors in respect of cases of encouraging or assisting suicide' (February 2010): www.cps.gov.uk/publications/prosecution/assisted_suicide.html.
[11] See ch 9.
[12] *B v An NHS Trust* [2002] 2 All ER 449.

to keep alive a PVS patient because their relatives and carers wish it? In theory, and subject to the important question of resources, yes. First: the patient's own dignity interests are not necessarily in a negative balance, and relatives'/carers' dignity interests might weigh heavily. Dignity will score relationships very high. And, to be real, relationships don't necessarily require reciprocation. The fact that a patient cannot and never will thank a carer for dressing his bedsores doesn't mean that the patient is not in a real relationship with the dresser. That relationship is potentially worth preserving indefinitely.

What if the PVS patient has made an advance directive requiring life-sustaining treatment to be withdrawn in the event of him entering a permanent vegetative state? Can his own persisting dignity interests, or the countervailing dignity interests of any other stake-holders, ever trump that advance directive? Well, as a matter of ethics rather than law, it is not inconceivable. But in practice it is very unlikely. Any decent dignity analysis will regard autonomous prior expressions of will very highly indeed.[13]

It may be very different in both ethics and (I have contended elsewhere) in UK law, in the case of personality-transforming disease. Say that a patient, X, makes an advance directive refusing life sustaining treatment in the event of, say, Alzheimer's dementia. X gets dementia. Its effect in him is, so far as his general well-being is concerned, apparently wholly benign. It has annihilated the old person, X—the one who made the directive—replacing him with a new one, whom we will call Y. As well as decimating the cortex, the merciful dementia has also decimated the horrors and neuroses that make miserable the lives of so many with functioning cortices. Imagine, then, the blissfully demented Y, beaming at his fellow patients and rejoicing in the very worst of daytime TV. Y gets a chest infection. It is easily treatable with antibiotics. X/Y's daughter, who happens to be the sole beneficiary under his will, produces the advance directive and asserts that it would be unlawful to give the antibiotics. Should they be given? There is a biological connection between X and Y, but it seems of little real significance. Y wants to watch next week's instalment of an appalling soap. Should a document signed by an entirely unrelated person, X, be Y's death warrant?

I suggest that the ethical answer, based on Y's evident thriving (and assuming that it is not possible to speak meaningfully about his autonomy), is no. And, further, that despite the stern words of s 26(1) of the Mental Capacity Act 2005, which indicates that if a patient has made an advance decision that is valid and applicable to the relevant treatment, the decision 'has the effect as if he had made it, and had had capacity to make it, at the time when the decision arises whether the treatment should be carried out or continued', it is not only not unlawful to give the antibiotics but (because the best interests determination required by the overarching s 4 of the Act is a determination of the best interests of the patient

---

[13] Jonathan Herring comments that attaching weight to patients' wishes respects their dignity: J Herring, *Medical Law and Ethics* (Oxford, OUP, 2010) 179.

facing the clinician at the time of the decision—not a notional, hypothetical, vanished patient), it would be unlawful not to give them.[14]

We have already seen, courtesy of Munby J's survey in *Burke v General Medical Council*,[15] how many English and other English-speaking judges have dealt with dignity in end-of-life cases. But more usually dignity is used as a slogan—often at the instance of the lawyers, who often, no doubt, find that a mention of dignity palliates the fears of relatives.

A typical example is in *An NHS Trust v Ms D and Mr and Mrs D*,[16] a first instance Family Division case concerning a 32-year-old woman with mitochondrial cytopathy, in a vegetative state, with a life expectancy in the region of six to twelve months.[17] The Trust responsible for her care sought declarations that (inter alia) it was not in her best interests to be resuscitated, ventilated, or have a central venous line placed, if she needed these interventions, and that:

> It shall be lawful as being in Ms. D's best interests for the claimant or the responsible attending practitioner nurses and healthcare staff generally to furnish such treatment and nursing care as may be appropriate to ensure that Ms. D suffers the least distress, discomfort and invasion of her autonomy as is consistent with giving the appropriate treatment and that she retains the greatest dignity.[18]

Coleridge J, concluding that the declarations should be granted, referred to Hoffman LJ's much-cited judgment in *Airedale NHS Trust v Bland*,[19] and went on:

> A few extra months will not be of any benefit to her. In my judgment she should be allowed as dignified a passing as is achievable. Some might say that her dignity has already been severely compromised by the progress and incidence of this awful disease. To subject her body to further grossly invasive procedure[s] can only further detract from her dignity. That would, on the contrary, in my judgment, be a real disadvantage to her.[20]

---

[14] The full argument is in Foster, *Choosing Life, Choosing Death* 151–58. Of course very often it may be possible in such circumstances to say simply that the advance directive is not 'valid' and/or 'applicable', without having to plumb any deep ontological waters.

[15] *Burke v General Medical Council* [2005] QB 424. See ch7 above.

[16] *An NHS Trust v Ms D and Mr and Mrs D* [2005] EWHC 2439 (Fam).

[17] Another very similar example is *An NHS Trust v (1) A (2) SA* [2005] EWCA Civ 1145, a Court of Appeal case about the withdrawal of life-sustaining treatment from an incapacitate adult. Waller LJ seemed content to be helped to his conclusion by the idea of dignity, without defining what was meant by that idea. His closing words included: 'I hope that [the family] can now accept that Mr. A should be allowed to die peacefully and with dignity and without further suffering'. Another example, this time from Italy, is the Supreme Court of Italy PVS case of *Englaro* (2008) Sentenza: 21748. Stefano Bondi, commenting on the judgment, says: 'The decision's most remarkable aspect is the fact that no universal idea of human dignity was endorsed, leaving it to individuals to assess the standards of what constitutes a meaningful existence.' S Bondi, 'Can Good Law Make up for Bad Politics? The Case of Eluana Englaro' (2009) 17 *MLR* 447, 453.

[18] *An NHS Trust v Ms D and Mr and Mrs D* (n 16) para 7.

[19] Ibid para 41. See ch7 above.

[20] Ibid para 44.

It is unfair to subject this to too much analysis.[21] The instinct behind it—to go to dignity when there is nowhere else to go—is absolutely right. The fact that dignity would be the language most palatable to the relatives is also significant: it resonated in them at a level that autonomy, respect or any other principle could not begin to reach. But it is hard to extract this meaning of dignity from Hoffman LJ's discussion, and dangerously repercussive to say that dignity is eroded by disease itself.

The salient parts of *Bland*, together with *Pretty v UK*, have already been cited (in Munby J's judgment in *Burke*). The ECtHR in *Pretty v UK* relied heavily on the Supreme Court of Canada case of *Rodriguez v Attorney General of Canada*,[22] which concerned the legality of a blanket prohibition on assisted suicide. Even a judgment as influential as *Rodriguez*, and which purported to make its decision on, inter alia, dignity grounds, had little to say about it. Here is the judgement of the majority:

> There is no question, then, that personal autonomy, at least with respect to the right to make choices concerning one's own body, control over one's physical and psychological integrity, and basic human dignity are encompassed within security of the person, at least to the extent of freedom from criminal prohibitions which interfere with these. The effect of the prohibition in section 241(b) is to prevent the appellant from having assistance to commit suicide when she is no longer able to do so on her own ... In my view, these considerations lead to the conclusion that the prohibition in section 241(b) deprives the appellant of autonomy over her person and causes her physical pain and psychological stress in a manner which impinges on the security of her person. The appellant's security interest (considered in the context of the life and liberty interest) is therefore engaged, and it is necessary to determine whether there has been any deprivation thereof that is not in accordance with the principles of fundamental justice.[23]

McLachlin J said:

> In the present case, Parliament has put into force a legislative scheme which does not bar suicide but criminalises the act of assisting suicide. The effect of this is to deny to some people the choice of ending their lives solely because they are physically unable to do so. This deprives Sue Rodriguez of her security of the person (the right to make decisions concerning her own body, which affect only her own body) in a way that offends the principles of fundamental justice, thereby violating section 7 of the Charter ... It is part of the persona and dignity of the human being that he or she have the autonomy to decide what is best for his or her body.[24]

---

[21] It is considered by Jonathan Herring, who sees it as possibly illustrating that dignity is the overarching criterion governing the extent of a doctor's obligation to prolong life: J Herring, *Medical Law and Ethics* (Oxford, OUP, 2010) 465–66.

[22] *Rodriguez v Attorney General of Canada* [1994] 2 LRC 136.

[23] Sopinka J, with La Forest, Gonthier, Iacobucci and Major JJ concurring: ibid 177–78.

[24] At ibid 195: L'heureux-Dubé J concurred.

In *Pretty v United Kingdom* the ECtHR moved directly from these passages to conclude that: 'The very essence of the Convention is respect for human dignity and human freedom',[25] and:

> The applicant in this case is prevented by law from exercising her choice to avoid what she considers will be an undignified and distressing end to her life. The Court is not prepared to exclude that this constitutes an interference with her right to respect for private life as guaranteed under Article 8(1) of the Convention.[26]

If one were to read only *Rodriguez* and *Pretty*, one might think that dignity at the end of life was co-extensive with autonomy. That is of course a consequence of the fact that both of those claimants were capacitate, but it is regrettable that those courts should have spoken so openly about dignity without acknowledging that there is more to it than that. That there is more is plain from the authorities reviewed in *Burke*, and perhaps particularly from Munby J's incontrovertible observation that Article 3 of the ECHR must apply to patients in PVS.[27] Would there be a breach of Article 3 if patients in PVS were gang-raped? Of course. The same point is made in other jurisdictions.[28]

What more is there? As with judicial consideration of abortion, so here. Dignity matters. The judges use it compulsively, and when they do, it has an aura that nothing else has. If it is appealed to, there is no appeal from its decision. Whatever it is, you get to it when you are forced to tunnel into the bioethical depths beyond the help of other, shallower principles. No meaning has been forced on it by the judges that precludes the adoption of our definition.

---

[25] *Pretty v United Kingdom* (n 2) para 65.

[26] Ibid para 67.

[27] An observation that has laid definitively to rest a suggestion to the contrary by Butler-Sloss P in *An NHS Trust A v M* [2001] 2 WLR 942. See the discussion in C Dupre, 'Human Dignity and the Withdrawal of Medical Treatment: A Missed Opportunity?' (2006) *European Human Rights Law Review* 678; and J Coggon, 'Could the Right to Die with Dignity Represent a New Right to Die in English Law?' (2006) 14 *MLR* 219.

[28] Eg in the US Supreme Court case of *Cruzan v Director, Missouri Department of Health* 497 US 261 (1990) the Court noted, at para 41, and subsequently relied on, the fact that in *Superintendent of Belchertown State School v Saikewicz* 373 Mass 728, 370 NE2d 417 (1977), the Supreme Judicial Court of Massachusetts had relied on both the right of privacy and the right of informed consent to permit the withholding of chemotherapy from a profoundly retarded 67-year-old man suffering from leukaemia. The grounds given by the Court included: 'an incompetent person retains the same rights as a competent individual "because the value of human dignity extends to both."'

12

The Use and Abuse of Body Parts

This chapter is mainly a vehicle for the final step in the argument in Chapter 1. It is a step that can only properly be taken by those who have persevered to this point. It is the step back—the step that gives perspective and, for the first time, allows us to use the intuitions about dignity that, in the name of argument, we have done our best to suppress. The function of those intuitions, if the argument has brought us this far, is only to reassure us. They provide cross-bearings which might help to confirm that the other compass that has brought us to this destination was telling the truth.

The judges don't have to be so rigorous. And, as we have seen, the way in which they often express themselves suggests strongly that, most of the time, they are not so rigorous. They follow their intuitions, giving them the name 'dignity'. The fact that their judgments are, for the most part, so inexplicit about what they mean by dignity tends to give the game away.

There are no new analytic points about dignity in this chapter.[1] Anyone who has read so far will be able to guess how I would put the argument about the use of body parts for transplants, for dissection, for the establishment of patentable cell lines[2] and for ashtrays. But (and the pun's enlightening), there's nothing like body parts to show us our own visceral feelings.

Suppose I look out of my window and see boys kicking something in the road. I look more closely, and see that it is a human head. I'm horrified. But why? The pain receptors in that head's skin were no longer broadcasting to any station that could do anything with the signals. The previous owner of the head has

---

[1] There is a useful overview of the way that dignity arguments might relate to disputes about the ownership and use of body parts in S Wheatley, 'Human Rights and Human Dignity in the Resolution of Certain Ethical Questions in Biomedicine' (2001) 3 *European Human Rights Law Review* 312, 316–18.

[2] On the question of DNA patents I broadly adopt the position of David Resnik, who argues that 'patents on human DNA do not *violate* human dignity because they do not treat human beings as complete commodities. However, since human DNA patenting uses market rhetoric to describe human body parts, it does treat human beings as incomplete commodities and, therefore, may *threaten* human dignity by taking us further down the path of human commodification.' D Resnik, 'DNA Patents and Human Dignity'(2001) 29 *Journal of Law, Medicine and Ethics* 152; cp B Brody, 'Protecting Human Dignity and the Patenting of Human Genes' in A Chapman (ed), *Perspectives on Gene Patenting* (Washington DC, American Association of the Advancement of Science, 1999) 111.

no way of knowing. I'm compelled to describe my reasons in terms of dignity. Of violation. But whose dignity is at stake? Who is being violated?

Am I worried that, if the boys aren't stopped and punished, they or their like might do the same to me one day? It can't really be that. I know that it is very unusual, and likely to remain so, for heads to be kicked around in central Oxford. But all the same, I wouldn't like it to happen to me, although I know that I wouldn't be physically hurt by it, or capable of being embarrassed by it. It's not about reputation, either. Nobody whose opinion matters to me would think any the less of me for being the innocent post-mortem subject of a game of football. It wouldn't worry me in the slightest that the notoriety of that involvement would overshadow very significantly what I'd done in my lifetime. As a matter of fact I'd be prospectively quite amused to know that I'd be known primarily as the man whose head was booted around. Let's keep the distinction clear: I don't mind the idea of being known that way: but I still wouldn't want the kicking to happen.

It's not that I have any settled thoughts about where I'd like my body to be. The footballers wouldn't be violating a romantic dream of rotting quietly in a sunlit country churchyard. I have no relevant religious convictions. I don't think that I'll be denied any afterlife that there might be if my head isn't united with my torso. At some level I'm glad that boys are having fun, instead of maggots having a feed.

A part of it, I suppose (but only, I'm embarrassed to admit, a small part) is due to my concern about other people who've known me being upset. But that just begs the same question of them: why are they upset? Upset about other people's upset isn't a complete answer.

It's not to do with control. I'm not proprietorial about bones and decomposing fat, even if they happen to be mine.

But still, I don't like the idea. I can't get much beyond inarticulate observations such as: 'It's not right'; or 'That's not what heads are for'.

And in those two blundering statements we have a potentially very fecund marriage of virtue ethics and dignity.

Heads are 'for' the business of human *being*. Most obviously, of course, when they are attached to a neck and lit up electronically with all the wonderment of the world. But even when they're not working like that, they're still for that part of human being that has nothing to do with cognition or pain or enjoyment; for that part that persisted in Tony Bland when his cortex gave up. That part of 'being' doesn't just exist in prospect—in my hopes of how I'll be remembered when I'm biologically no more; and it doesn't just consist in memories.

I note, too, that it doesn't matter at all that I don't know whose head is being kicked around. If it were the head of an enemy, I'd still be disgusted. The disgust would come from the same place, and be of a similar magnitude, as if the head were that of a member of my family. There would be other types of outrage laid on top of the basic disgust in the case of a family member, of course, but the dignity-type outrage would be much the same in each case.

I also note that I would feel similar things, of similar origin but lesser in magnitude, if the boys were kicking round a dog's head.[3] That observation is helpful. It lets me locate my disgust more confidently in the 'That's not right' and 'That's not what heads are for' area.

I'm concerned about the boys, too. A corollary of my feelings about the purpose of heads is that the boys are beyond the pale. That's not what boys' feet are for. I'm not primarily concerned that the sort of callousness revealed by their game is going to show up in a rise in violent crime down the Cowley Road. It sounds pompous and sanctimonious, but I'm ontologically worried for them. They're not being what they ought to be. They are acting in a dehumanised way. They're diminishing their dignity by behaving towards another human in a way not compatible with that other person's dignity. The reciprocity that comes from being human—and therefore, necessarily, from being part of the gigantic human web—is terrifying as well as glorious.

Ethic and being should dance together, and when they dance well it is quite a sight. A good motive can make splendid an otherwise unacceptable act—an act inconsistent with proper human *being*. What distinguishes post-mortem organ harvesting from cannibalism? Well, permission from the donor, possibly, depending on whether there's an opt-in or opt-out system. But certainly a good motive on the part of the harvester.

Autonomy is one of the principal draftsmen of much law relating to the use of body parts. The Human Tissue Act is a good example.[4] But, as we have seen before, so many times, autonomy often begs far more questions than it answers, and it is never the fundamental principle. So the statute gives you the right to choose what happens to your liver after you die. Why should you be concerned about that? We're straight back to human heads in the street, and hence straight back to dignity.

Sometimes the law has recognised this.

Mr Kestenbaum, who lived in Israel, asked the local Jewish Burial Society to allow him to inscribe his late wife's name on her tombstone in Latin letters, and her birth and death dates according to the Gregorian rather than the Jewish calendar. The Society, after due rabbinic consideration, refused, saying that this affronted Jewish law. The matter found its way to the Supreme Court of Israel, which rejected the appeal of the Society. Justice Barak said that the Society's decision violated public policy because it struck at human dignity—the dignity both of the living and the dead.[5]

---

[3] Thanks to Tony Hope for this observation.

[4] See C Foster, *Choosing Life, Choosing Death* (Oxford, Hart, 2009) 173–80.

[5] *Jerusalem Community Burial Society v Kestenbaum* CA 294/91: 46(2): 464, 524. See too *Fredrika Shavit v Rishon LeZion Jewish Burial Society* (Supreme Court of Israel 1999: CA 6024/97). Note too the decision of the French Conseil Constitutionnel, which saw dignity as the key guiding principle when considering the constitutionality of laws relating to the use of body parts and products derived from human bodies: Decision de 27 juillet 1994, nos 94-343-344, DC: relative au respect du corps humain

That, we can now see, is what many courts actually recognise, and how they act. Not only can dignity work in the wards, the mortuary and in the courts, but it does and it must. Sometimes in bioethics you're wading so deep in the human condition that to make progress, you've got to go right down to the bed rock.

et a l'utilisation des elements et produits du corps human, a l'assistance medicale a la procreation et audiagnostique prenatal (lois no 94-653 et no 94-654 du 29 juillet 1994).

Epilogue

I have sought to make out the thesis articulated in Chapter 1. In so doing I have ranged widely. Whether I have ranged successfully can be decided by revisiting Chapter 1 in the light of what I have said. There is no point in reiterating the thesis and then asserting: 'It's been proved.' But the argument can be summarised in the course of apologising, as I now do, for the constant and no doubt tedious reference to Article 8 of the ECHR.

The purpose of this reference was not to suggest that the Strasbourg jurisprudence was impeccable so far as dignity was concerned, but simply to show that:

(a) in difficult situations, the court resorts to dignity; and
(b) that is because there is no other resort; and
(c) the substantive account of dignity used by Article 8 is akin to the one I advocate; and
(d) the structure of Article 8, leading as it does with individual interests and then weighing those interests against those of all other stakeholders, procedurally embodies the 'transactional' approach to bioethics that I suggest is necessary when using dignity properly; and
(e) the results that dignity gives are acceptable; and
(f) Article 8 is wide. It can cover all conceivable bioethical conundrums. It must be the primary procedural lens, for instance, through which human enhancement problems are examined. It will use dignity in that examination; and
(g) Article 8 resorts to dignity in hard situations because hard situations force one to fundamentals, and philosophical and forensic experience shows that there is nothing more fundamental than dignity; and
(h) if that's right, we should not be satisfied with solutions in less obviously hard situations (such as typical informed consent cases, or clinical confidentiality cases) that cannot be demonstrated to be derived from dignity. There is a real practical value in intellectual consistency. In many places the law has been disfigured by piecemeal development. A shallow, make-do solution in an easy case might be dangerously repercussive in an area far distant factually, philosophically and in terms of gravity from that easy case. It's worth getting things fundamentally right.

Many will remain sceptical about the utility of dignity. I have acknowledged the force of their reasons. But dismissing the idea completely is not an option: everyone involved in bioethics and bio-law will have to come to terms with the fact that dignity is going to be the ruling paradigm. It (whatever *it* is) is ubiquitous in the guidelines, professional codes of conduct, and authoritative declarations, and the judges will find dignity increasingly unavoidable.

This ubiquity is not, as the cynics suggest, an indication that dignity means whatever anyone wants it to mean. Dignity is ubiquitous because dignity is at least as old as man, and is to be found wherever there is a real human being or a question about one.

INDEX

Printed in Great Britain
by Amazon